RADICAL *of*
RADICALS

Publications of the
Michigan Civil War Association

Heart in Tatters: Eunice Hunt Tripler and the Civil War
His Sword a Scalpel: General Charles Stuart Tripler, MD, USA
Warriors for Liberty: William Dollarson & Michigan's Civil War
African Americans
Radical of Radicals: Austin Blair: Civil War Governor—
In His Own Words

Praise for *Radical of Radicals*

"*Radical of Radicals: Austin Blair: Civil War Governor—In His Own Words* is an essential work that brings to light the extraordinary leadership and vision of Michigan's 'War Governor.' Blair's commitment to emancipation and equality, paired with his unyielding support for the Union cause, exemplifies the spirit of Jackson, the city that shaped his political rise. This volume preserves his legacy for future generations, offering a profound insight into the man whose radical convictions helped define both Michigan's and America's path to justice and freedom. A must-read for those seeking to understand the Civil War's impact on the Wolverine State and beyond."

—**Maurice Imhoff**, president, Jackson County
Michigan Historical Society

"Once again, the Michigan Civil War Association has performed an exemplary service by publishing an annotated collection of important primary sources, the works of Michigan's Civil War governor, Austin Blair. The MCWA's work ensures that Blair's contributions to ending slavery and preserving the Union remain accessible and appreciated."

—**Tom M. George**, MD, former state senator and past
president of the Historical Society of Michigan

"Austin Blair was a gifted public servant who stood with President Lincoln in the heroic task to save the Union. As Lincoln guided the nation, so Governor Blair guided Michigan. A retrospective on Michigan's Civil War governor is overdue. Kudos to Jack Dempsey for opening that door using Governor Blair's own words."

—**Cameron S. Brown**, president of the Kalamazoo Abraham
Lincoln Institute and former Michigan state senator

"We all know how President Lincoln ended slavery, but most Michiganders probably have no idea that our state's Civil War governor was a radical who fought for not only emancipation but also women's suffrage, racial equality for Black Americans, and abolishing the death penalty. This volume does a real service to his legacy."

—**Maria Taylor**, former editor, *Michigan History* magazine

"Civil War Governor Austin Blair is barely remembered today. A remarkable man, he was the right person in the right place at the right time. His loyal support was critical to the preservation of the Union. The MCWA deserves praise for its treatment of one of the most beloved and effective leaders Michigan ever produced."

—**Kerry Chartkoff**, emeritus Michigan State Capitol historian

Praise for *Warriors for Liberty*

- "a veritable treasure-trove ... fascinating and important book" —Michigan in Books
- "a multifaceted gem that sparkles" —Dr. Chandra Manning
- "exhaustively researched and extremely well-written" —Dr. Douglas R. Egerton
- "engaging and inspirational" —Amy Elliott Bragg
- "a complete recounting of the critical roles played by African Americans" —*BridgeDetroit*
- "well written and very impressive" —Bryan Cheesboro
- "a most compelling story" —Steve Spreitzer
- "expertly researched and vividly rendered" —Dave Dempsey
- "inspiring and thought-provoking ... provides readers with important stories" —*Emerging Civil War*

Praise for *His Sword a Scalpel*

- "fabulous work ... A really wonderful read presenting a lot of new insights" —John Lustrea
- "beautifully written and fact filled. A great job" —Dr. John L. Cameron
- "thoroughly researched and well-documented ... a masterful job" —Dennis A. Rasbach

- "compelling … done history, Michigan, and all of us an enormous favor" —Jack Lessenberry
- "thorough and cogently argued treatment" —Dr. Martin J. Hershock
- "fantastic book" —Nancy Hancock-Cullen
- "a major contribution to the history of Michigan in the Civil War" —*Michigan in Books*
- "This is a great read!" —Amazon reviewer

Praise for *Heart in Tatters*

- "This exciting inaugural volume stands as a tremendous contribution and sets the stage for the series of MCWA publications to follow" —Dr. Martin J. Hershock
- "fascinating reading for anyone interested in America's past" —Dr. Steven E. Woodworth
- "candid insights into some of the war's most famous men and fascinating details of life during that era that I have not seen anywhere else before" – Candice Shy Hooper
- "compelling book" – Bonnie Johnson
- "a welcome addition to the shelves of anyone who enjoys reading about the lesser-known stories surrounding the Civil War" – Patricia Majher
- "enlightening and entertaining. The MCWA has done a real service to Civil War scholarship" – Dr. Gerald J. Prokopowicz
- "Huzzah to Jack Dempsey and the Michigan Civil War Association on the first in a series of books that you'll want in your library!!" – Amazon reviewer

RADICAL *of* RADICALS

Austin Blair

CIVIL WAR GOVERNOR–IN HIS OWN WORDS

 Mission Point Press

Readers are encouraged to go to MissionPointPress.com to contact the author
or to find information on how to buy this book in bulk at a discounted rate.

Published by Mission Point Press

 Mission Point Press

2554 Chandler Rd.
Traverse City, MI 49696
(231) 421-9513
MissionPointPress.com

Hardcover: 978-1-965278-54-3
Softcover: 978-1-965278-55-0
LOC: 2025903559

Printed in the United States of America

Fourth in a series

★ ★ ★

Proceeds from this volume benefit the Michigan Civil War Association in preserving and sharing Michigan's role during the American Civil War.

At the time of this publication, the MCWA is raising funds to erect a Monument honoring Michigan's contributions to victory and to Emancipation at the Battle of Antietam, Sept. 17, 1862.

Donations supporting the Monument project are received at https://michigancivilwarassociation.org

★ ★ ★

The Michigan Civil War Association is a Michigan 501(c)(3) non-profit corporation.

Its corporate purpose is to pursue cultural, historical, and economic development opportunities to preserve and promote the history of Michigan's role in the American Civil War.

Founded in 2013, the MCWA has acted as a careful steward of all donations received.

More information is available at https://www.michigancivilwar association.org

Contents

Illustrations Follow Part Two

I confess myself one of those who have an abiding faith in the final success of American institutions and the perpetuity of American independence

Only an inspired tongue could properly portray
his lofty patriotism and unwavering courage,
his unsullied integrity and consecration to duty,
and his heroic services in those hours of trial when,
with the mightiest things in his keeping,
he was faithful and true.[1]

1.   *An Address by [former U.S. senator] John Patton, Delivered at Lansing, Mich.,*
October 12, 1898, at the Unveiling of the Statue, Erected by the State of Michigan,
in the Capitol Grounds, to the Memory of Austin Blair, War Governor (Lansing:
1898), 4.

Preface

The adage of "hard times create strong people" cannot be more applicable when looking to the history of the United States. During the most trying times, people have stepped forward, often at their own personal sacrifice, to face those circumstances. The "great experiment" of the United States has been tested and brought to near extinction at times in our country's history. American Democracy is a fragile commodity that needs care and feeding. As a major work in progress, the significant achievements in fulfilling the promises of the Declaration of Independence must be used as a catalyst to sustain that form of government.

One often hears in the news, editorial commentary, and in conversations with colleagues and friends that we are in hard times now. As we witness the country in severe strife, ugly divisiveness, and fracture, there is a tendency to feel this the worst time in our history and the country is on the precipice of catastrophic demise—"losing America."

Not dismissing or marginalizing the struggles and challenges of today, but we must look to the past and take stock that we have been through the darkest of times. Whether it was the Great Depression, world wars, nuclear arms threats, domestic terrorist attacks, and pandemics, the United States has seen hard times, and those times reveal strong people who persevere.

At no time in our history did we come to near complete dismantling of the United States than during the Civil War. The decades-long pressure cooker of tension prior to 1861 proved cataclysmic as nearly 750,000 lives were lost over the following four years. That ratio to the

2024 population would equal an unfathomable 8.375 million lives lost today. The fabric of the United States was severely torn, but did not sever.

The years 1861–1865 saw the hardest of times in our country's history. With the United States on the precipice of disaster and a tsunami of devastating grief gripping nearly every aspect of the country, strong people emerged. Arguably those engaged on the battlefield produced strong men to achieve military success, but this time also produced many strong people in the civilian population to face the devastating effects of war. One of those strong people to emerge was Michigan's war-time governor, Austin Blair.

Though Blair was admitted to the bar and having had experience in politics first serving as the county clerk in Eaton County, Michigan, and as a state representative and senator, his dissenters claimed he "lacked political acumen." Notwithstanding, in the early 1850s he served on the committee that drafted the new Republican platform. In 1860, Blair served as delegate to the Republican national convention nominating Abraham Lincoln. The fall of that year, he was elected to hold the highest executive seat in the state, Michigan's thirteenth governor.

Commitment, dedication, and strong personal conviction fueled his ascendancy as Michigan's top executive. His tireless drive and commitment to the Union, and firm belief in the Constitution and Declaration of Independence, guided his actions as the war clouds gathered in the winter of 1861.

The mounting powder keg of tension since the American Revolution finally detonated on April 12, 1861, when South Carolina artillery batteries fired upon the federal garrison at Fort Sumter in Charleston harbor. Awareness of the bombardment and ultimate surrender of the fort spread across the country rapidly as telegraph lines carried the news that the anticipated war had commenced.

North and South alike, the enthusiastic fevered pitch of vengeance and rebellion permeated every community. The sentiment expressed in Monroe County, Michigan's *Monroe Commercial* newspaper was nearly the same throughout the north:

> There is but one feeling, one sentiment, one voice; and that is, the administration must be sustained, the Stars and Stripes defended, and our government preserved. Howevermuch [sic] political opinion may have divided us there are no differences now. Our country sounds the bugle note of alarm, and the people respond as one man.

Almost immediately, Lincoln put out a call for 75,000 three-month volunteers to suppress the unfolding rebellion. Governor Blair, in a prophet-like moment during his inaugural address in January of that year, urged that Michigan should convey all its military assets to the Lincoln administration in defense of the Union. With the call from Washington for voluntary enlistments, Governor Blair was equal to the task in raising ten companies as the 1st Michigan regiment was mustered into service.

Proactively, Governor Blair continued to raise Michigan regiments as well as other supportive legislative actions. A $1,000,000 war loan was authorized as well as a Soldiers' Relief Law. The newly passed law required Michigan counties to look after the families who had soldiers on the front lines. Though all states north and south sprang into action with volunteer enlistments and community groups organizing for the war effort, Governor Blair's alacrity in formalizing such efforts was unprecedented.

Governor Blair continued to raise regiments maintaining mobilization momentum. The massive influx of troops pouring into Washington from all over the north caused Secretary of War Simon Cameron to inform the states to halt further enlistments. By the time word had been sent to the states, the 3rd and 4th Michigan Infantry regiments were being raised. Not skipping a beat, and knowing the initial three-month enlistments would soon expire, Blair continued to raise additional units. By early fall, the 5th, 6th, and 7th Michigan infantry regiments were deployed into service.

During the war, Governor Blair led Michigan furnishing more than thirty regiments of infantry (including the 1st Michigan Colored Infantry that would become the 102nd U.S. Colored Infantry), eleven regiments of cavalry, twelve six-gun light artillery batteries, two batteries of medium artillery, a regiment of engineers and mechanics, and a regiment of sharpshooters. Amazingly, of a population of nearly 800,000, approximately 90,000 of the 110,000 able-bodied men capable of enlistment would serve. The per capita enlistments of many Michigan counties rank among the highest of any other state.

Governor Blair led by example. His own personal commitment to the war effort and support of aid to the soldiers' families left him nearly penniless when he left office in 1865. He used much of his meager annual salary of $1,000 on behalf of directly aiding soldiers. He built a tremendous rapport with the soldiers during the conflict and then with the veterans after the war. And he strove to provide Michigan units with the best arms and equipment for their success.

"Radical of Radicals" is an apropos title of this work. Austin Blair was far ahead of his time with his progressive ideals and beliefs. Lacking military background or experience he very successfully led Michigan's war efforts both on the front lines and at the home front. He spurred Michigan's industry, mining, and agriculture to meet the demands of the national crisis. Michigan's exports to fuel the northern war machine aided substantially to ultimate victory.

In 2026, the United States will celebrate its Semiquincentennial. The American Association for State and Local History has created a program handbook and five distinct themes that is guiding the national and many state efforts to commemorate "America 250." Unlike the bicentennial in 1976, the 2026 themes are not only commemorative, but also a retrospective look since 1776 through the lens of all voices and perspectives. One theme in particular, "Unfinished Revolutions," embraces the work we as a nation are in and the work yet to do in fulfilling the promises of the Declaration of Independence.

Governor Blair was truly a strong person and an integral part of the northern war effort. He did not have military experience and was a politician ahead of his times. Blair was a staunch abolitionist and an advocate of suffrage for women and black citizens. The armies of the Civil War were primarily made up of citizen soldiers, especially in the beginning. Although Blair had years of political experience, he could be characterized as a citizen politician believing representation was for all people, not just the wealthy segments and classes.

As historians we have an obligation to bring a voice to those in the past who can no longer speak. The sacred trust of this task not only serves as an educational component but also as a reservoir of inspiration for us today and those of tomorrow. With "Radical of Radicals" we have the incredible opportunity to do so with Austin Blair's story. The subtitle, "In His Own Words" is purposefully designed to let readers know him firsthand through his own speeches and writings. History may not exactly repeat itself, but it certainly remixes itself and we have only to look back to see a clearer path forward.

The Michigan Civil War Association's purpose is to share Michigan's stories of sacrifice, contribution, and impact during the Civil War era. Exploration of the military, social, political, and economic histories of Michiganders, especially those whose stories may have been traditionally marginalized and previously under-told, will be shared. In this volume, the MCWA's Publication Division has delivered another mission-fit work on a story not previously explored.

As you read through this book, think of how the hardest of times created the strongest of a person in Austin Blair. Think of how he was ahead of his time as a true advocate for a color-blind society. Think of the unfinished revolutions we may be facing currently and how his leadership would be instrumental today. Learn from his leadership model and apply that in your life.

Comparatively little has been written about the Union Governors during the Civil War. It is our sincere hope that you are inspired by hearing Governor Blair's own words and seeing someone whose commitment and personal sacrifice was vitally crucial in preserving the

Union and providing freedom for millions of enslaved Americans. Through this book, he is brought to life with perspectives that reach far beyond the "War Governor" narrative he is traditionally known by.

Hard times create strong people and Austin Blair defines that adage perfectly. His inspirational leadership during the nation's greatest crisis is truly an aspirational benchmark for Michiganders and citizens today.

Tuebor!

—Brian James Egen
President, Michigan Civil War Association

Introduction

Leadership is important in all walks of human life, none more so than in public service and administration. A leader's voice is "the expression of one's beliefs."[2] This book reveals the voice of Austin Blair, Michigan's chief executive during 1861–1865.

For nearly a century after the guns of the Civil War went silent, governors of the loyal states—an office where "the buck stops"[3]—were largely ignored by historians. Not until the ending of the Second World War did an expert in mid-nineteenth century American history delve thoroughly into their "significant, hitherto neglected" role. This Midwest professor penned "an arresting interpretation" of the Lincoln presidency, claiming the loyal governors were conciliated, cajoled, and manipulated by the much cagier politician who occupied the White House.[4] Not only had the president won the war, his achievement came "as much by Lincoln's political victories over the Northern governors as by the military victories over the Southern secessionists."[5]

---

2. Max De Pree, *Leadership Jazz* (New York: Dell Publishing, 1992), 5.
3. https://www.trumanlibrary.gov/library/public-papers/378/presidents-fare-well-address-american-people
4. Reinhard H. Luthin, *The American Historical Review*, Vol. 54, No. 4 (Jul. 1949), 887-889, reviewing Hesseltine, *infra*.
5. William B. Hesseltine, *Lincoln and the War Governors* (New York: Alfred A. Knopf, 1948), quote from inside dust jacket; front cover highlighted this "little-known but dramatic story." Another interpretation is that Congress brought about victory more than Lincoln or the governors. Leonard P. Curry, *Blueprint for Modern America: Nonmilitary Legislation of the First Civil War Congress* (Nashville: Vanderbilt University Press, 1968).

Lincoln was the giant; the governors were pint-sized; he and his Administration downplayed appreciation for the state executives.[6]

Lincoln had not come to the presidency as an abolitionist.[7] He ran in 1860 on a party platform that opposed the extension of slavery in America rather than to abolish it. In August 1862, he announced: "If I could save the Union without freeing any slave I would do it." Other Republicans were decisively in favor of abolition—Blair among them. And Blair believed it a military necessity to emancipate the millions of black workers who were forced to labor on behalf of the secessionist cause.

The *War Governors* labeled Austin Blair as "extremist" in 1859 and in the next year as a "rising Republican radical and old abolitionist." It said Blair "was even more radical than his [fellow Republican] predecessor" and "a fanatic lacking in political acumen." A Civil War classic described him as "a man of radical temper who favored prompt, sweeping, and aggressive policies."[8] Abolitionists were "fractious" and uncompromising,[9] and Blair fit in as "an anti-slavery extremist

---

6. The descriptive term in John Stauffer, *Giants: The Parallel Lives of Frederick Douglass and Abraham Lincoln* (New York: Twelve, 2008). Perhaps only once during the war, in late 1862 after the Altoona conference (see *infra*), did the U.S. War Department laud: "The patriotic zeal and efficient aid cordially rendered by the respective governors of the loyal States in the laborious and complicated duties pertaining to raising the volunteers and making the draft." Report of the Secretary of War, Dec. 1, 1862, 10, in *Message of the President of the United States to the Two Houses of Congress at the Commencement of the Third Session of the Thirty-Seventh Congress*, Vol. IV (Washington: Government Printing Office, 1862). Doris Kearns Goodwin, *Team of Rivals: The Political Genius of Abraham Lincoln* (New York: Simon & Schuster, 2005), highlighted Lincoln working through diverse viewpoints, without a treatment of governors.
7. Bruce Catton, *Reflections on the Civil War* (Garden City: Doubleday & Co., 1981), 8-9 (John Leekley ed.). Lincoln, an antislavery moralist, "detested abolitionism" according to Fred Kaplan, *Lincoln and the Abolitionists: John Quincy Adams, Slavery, and the Civil War* (New York: Harper, 2017), xi.
8. Hesseltine, 48, 116, 391; Allan Nevins, *The War for the Union, Vol. I, The Improvised War: 1861-1862* (New York: Charles Scribner's Sons, 1959), 170.
9. See Frank J. Cirillo, *The Abolitionist Civil War: Immediatists and the Struggle to Transform the Union* (Baton Rouge: Louisiana State University Press, 2023).

of his day."[10] Lincoln's secretary branded radicals and abolitionists as "Jacobins," the French revolutionaries who had brought about a bloody reign of terror.[11]

The opposition heaped scorn on Blair as the "darling of the radical Republican wing" of his party—the "Black Republican Party" concerned more with the welfare of Blacks than Whites. Worse than just "a briefless, witless lawyer," he was an unmitigated "Negro worshiper." He was controlled by "the spirit of fanaticism," an "arch demagogue" whose speeches sought to spread "his fanatical effusions." His utterances suffered because he was an "uninspired" communicator, "gaunt, wizen-faced," unattractive for being "slightly built, intense and nervous in manner."[12]

Blair was nothing less than "the radical of radicals."[13]

The popular 2012 motion picture *Lincoln* portrays an argument among congressional Republicans in the office of Representative Thaddeus Stevens.[14] Mary Lincoln labeled them "demented radicals,"

10.   George Weeks, *Stewards of the State: The Governors of Michigan* (Ann Arbor: Historical Society of Michigan, 1991), 45. In other surveys: Willah Weddon, *Michigan Governors: Their Life Stories* (Lansing: NOG Press, 1994), 42-46; Raymond Sikkenga, *Doers & Dreamers: The Governors of Michigan* (Spring Lake: River Road Publications, 1987), 40-41; George N. Fuller ed., *Governors of the Territory and State of Michigan*, Bulletin No. 16 (Lansing: Michigan Historical Commission, 1928), 90-97; Nevins, 177.

11.   T. Harry Williams, *Lincoln and the Radicals* (Madison: University of Wisconsin Press, 1941), 5-6. See that author's "Lincoln and the Radicals: An Essay in Civil War History and Historiography" in Grady McWhiney ed., *Grant, Lee, Lincoln and the Radicals: Essays on Civil War Leadership* (Baton Rouge: Louisiana State University Press, 2001).

12.   Martin J. Hershock, *The Paradox of Progress: Economic Change, Individual Enterprise, and Political Culture in Michigan, 1837-1878* (Athens: Ohio University Press, 2003), 209; *Democratic Free Press*, May 15, 1846, 2, hoping "the end of the [legislative] session will see the end of" Blair; Mar. 28, 1856, 2; Apr. 3, 1856, 2 ("*DFP*"); Ezra C. Seaman, *Gov. Blair's Speech*, reprint of *Ann Arbor Journal*, Nov. 1866, 1, 2 (Library of Congress Control Number 11030886); Hesseltine, 48, 116, 310, 391.

13.   *DFP*, Aug. 28, 1866, 4.

14.   A kindred spirit to Blair. See Bruce Levine, *Thaddeus Stevens: Civil War Revolutionary, Fighter for Racial Justice* (New York: Simon & Schuster, 2021);

but in January 1865 the President needs their help to secure passage
of a proposed Thirteenth Amendment to abolish slavery. One of the
members urges non-cooperation: "Withdraw radical support, force
him to abandon this scheme, whatever he's up to ...." That hostility
is matched in the Hampton Roads conference on February 3, 1865,
with the president and secretary of state William H. Seward when
Confederate vice-president Alexander H. Stephens speaks about the
amendment:

> Which now extinguishes slavery. And with it our economy.
> All our laws will be determined by a Congress of venge-
> ful Yankees, all our rights'll be subject to a Supreme Court
> benched by Black Republican radicals. All our traditions will
> be obliterated. We won't know ourselves anymore.[15]

This volume is published during the 160th anniversary of the end
of the Civil War, when some contend that Americans don't know
themselves anymore. Surveys reveal significant ignorance of fundamental civics facts. Once-respected historical monuments have been
vandalized; authors who grew up revering Southern icons now repu-
diate them; and generations of "Lost Cause" histories have been rele-
gated to the dustbin. Military history studies, once so important for
understanding this conflict, are on the decline. The "unhappiest field
of study" is the humanities, i.e., history, literature, and the human
condition.[16]

Fawn M. Brodie, *Thaddeus Stevens: Scourge of the South* (New York: W.W. Norton & Co., 1959).
15.   Tony Kushner, *Lincoln: The Screenplay* (New York: Theatre Communications Group, 2012), 13, 40-41, 153.
16.   E.g., Ty Seidule, *Robert E. Lee and Me: A Southerner's Reckoning with the
Myth of the Lost Cause* (New York: St. Martin's Press, 2020); Peter S. Carmichael,
Lorien Foote, Jennifer M. Murray & Craig L. Symonds, "The Fortenbaugh Lecture: A Panel Discussion on Military History" in *The Journal of the Civil War
Era*, Vol. 14, No. 3 (Sept. 2024), 293, 295, 298; Matthew Stewart, *An Emancipation of the Mind: Radical Philosophy, the War over Slavery, and the Refounding of*

Austin Blair knew himself, made clear what values he stood for, and followed those moral principles even if personal unhappiness resulted. "That is what he said" is a vital motif to Copland's great *Lincoln Portrait* orchestral work. This volume relies on what Blair said, revealing as never before a fuller story of an interesting and complex leader. To the extent Blair is remembered, it is as "the War Governor" whose statue holds central stage in front of Michigan's capitol. The label signified much:

> The name indicates that something had been added to the office as it had been known in the ordinary civic routine of the States. They were indeed detached but assimilated War Ministers, wielding the resources of their governments, not only in execution of the law, but by mustering all the powers of the States according to the need, and under the requisitions, of the national government. Their energies in most instances were unbounded, while their executive resource and tact were unfailing.[17]

It only lacked completeness.

Watching his performance, the people of Michigan "placed great faith" in and, "by their expressions and support, advanced significant power to the governor." His force of personality and untiring work became "the nucleus of patriotism" as the war escalated and lengthened. The governor, by one estimate, "practically ran the state single handedly."[18]

The title did not disclose its full cost. Personal tragedy and career disappointments wounded Blair: he "felt my hopes sinking and my

America (New York: W.W. Norton & Co., 2024), ix. "Lost Cause" refers to the war as having origins other than slavery.

17. William B. Weeden, *War Government, Federal and State, in Massachusetts, New York, Pennsylvania and Indiana, 1861-1865* (Boston: Houghton, Mifflin & Co., 1906), xi-xii.

18. Stephen Engle, *All the President's Statesmen: Northern Governors and the American Civil War* (Milwaukee: Marquette University Press, 2006), 11.

ability to battle the storms of life giving way." He struggled "to believe that life had yet something in store for me."[19] A cruel statistic, this: for each of the 1,460 days that Blair served in the state's highest office, ten Michigan soldiers died. In such a toll is revealed the great and bloody sacrifice he presided over, of faces he saw for the last time as they left for the front or during his many trips to the front lines. These men his heart had "followed with increasing anxiety & care after they were in the field, through their battles, in the hospitals & prison pens & every where when the exigencies of the war carried them."[20] Leaving office, his first task was "to recover the financial losses he had endured as governor," which included aid to soldier families.[21]

Blair's words in public life, dating from 1845, originate from a human rights activist: opponent of capital punishment; advocate for expanded voting rights; a conscience that could not countenance the "great moral, social and intellectual evil" of human bondage; a commitment to destroy that "relic of barbarism."[22] His defense of liberty and equal opportunity extended outside the four years of war. He had chosen to relocate to Michigan in 1841, "his enthusiasm for the West"[23] arising out of several factors, including the foundation laid by the Northwest Ordinance of 1787, a system of governance replete with "humanitarian provisions" under a "law of highest hope and modern ideals."[24] This "idealistic charter" yielded "a new and unique democratic order in the future Midwest, one unequaled in world

19.   Robert C. Harris, *Austin Blair of Michigan: A Political Biography* (East Lansing: Michigan State University, 1969) (Ph.D. dissertation), 41.

20.   Austin Blair, *Address in Honor of Loyal Governors: Their Claim to Grateful Remembrance*, Reunion, New York, Grand Army of the Republic, February 1888.

21.   Stephen D. Engle, *Gathering to Save a Nation: Lincoln and the Union's War Governors* (Chapel Hill: University of North Carolina Press, 2016), 440.

22.   John W. Quist ed., *Michigan's War: The Civil War in Documents* (Athens: Ohio University Press, 2019), 14, presenting the 1854 Republican party platform written in Blair's hometown and to which he contributed such phrases.

23.   Harris, *Austin Blair*, 17, the term coming to mean the Midwest.

24.   *History of the Ordinance of 1787 and the Old Northwest Territory* (Marietta: Northwest Territory Celebration Commission, 1937), 15, 83.

history."[25] At its centennial, Blair referred to this measure as "[t]he great Ordinance," one built on the bedrock truth in the Declaration of Independence that "all men are created equal."[26] His life's service sought to extend its greatness throughout America and defeat slavery advocates, such as John C. Calhoun of South Carolina who held that the proposition was "the most false and dangerous of all political errors."[27]

Calhoun was known as a powerful orator. Blair was equally so but consistently on behalf of equal rights, beginning with his first appearance on a statewide platform in 1846: "He made an earnest report in favor of abolishing the color distinction as related to the elective franchise."[28] Two years later, he "refused longer to affiliate with the Whig party, because of its refusal to endorse in convention any anti-slavery sentiment. He joined the Free-soil movement, and was a delegate to their convention."[29] He "was one of the few who offered support" for women's suffrage during this era.[30] His charismatic speaking was regularly reported: "The people were always eager to hear him. He was fervid in manner and clear and cogent in argument.[31] Typical was

25.   Jon K. Lauck, *The Good Country: A History of the American Midwest, 1800-1900* (Norman: University of Oklahoma Press, 2022), 20.

26.   *The Semi-Centennial Celebration of the Organization of the University of Michigan, June 26-30, 1887* (Ann Arbor: University of Michigan, 1888), 75ff. For his view of the ordinance, see Abraham Lincoln, Speech at Peoria, Illinois, Oct. 16, 1854, in Roy P. Basler ed., *The Collected Works of Abraham Lincoln*, Vol. II (New Brunswick: Rutgers University Press, 1953), 247, 249 ("*CW*").

27.   Richard K. Cralle ed., *The Works of John C. Calhoun*, Vol. IV (New York: D. Appleton & Co. 1854), 507.

28.   S.D. Bingham, *Early History of Michigan with Biographies of State Officers, Members of Congress, Judges and Legislators* (Lansing: Thorp & Godfrey, 1888), 105.

29.   *Portrait and Biographical Album of the Members of the Legislature of the State of Michigan (1883). Thirty-Second Session* (Chicago: Chapman Bros., 1883), 145.

30.   Elizabeth A. Homer, *Pioneers, Reformers, & Millionaires* (Saline: McNaughton & Gunn, 2014), 56.

31.   Samuel W. Durant, *History of Ingham and Eaton Counties, Michigan, with Illustrations and Biographical Sketches of Their Prominent Men and Pioneers* (Philadelphia: D.W. Ensign & Co., 1880), 373.

the report at one mass meeting: "Hon. Austin Blair, of Jackson was then called for, who responded; and eloquently addressed the multitude two hours, being frequently interrupted by cheering applause."[32] Successor governor Henry H. Crapo believed he would suffer by comparison, since Blair was "one of the most eloquent and gifted men of our state."[33] Blair's obituary would cite how he "stood in the first rank" of orators and "to that gift he owed much of his success in public life."[34]

Coincident with the debut of *Lincoln*, a more complex thesis about the Union's war governors emerged. Sometimes obstructionist, sometimes petty, the chief executives generally worked with the Administration to win the war. The thesis posited that Lincoln did not so much outsmart these men as enlist them as partners. This characterization restored Blair and his peers to a semblance of competence.[35] On its heels appeared a rich study of how state leaders were pivotal to victory by cooperating with and "pushing" the president "toward greater national efforts." Blair, it offered, "the darling of the Michigan radicals," had given "Republicans their largest victories of any Northern state" at a crucial stage in 1862 and, declining a third term in 1864, left office no less popular, endorsed by the people for "his radicalism and his attention to the soldiers."[36] Perhaps, even, the loyal governors "were more important than generals."[37] Their reward: fading from memory into obscurity.[38]

The American Union held sacred space in Blair's heart. Secessionists contended that the states had united to form a national

---

32. *Hillsdale Standard*, Sept. 23, 1851, 2.

33. Martin D. Lewis, *Lumberman from Flint: The Michigan Career of Henry H. Crapo 1855-1869* (Detroit: Wayne State University Press, 1958), 162.

34. *DFP*, Aug. 6, 1894, 1.

35. William C. Harris, *Lincoln and the Union Governors* (Carbondale: Southern Illinois University Press, 2013), 1-3.

36. Engle, *Gathering*, 2, 248, 454,

37. Nigel Hamilton, *Lincoln vs. Davis: The War of the Presidents* (New York: Little, Brown & Co., 2024), 231.

38. Engle, *Gathering*, 481.

government in 1787–1789, and, thus, the states had the right to end this union if necessary. Blair countered that the Union was not a creation of the states but of the people. Indeed, he argued, the Founders made this self-evident in the Constitution when it affirmed how "We, the people," sought to form a more perfect Union. That Union was not a compact between autonomous political entities severable by the action of any one or number of them. The states were important, Blair affirmed, in that they were instruments by which the people governed themselves. But they were not of first rank; the Union of the people held that priority. Blair did not stand alone in this view, but no one else had more devotion to the idea of the indivisibility of the nation.

Blair's views on liberty and equality are now embedded in America's public policy. His unequivocal loyalty to Union is a clarion call to an intensely divided populace. This "radical of radicals" now stands in a different light on the 160th anniversary of the war for freedom he helped win. The Civil War master of irony best summarizes Blair's extremism:

> RADICALISM, n. The conservatism of to-morrow injected into the affairs of to-day.[39]

---

39. Ambrose Bierce, *The Collected Works of Ambrose Bierce, Vol. VII: The Devil's Dictionary* (New York: Neale Pub. Co., 1911), 275.

Editorial Note

This first of two volumes tracks Austin Blair from his first public statement until the end of the Civil War. It concludes with his reaction to the assassination of Abraham Lincoln, a blow that struck Blair personally. Volume II, scheduled for September 2026, will continue the story until the War Governor's voice went silent. Interspersed among these pages are selected quotations of Blair's. Little of his correspondence survives; sources have been sought far and wide. We are honored to have located and now publish more of his words than ever before.

As with all books in the series, this volume is available in hardcover (for durability), with a full index (to aid accessibility and reference) and bibliography (documenting all sources), footnoted (on the same page), with appendices that add supplementary material (a history lover's delight). They are to be readable while also maintaining standards of the highest scholarship, reflecting a kind of craft that does not sacrifice to commercialism. They each appear in proximity to the anniversary of the Battle of Antietam, where Michigan contributed mightily.[40]

Because such changes are inconsequential to the purpose, misspellings typically have been silently corrected and words in all caps generally revised. Brackets supply necessary explanations with conservative use of sic.

All errors are the responsibility of the undersigned.

—Jack Dempsey, editor

---

40.   Jack Dempsey & Brian James Egen. *Michigan at Antietam: The Wolverine State's Sacrifice on America's Bloodiest Day* (Charleston: The History Press, 2015).

RADICAL *of*
RADICALS

Part One

Austin Blair: Early Life

A ustin Blair (no middle name) descended from immigrants who first came from Scotland in 1718. His parents were George Blair, born November 29, 1786, in Massachusetts, a farmer by occupation, and Rhoda (Blackman), born October 5, 1790, in Peru, Berkshire County, Massachusetts. Austin was the oldest of four siblings: Sarah, born on March 21, 1821; Robert on April 2, 1825; and William Henry on January 22, 1831.[1] His paternal grandfather, "Capt[.] Robert Blair," was among the prisoners "taken in the sloop 'Retrieve' (privateer) off Casco Bay by the British ship 'Milford'" in 1777.[2]

Austin was born in a log house near Caroline, Tompkins County, New York, on Sunday, February 8, 1818. He attended the local "Common School" for four months during fall and winter, the remainder of the year spent doing farm work. At sixteen, he attended a "select school" in neighboring Tioga County, learning Latin and the

1. Emily Wilder Leavitt, *The Blair Family of New England* (Boston: David Clapp & Son, 1900), 24, 82, 113-117; U.S. Census, 1850, Caroline, Tompkins County, New York, 22. William's son, Austin J., born January 24, 1857, died February 1, 1862. George died December 20, 1869, Rhoda on July 8, 1874. They married on May 7, 1817, after her first husband died in the War of 1812. Leavitt, 82; findagrave.com; and https://www.tcpl.org/sites/default/files/content/archive/1860-74.pdf Their graves, "in the soil of the old homestead," *Portrait and Biographical Record of Genesee, Lapeer and Tuscola Counties, Michigan* (Chicago: Chapman Bros., 1892), 145; Leavitt, 114, appear to be at GPS coordinates 42.32015, -76.28173, on Smith Road west of Old 76 (County Road 115), Speedsville N.Y. The marker for George: "He came to this place in A.D. 1808 among the Pioneers and settled on the farm where he resided until his death, leaving a name unspotted in social and domestic life. This pillar was placed over a Father's grave by his grateful sons, Austin, Robert and William Henry Blair, A.D. 1872." http://tompkins.nygenweb.net/cemeteries/blair_cem.htm
2. *Massachusetts Soldiers and Sailors of the Revolutionary War* [Vol. 2] (Boston: Wright & Potter Printing Co., 1896), 120; *Lineage Book, National Society of the Daughters of the American Revolution*, Vol. XLVII (Washington: Judd & Detweiler, 1919), 369; Charles E. Claghorn, "Maine Privateers during the Revolutionary War" in *Maine History* 28, 4 (1989), 214; findagrave.com

natural sciences. In fall 1834, he began college preparatory studies at Cazenovia Seminary (later College), then entered Hamilton College in Oneida County. In the middle of his junior year, he transferred to Union College in Schenectady and graduated in 1839 with an LL.D. degree. He excelled academically; a grade report specifies ninety-nine percent attendance, perfect conduct, and one hundred in each of three courses including Intellectual Philosophy. The college was led by president Eliphalet Nott, a known abolitionist.[3] Entering the law office of Sweet & Davis at Owego, New York, he was admitted to practice in Tioga County in 1841.[4]

Both parents were "active opponents of slavery." George was of a "thinking turn of mind" and "a man of great mental power," "eminently religious" and "thoroughly conscientious in everything." He was "a constant reader of history and all the best literature." Rhoda "was full of benevolence and kindness of heart" and "more vigorous and more ambitious." Their eldest child enjoyed "the simple and unalloyed pleasures of rustic life" and remembered his boyhood as "happily and innocently spent."[5] The Blair family imbued the religious fervor of the "Burned-over District," the area of western New York where religious fervor spawned new sects (Mormons) and renewed emphasis on moral and religious improvement. Evangelical enthusiasm embraced abolition, and no other part of America would "prove to be so thoroughly and constantly sensitive to antislavery agitations." Unitarianism flourished. The Erie Canal invited newcomers; it also

---

3. C. Van Santvoord, *Memoirs of Eliphalet Nott, D.D. LL.D. For Sixty-Two Years President of Union College* (New York: Sheldon & Co., 1876), 211-215.

4. *The Red Book for the Thirtieth Legislature of the State of Michigan, 1879-80*, 493; Jean J.L. Fennimore, "Austin Blair: Pioneer Lawyer, 1818-1844" in *Michigan History*, Vol. 48, No. 1 (Mar. 1964), 1-5 ("Fennimore I"); *First Fifty Years of Cazenovia Seminary, 1825-1875* (New York: Nelson & Phillips, 1877), 84; Thomas H. Fearey, *Union College Alumni in the Civil War, 1861-1865* (Schenectady: n.p., 1915), 4; Biographical Sketch, Union College Sheet No. 127, Austin Blair Papers, Burton Historical Collection, Detroit Public Library. William H. Seward was an 1820 Union graduate.

5. Biographical Sketch; Fennimore I, 1-2.

carried them farther west when opportunity grew scarce. As economic conditions tightened, the next generation found security elusive and "were making for Michigan or Illinois" to build the kind of life their parents had founded.[6]

Austin became restive; Illinois seemed attractive; but an uncle's move with family to Jackson, Michigan, where the first settler came from Tioga County, proved most appealing. The state was "then very new" with fresh opportunity, and Jackson was home to Michigan's first antislavery newspaper, the *American Freedmen*, founded in 1838. After marrying Persis Lyman, a humble farmer's daughter, on February 18, 1841, the couple moved in June. He was immediately admitted to the bar in all the courts of the state and commenced practicing. Within a year they relocated twenty-five miles northwest to Eaton Rapids. Here, in 1842, he was first elected to public office, as county clerk.[7]

Here, also, he encountered the first in a succession of profound personal tragedies. He had felt "the better and the happier man" for having met and married Persis. Their union was "the fulfilling of my brightest hopes." They lost baby Gertrude to illness in September 1842. Then, his wife died on January 29, 1844, at age twenty-four, after an illness of three months. He was left with "regrets for the loss of her whom I loved more than myself."[8]

Blair returned to Jackson, resumed practicing law, and became an instructor at Michigan Central College in nearby Spring Arbor.[9]

6.   Whitney R. Cross, *The Burned-over District: The Social and Intellectual History of Enthusiastic Religion in Western New York, 1800-1850* (New York: Harper & Row, 1950), 141, 226. For Unitarianism in America, see Sydney E. Ahlstrom, *A Religious History of the American People* (New Haven: Yale University Press, 2004), 388-402; also see W.C. Harriman, "The Late Gov. Blair of Michigan" in *The Unitarian: A Monthly Magazine of Liberal Christianity*, Vol. IX (Boston: George H. Ellis, 1894).

7.   Biographical Sketch; Fennimore I, 5-6, 8, 10-12, 15; Durant, 363.

8.   Fennimore I, 11, 17; Blair Papers, Burton.

9.   Because of the school's "strong abolitionist stance" and admission of women and blacks. The college was renamed upon its move to Hillsdale. As state senator, Blair is credited with sponsoring legislation that enabled the institution to exist.

He dove deeper into politics, rejecting the Democratic party position on slavery.[10] In the 1844 presidential election, he supported Whig party candidate Henry Clay of Kentucky in a losing race with Democrat James K. Polk of Tennessee. Despite the outcome, the campaign launched Blair's "reputation as an effective public speaker."[11] His growing notoriety gained him a spot on the Whig ticket for a seat in the Michigan House of Representatives in fall 1845. Victorious, he attended the opening session of the legislature in January 1846 in Detroit, then the state capital, in the capitol located at Griswold and State streets. Blair was among the legislators who could brag of having attended the final session prior to relocation of the capital to Lansing. He was named a member of the Committee on the Judiciary, with the primary task of statutory revision. One of those changes was elimination of capital punishment, giving Blair another bragging right. Ever since, Michigan has staked its claim to be the first English-speaking jurisdiction to eliminate the death penalty.[12]

The House had twice rejected such legislation, and Blair played a key role when the measure came over from the Senate. He proposed an amendment to require the penalty for first degree murder to be solitary confinement for life at hard labor. It passed 25-9, heading off an amendment to restore death as a penalty "as the jury in their verdict shall designate." He was named to the conference committee, which made no further changes before final approval. Blair had "refused to

Arlan K. Gilbert, *Hillsdale College: The Civil War Experience* (Hillsdale College Press, 1994), xv, 16, 22-23 n.16, 50, 120ff. Blair was professor of law on the 1850 faculty. *Catalogue of the Officers & Students of the Michigan Central College at Spring Arbor, for the Year Ending July 1850* (Jackson: R.S. Cheney, 1850), 4.
10.   The 1844 platform asserted "that all efforts, by abolitionists or others, made to induce Congress to interfere with questions of slavery" were to be opposed. https://www.presidency.ucsb.edu/documents/1844-democratic-party-platform
11.   Charles V. DeLand, *DeLand's History of Jackson County, Michigan* (n.p.: B.F. Bowen, 1903), 275; *Portrait and Biographical Record of Genesee, Lapeer and Tuscola Counties*, 145.
12.   Bryan Vila & Cynthia Morris eds., *Capital Punishment in the United States: A Documentary History* (Westport: Greenwood Press, 1997), xxxviii.

be beaten and finally achieved victory." He counted it "among the best pieces of work to which it has been my good fortune to contribute."[13]

Blair also made a report on behalf of the Judiciary Committee in favor of striking "white" from the state constitution as applied to qualification to be an elector. He argued (*infra*): "the time has come when the colored men of America should be allowed to assume their rightful position as citizens of the republic, upon an equality in all respects with their white brethren."

As voting by women, Blair was quoted as saying "he should make no objection to females voting if the right was asked for."[14] In March 1846, Blair attended a lecture in the capitol by Ernestine Louise (Potowski) Rose of New York City. Born in Poland to a Jewish rabbi, Rose was one of America's leading suffragists. Blair took the opportunity to speak out in favor of women's suffrage—one of the first Michigan leaders to publicly offer support.[15]

These were high points, as was his marriage to Elisabeth Pratt on May 25 as the session concluded. She died eleven months later on April 28, 1847, followed in August by their four-month-old child, James Hunter Blair. In the 1848 election, Blair lost his seat to the Democrat candidate. When the Whig party chose slaveholder Zachary Taylor as its presidential choice, Blair joined the Free Soil party.[16] He attended its national convention in Buffalo in August, was appointed among

---

13.   *Journal of the House of Representatives of the State of Michigan, 1846* (Detroit: Bagg & Harmon, 1846), 575-577; Paul Finkelman & Martin J. Hershock eds., *The History of Michigan Law* (Athens: Ohio University Press, 2006), 31; Autobiography, Blair Papers, Burton, 5 (written between 1877-1881); Vivian Thomas Messner, *The Public Life of Austin Blair, War Governor of Michigan (1863-1894)* (Detroit: Wayne State University) (Master's thesis), Appendix.

14.   Jean Joy L. Fennimore, Austin Blair: Political Idealist, 1845-1860" in *Michigan History*, Vol. 48, No. 2 (June 1964), 130, 135 ("Fennimore II"), quoting *Detroit Daily Advertiser*, May 4, 1846 ("*DDA*").

15.   Homer, 56.

16.   He also ran as Free Soil candidate for lieutenant-governor. Theodore C. Smith, *The Liberty and Free Soil Parties in the Northwest* (New York: Longmans, Green & Co., 1897), 201-202. Walt Whitman was delegate to the 1848 convention of the Free Soil party.

the twelve official delegates from Michigan, and served as a member of the committee that nominated Martin Van Buren for president.[17] Taylor won, and Blair was defeated for election as probate judge on the Free Soil ticket.[18] One in seven Michigan voters, however, chose Van Buren, a major increase from the 6.53 percent garnered four years earlier by the Liberty Party.

Fortunes turned for the better. He married widow Sarah Louisa Horton (Ford) on February 16, 1849, in a marriage that would last till death. They were blessed with five children:

- George Henry, born on April 10, 1850, died April 11, 1904
- Nelly, born in 1852, died after 10 months
- Charles Austin, born April 10, 1854, died August 30, 1912
- Frederick Johnson, born in December 1860, died in 1943
- Austin True, born on January 27, 1864, died in 1944

On August 15, 1850, a convention concluded its two-month long proceedings with a proposed new constitution; the voters approved it on November 5, 1850. Blair had been a Whig party candidate for delegate from Jackson County, but Democrats elected their full slate. He ran for attorney general but lost to the Democrat.[19]

At the national level, the "Compromise of 1850" failed to settle sectional differences over slavery. That congressional package strengthened fugitive slave recovery procedures; abolitionists such as Blair detested it. He was elected county prosecutor in 1852, the year of Nelly's death, serving from 1853–1854.[20] Despite the new federal law, he did nothing to aid the return of escapees into bondage. His reputation and influence with the public in Jackson County continued to grow. A state senator from the area wrote:

---

17. *Michigan Liberty Press*, Aug. 25, 1848.
18. *History of Jackson County, Michigan* (Chicago: Inter-State Pub. Co., 1881), 334; *Deland's History*, 296.
19. *DeLand's History*, 145, 296.
20. Id. 297, 335.

He has great weight with the people [and] from his character and position can do more, probably, than almost any other man to quiet or inflame the public mind .... [H]is ambition far exceeds his avarice and he is honest. Satisfy him a thing is right and you have gone far to get his cooperation.[21]

Events in 1854 proved significant. On January 23, the "Kansas-Nebraska bill" repealing restrictions on slavery in the federal territories made its debut in the U.S. Senate. It passed in March; the House of Representatives approved it in May;[22] and President Franklin Pierce signed it on May 30. Friends of liberty were outraged.[23]

In Michigan, the law prompted a fusion among those of differing party identities who opposed any extensions of slavery. A key step occurred on February 21, 1854, in an evening meeting held in Blair's office in Jackson among leaders of the Free Soil movement. Present besides Blair were Whig editors and figures who would rise to prominence, including Kinsley S. Bingham, as governor, and Isaac P. Christiancy, as U.S. senator. They agreed to prepare the ground for merger of the party into a new "fusion" organization for the fall canvass.[24]

---

21. Hershock, *Paradox*, 89, 248 n.23.
22. Blair met with leading citizens in Detroit on May 23, the day after House passage, advocating a coalition to oppose slavery's extension. Fennimore II, 147.
23. Blair "in a masterly and convincing manner" spoke on March 3 at the Jackson courthouse on "the falsity and danger" of the measure, prompting "frequent applause of the audience." Id. 144, quoting the antislavery *Jackson Citizen*, Mar. 4, 1854. See Floyd Benjamin Streeter, *Political Parties in Michigan, 1837-1860: An Historical Study of Political Issues and Parties in Michigan from the Admission of the State to the Civil War* (Lansing: Michigan Historical Commission, 1918).
24. William Stocking ed., *Under the Oaks: Commemorating the Fiftieth Anniversary of the Founding of the Republican Party at Jackson* (Detroit: Detroit Tribune, 1904), 26; *Livingstone's History of the Republican Party*, Vol. I (Detroit: Wm. Livingstone, 1900), 21. William Livingstone attained prominence in business and political affairs in Detroit and is commemorated by the lighthouse on Belle Isle. In this account of the meeting, he indicated "I remember ..." but would then have been a minor. In 1860, Loomis & Whitwell's Bank Building on the south side of Main Street housed the Blair & Gibson law office. *Loomis &*

Calls for joinder culminated at a meeting in Blair's hometown of Jackson on July 6. He served as chairman of the reception committee, called the session to order, and served on the platform committee alongside Jacob M. Howard, its chairman. Other advocates for freedom who were present included Zachariah Chandler and Thomas W. Ferry—all three would become U.S. Senators. The committee's work product, grounded on anti-slavery principles, began by asserting the institution of slavery "is a great moral, social, and intellectual evil" and a "violation of the rights of man." It contended that the founders sought in the Constitution "not to promote but to prevent the spread of slavery." Blair also presented a report supporting more economical administration of state government and greater accountability for public officials. The assembly approved the platform, including "Republican" as the party identity, and approved a slate for November. Blair was "an active member" and "one of five prominent men" who helped cement unity through his speeches.[25]

After the founding of the Republican party, a call went out for a convention to be held in Marshall for the purpose of nominating a Whig ticket. Blair and others who supported the outcome of the Republican convention attended this October meeting, helping to quash a rival slate. Instead, the delegates adopted an address that appealed for support by Whig voters of the new ticket, including these sentiments:

> We do now declare that we regard slavery as an evil from every point of view, debasing to free labor, antagonistic to free institutions, a barrier to high progress and advancement, and a blot upon our country's escutcheon. We are unalterably opposed

Talbott's Jackson City Directory, and Business Mirror, for 1860-61 (Detroit: George W. Hawes, 1860), 16.

25.   George N. Fuller ed., *Michigan, A Centennial History of the State and Its People*, Vol. I (Chicago: Lewis Pub. Co., 1939), 309; Fennimore II, 148, 150-151; Hershock, *Paradox*, 128; Henry M. Utley & Byron M. Cutcheon, *Michigan as a Province, Territory and State, the Twenty-Sixth Member of the Federal Union* (New York: Publishing Society of Michigan, 1906), 381-382.

to its extension over one inch of territory now free. ... We declare our opposition to the admission of another Slave State into the Union. We avow our solemn determination to exercise every constitutional right to check the encroachments of slavery and to spread far and wide the blessings of humanity and freedom.

Blair subscribed his name to this statement.[26]

Bingham won the fall election as governor, and both houses of the legislature seated Republican majorities. Blair was elected state senator. His committee assignments included Enrolled Bills, Public Instruction, and State Affairs, and he became majority leader. An avowed foe of the 1850 Fugitive Slave act, he sought to undermine its effectiveness by voting for two measures that became law on February 13, 1855. One, "An act to protect the rights and liberties of the inhabitants of this State," was colloquially known as the Personal Liberty law (the text is provided in *Michigan's War*, 17-18). The other sought "to prohibit the use of the common jails and other public buildings in the several counties for the detention of persons claimed as fugitive slaves." Under these statutes, it became the duty of the county prosecutors "whenever any inhabitant of this State is arrested or claimed as a fugitive slave ... diligently and faithfully to use all lawful means to protect and defend every such person so arrested or claimed as a fugitive slave" in order that "all persons so arrested and claimed as fugitive slaves, shall be entitled to all the benefits of the writ of habeas corpus and of trial by jury." Fines and jail time were levied for anyone who would falsely claim a person to be enslaved. A joint resolution

---

26. General Committee, *Proceedings at Celebration of the Fiftieth Anniversary of the Birth of the Republican Party at Jackson, Michigan, July 6, 1904; together with a History of the Republican Party in Michigan* (Detroit: Detroit Tribune, 1904), 60 (paragraphs omitted). For an earlier account, mentioning Blair spoke to the convention, see Hovey K. Clark, *Under the Oaks. The Record of the First Republican State Convention. Which Was Held in Jackson, July 6, 1854. The Events Which Led To It, and the Results That Followed. Republished from the Detroit Post and Tribune of July 6, 1879*, 16.

"respecting Slavery in the Territories" also passed, which Blair helped craft (see Appendix). A law to protect women's property rights in marriage was also enacted.[27]

In 1856, Blair supported John C. Fremont as the unsuccessful Republican candidate for president. From 1856 to 1860, the Jackson lawyer was out of public office and not a candidate. He was too busy maintaining a practice and serving as an active party leader. He was a delegate and twice a speaker at the Republican state convention in Marshall in July 1856. When prominent Republican speakers gave addresses at a Kalamazoo gathering in August, Blair was there along with Chandler and Howard—and a lawyer from Illinois, Abraham Lincoln.

Blair served as both temporary and permanent chairman of the state party convention in Detroit in August 1858. His views remained consistent: "No more Slave Territories and no more Slave States." He paved the way for Republican Moses Wisner to win nomination for governor. The first substantive action by the convention was an informal ballot for the top post. Blair received thirteen votes, prompting the next recorded action:

> On the announcement of this result, Mr. Blair assured the Convention that he was not, and did not desire to be, a candidate for the nomination, and requested that his name be withdrawn. The Convention then proceeded ....

Other candidates allowed their names to remain in contention, but Blair's decision helped increase Wisner's tally from fifty-five to ninety-eight in the next count. The "formal ballot" then selected the Pontiac native, who went on to win that fall.[28]

Republicans swept control, holding majorities in the legislature,

---

27. *History of Michigan Law*, 54. Blair also managed a major railroad reform bill that addressed constituent concerns. Hershock, *Paradox*, 136-138.
28. Stocking, 78; Fennimore II, 161; Lansing State Republican ("*LSR*"), Aug. 24, 1858, 2.

the governor's office, and every seat in the congressional delegation. Blair did "yeoman's service in this campaign" by contributing
his eloquence and energy. As a "popular orator" he had no superior.
Michigan, said a friendly newspaper, "has no more effective or gifted
son."[29] Internal party politics caused him to be passed over in January
1859 when the Republican-controlled legislature chose ex-Governor
Bingham as U.S. senator. Biding his time, Blair continued to practice
law in Jackson and serve as a loyal party member.[30]

At the Republican National Convention at Chicago in May 1860,
Blair attended as delegate and chairman of the Michigan delegation.
He was named to the Committee on Resolutions, reflecting his prominence as a leader and communicator. The delegation had pledged
its support to presidential nominee William H. Seward of New
York, whose abolitionist credentials were undisputed. Blair seconded
Seward's nomination.[31] The delegation delivered all its votes faithfully
to Seward on three consecutive ballots until Abraham Lincoln secured
a majority. As the delegations fell in behind the new nominee, Blair
announced to the convention that Michigan would provide Lincoln
a 25,000-vote majority in November.[32] He was appointed to the
National Committee.[33] His leadership and loyalty to the Republican
cause won him the party's gubernatorial nomination on the first ballot
at its Detroit convention on June 8. Joining him for lieutenant-governor was James Birney of Bay City, son of the noted abolitionist.[34]

Blair held qualifications to serve as governor in certain respects:

---

29. Fennimore II, 159, quoting *DDA*, Oct. 4, 1856.

30. Id. 161-162.

31. Stocking, 79; *Proceedings of the First Three Republican National Conventions of 1856, 1860 and 1864* (Minneapolis: Charles W. Johnson, 1893), 148.

32. Actual margin of 23,323 was close to Blair's prediction. *Manual for the Use of the Legislature of the State of Michigan, 1875-76* (Lansing: W.S. George & Co., 1875), 230.

33. *Proceedings of the First Three Republican National Conventions*, 166.

34. George S. May, *Michigan and the Civil War Years 1860-1866, A Wartime Chronicle* (Lansing: Michigan Civil War Centennial Observance Commission, 1964), 2.

as administrator at the county level; service in both houses, familiar with the legislative process; and excellent communication skills. On the other hand, at forty-two he had no experience in administration of a large organization. Familiarity with military affairs—an attribute not seen as relevant in 1860—was perhaps his greatest shortcoming.

Voters could see similarities between Lincoln and Blair: born in log cabins; lawyers by profession; tall and gaunt; good communicators; former Whigs; Midwesterners. Both had gained renown for their opposition to extending human bondage in America. Blair went further and had publicly supported equal rights for African Americans. A party newspaper called him "as devoted a friend of freedom as breathes."[35]

Campaigning for personal office in that era was typically viewed as the realm of demagogues, not statesmen. But Blair was committed to a full airing of the pressing issues of the day, hoping the people would share his principles and vote for him. He did not shy away or hide behind a tradition of letting others do electioneering. He personally visited "every important county in the state." Chandler and Blair often appeared together: "[e]arly in the season they commenced stumping the State, and their efforts have been continued and indefatigable," speaking up to six times per week. The Detroit *Daily Advertiser* singled out Blair:

> During the campaign he has endeared himself still more strongly by the courage, fidelity, and ability with which he has discussed all the questions at issue. He has made a gallant fight, and he should receive the approval of the people.[36]

An "October surprise" might have cost him the approval of some voters. On the 31st, the *Free Press* reported that Blair had spoken of

35. Fennimore II, 165-166, quoting *DDA*, Nov. 2, 1860.
36. Id. Blair's election was also a repudiation of nativism. Eric Foner, *Free Soil, Free Labor, Free Men: The Ideology of the Republican Party Before the Civil War* (London: Oxford University Press, 1971), 258.

a "class of people whom he called the 'dirty Dutch'" and would expel from the country. Blair issued a denial.[37] In the statewide results of November 6, he received 87,780 votes (56.7%) to defeat Democratic party candidate and former governor John S. Barry, who tallied 67,053 (43.3%). It was a resounding victory. The Republican ticket gained the majority in the Democratic stronghold of Detroit, with Blair winning 4,406 to 4,046. In the Michigan senate, the new governor would find his party holding a 30-2 majority.[38] Lincoln won the national electoral vote to become president, thus installing a fellow Republican in the White House.

Winning ushered in difficult challenges for both leaders. On December 20, South Carolina approved an ordinance of secession grounded on the right of property in slaves, the first of eleven states to withdraw from the Union and form the Confederate States of America. Blair entered office to find "an empty treasury and a scattered, ill-equipped militia." If civil war came, he would have the ultimate responsibility to raise manpower and send off troops adequately prepared. Under article 5 of the 1850 Constitution, Blair had overall martial authority:

> Sec. 4. The Governor shall be commander-in-chief of the military and naval forces, and may call out such forces to execute the laws, to suppress insurrections and to repel invasions.

Section 12 contemplated his service under fire:

> When the Governor shall be out of the State in time of war, at the head of a military force thereof, he shall continue commander-in-chief of all the military force of the state.[39]

37. *DFP*, Oct. 31, 1860, 2.
38. Martin J. Hershock, "Copperheads and Radicals: Michigan Partisan Politics during the Civil War Era, 1860-1865" in *Michigan Historical Review*, Vol. 18, No. 1 (Spring 1992), 37 n.13.
39. *The Revised Constitution of the State of Michigan, Adopted in Convention,*

Events would make clear that Blair never shrank from his role and took "great pride in marshaling for war, especially if it were to lead to slavery's abolition."[40] His inaugural address opposed acceding to Southern demands: "I am not willing that the State should be humiliated by compliance with this demand, accompanied by threats of violence and war. ... It is not concession that is needed now; it is patriotic firmness and decision."

War came with the attack and surrender of Fort Sumter in Charleston Harbor in mid-April. Lincoln called up the militia; Michigan's quota was one regiment. Blair believed that a broader effort was needed to marshal the Union's might and almost immediately began pressing Washington for authority to enlist more troops. He attended a meeting of governors in Cleveland on May 4, 1861, convened by Ohio's William Dennison, "to pressure Lincoln and the War Department to take more vigorous measures." Among the attendees was George B. McClellan, recently appointed to head Ohio's troops. At conference's end, the governors agreed to send their concerns on the conduct of the war to the president.[41] Anticipating a longer war than most thought would transpire, the governor "took independent action and established a camp of instruction at Fort Wayne in Detroit" to train additional units.[42]

Because of its proximity to Canada, some regarded the border and the Great Lakes as a frontier to be defended against hostile British and Confederate action. Blair recommended that the legislature appropriate enough funds for "a powerful war marine" to defend the state. His

August 15, 1850 (Lansing: R.W. Ingals, 1850), 11. Blair did not head up a military force but did inspect troops out of state.

40.   Engle, *Gathering to Save a Nation*, 28.

41.   Harris, *Lincoln and the Union Governors*, 23-26. McClellan confirmed the conference was "for the purpose of urging on military preparations." George B. McClellan, *McClellan's Own Story: The War for the Union* (New York: Charles L. Webster & Co., 1887), 46.

42.   Jean J.L. Fennimore, "Austin Blair: Civil War Governor, 1861-1862" in *Michigan History*, Vol. 49, No. 3 (Sept. 1965), 193, 202, 206 ("Fennimore III").

attentiveness to the needs of Michigan's units in the field did not flag, and he made appointments as officers regardless of party affiliation.[43]

Over the next four years, Blair would find his primary responsibility to be leading and fulfilling Michigan's commitment to the Union war effort. In 1862, he stood for reelection in a year of major setbacks on the battlefront, especially in the Eastern Theater. Union victory at the Battle of Antietam resulted in a new federal emancipation policy. Some voters chose to sit out the race in protest; deployed soldiers were not able to vote.[44] Blair's success at the polls, receiving 68,716 votes (52.5%) to Democrat Byron G. Stout's total of 62,102 (47.5%), enabled continued vigorous prosecution of the war. When he stepped down in January 1865, defeat of the Confederacy was at hand.

Blair's second term witnessed significant Union victories at Gettysburg and Vicksburg in July 1863, battles in which Michigan troops served with distinction. He received personal notice when elected to honorary membership in the Amphictyon Society, a literary group, at Hillsdale College.[45] The College awarded him the degree of Doctor of Laws on June 18, 1864.[46]

Financial challenges, the pressures of office, the prospect of being chosen by the legislature for the U.S. Senate, and precedent contributed to his decision not to run again. Republican successor Henry H. Crapo won election handily by a 55-45 margin, receiving over 91,000 votes. Voters had endorsed Blair's conduct of the war. What they did not comprehend was his financial sacrifice: Blair frequently advanced personal funds in aid of his duties out of an annual salary of $1,000.

Blair left office with one final speech to the legislature and the people. It was a triumphant valedictory, with prospects then bright for

43. Fennimore III, 210, 212.
44. Total 1860 gubernatorial tally: 154,833; for 1862 during deployment: 130,818.
45. *History of the Amphictyon Society of Hillsdale College, Hillsdale, Michigan* (Chicago: Smith & Colbert, 1890), 63. It appears to be the first such honorific, on Oct. 19, 1863.
46. *First Quinquennial Record of the Alumni Association of Hillsdale College* (Hillsdale: Frank Sands & Co., 1876), 33.

military triumph, aided by stellar performances of Michigan's troops, and the future of the nation more tangible than ever before as full embodiment of the values he held dear.

The murder of President Lincoln in April caused Blair to set down words infused with anger and vengeance. Whether he delivered them from a speaker's podium is unclear. What is definite: the assassination confirmed Blair's long-held views about a society based on racial supremacy and oppression: "let it perish," he vowed.

The war and its immediate aftermath left Blair's health "withered."[47] What of his appearance? No writing appears to be descriptive, so perhaps the best way to judge his physical presence is by studying Alvah Bradish's portrait in the Michigan Senate chamber and Edward Clark Potter's bronze statue of him on Capitol square. The Bradish portrait, painted from life during the war, is informative. He left office at nearly forty-seven, his black hair and beard streaked with gray, his eyes dark, probably dark brown. He appears to be a slender man. His height might be judged by a comparison to the furnishings in the portrait, including the sword. He was probably above medium height.[48] His "powerful voice" influenced how he was seen: "slightly built, intense and nervous in manner, Blair gave the appearance of a devout crusader."[49] Many described him as an impassioned, seasoned, and persuasive orator, so his voice likely carried without aid to the edges of large gatherings. One who first heard him in 1848 wrote: "Austin Blair was always a captivating speaker." His style depended upon but went beyond logic: "There was enough of the poet in his nature to make his words have a thrilling effect upon his sympathetic listeners."[50]

His faith sustained him during the dark days of the Civil War.

---

47.   Fennimore III, 208.
48.   Credit Kerry Kona Chartkoff, Emeritus Michigan State Capitol Historian.
49.   Hesseltine, 48, 84, 116 (without citation).
50.   E.W. Barber, *Reminiscences of Governor Austin Blair*, Blair Papers, Burton. Barber lived in Jackson, held many public offices, and was engaged on Michigan's first Free Soil paper.

Blair's religion "centered on the Golden Rule" as a Unitarian, admitting to connection "with a Society of that denomination, in which I take great interest." He "frequently delivered addresses from the pulpit in the absence of the minister." Embracing this branch of Christian theology, Blair found in it a home for his conviction that "truth is better than any fiction wherever found."[51] His public statements referred to Providence, Almighty God, Heavenly Father, "our Creator," "us as a Christian people," and "Thanksgiving and Praise." He held these beliefs constant during many dark days.

Blair's "penchant for candid honesty" and adherence to "strong convictions" about American society and government carried him to the summit of state power during the nation's deepest crisis. His devotion required personal sacrifice, affiliation based on principle "with five different political parties," and abiding faith in victories not easily achieved.[52] In important ways, Blair was truly a "radical of radicals." How would he and his reputation fare in the tumultuous post-war years?

That verdict will come in the forthcoming companion volume spanning from summer 1865 until Blair's passing at age seventy-six.

---

51.   Leavitt, 116; Biographical Sketch, final page, Blair Papers, Burton; dated between 1877-1881, "Descriptive List of the Papers of Governor Austin Blair" in *Michigan History Magazine*, Vol. I (Lansing: Michigan Historical Commission, 1917), 133.
52.   Messner, ii.

Chronology

1818 born February 8th, Caroline, Tompkins County, New York State

1839 graduation, Union College, Schenectady, New York

1841 married Persis Lyman, February 18th

1841 moved to Jackson, Michigan, in June, commencing law practice

1842 daughter Gertrude died September 13th, age 7 months
elected Eaton county clerk

1844 wife Persis died January 29th
moved back to Jackson

1845 elected to Michigan House of Representatives, November 4th, Whig party

1846 served in House of Representatives, January 5th–May 18th
married Elisabeth Pratt in Lorain County, Ohio, May 25th

1847 wife Elisabeth died on April 28th
son James Hunter Blair died, age 1 month
defeated in election for Michigan Senate, Whig party

1848 attended National Free Soil Convention, Buffalo, August 9th–10th
defeated in election for probate judge, Free Soil party, November 7th

1849 married Sarah Louisa Ford, February 16th

1850 son George Henry born on April 10th
defeated in election for attorney general, Free Soil party, May 6th

1851 daughter Nelly born on October 10th

1852 daughter Nelly died on August 14th
elected county prosecutor, Whig party, November 2nd

1854   hosted conference to discuss fusion, February 21st
        son Charles Austin born on April 10th
        attended anti-slavery convention at Kalamazoo courthouse,
        June 21st
        helped found the Republican party "under the oaks," July
        5th–6th
        elected to Michigan Senate, November 7th; elected majority
        leader
1855   served in eighteenth legislature, 1855–1856
1860   delegate, delegation chairman, Republican National
        Convention, Chicago, May 16th–18th
        nominated for governor, Republican ticket, June 8th
        elected governor, November 6th
        son Frederick Johnson born on December 15th
1861   sworn in as governor, January 2nd
1862   re-elected Governor
1863   elected to honorary membership, Amphictyon Society,
        Hillsdale College
1864   son Austin True born January 27th
        delegate, delegation chairman, National Union Convention,
        Baltimore, June 7th–8th
1865   stepped down from governorship after two terms, January
        4th
        resumed practice of law in Jackson

Works

July 1845 *Fourth of July Oration, Tecumseh*

April 1846 *Report on Suffrage for Blacks*

February 1854 *Mass Convention*

June 1854 *Appeal to the People*

May 1860 *Speech at State Convention*
Speech of the Hour

June 1860 *Speech Accepting Nomination for Governor*

January 1861 *Inaugural Address*

February 1861 *Transmittal on the Peace Conference*
Transmittal on Military Readiness

April 1861 *Proclamation on Formation of Volunteer Regiments*
Official Letter to Secretary of War
Proclamation Convening Legislature
Remarks at Campus Martius

May 1861 *Remarks to Cleveland Crowd*
Message to Special Session

May/June 1861 *Communications on Recruitment*

July 1861 *Reply to Serenade*

September 1861	*Proclamation: Day of Humiliation, Prayer, and Fasting*
November 1861	*Proclamation of Thanksgiving*
December 1861	*Proclamation Convening Legislature*
January 1862	*Message to Special Session* *Transmittal of Legislative Items* *Messages on Approval of Legislation*
June 1862	*Official Letter to Secretary of War*
June-August 1862	*Recruiting Communiques*
August 1862	*Welcoming Address on Return of POW Orlando B. Willcox*
September 1862	*Address of the Loyal Governors to the President* *Speech on Renomination* *Speech in Washington*
November 1862	*Proclamation of Thanksgiving* *Address to the People on the Federal Draft*
January 1863	*Second Inaugural Address*
February 1863	*Transmittal to Legislature on Desertion*
March 1863	*Messages on Approval of Legislation*
May 1863	*Speeches to the Soldiers*

November 1863   *Proclamation of Thanksgiving*
                    Proclamation for Volunteers

December 1863   *Speech to 1st Michigan Colored Regiment*
                    Proclamation Convening Legislature

January 1864   *Message to the Legislature*

February 1864   *Messages on Approval of Legislation*
                    Call for Convention

June 1864   *Union National Convention*

July 1864   *Proclamation on Conscription*

September 1864   *Remarks at Michigan State Sanitary Fair*

November 1864   *Proclamation of Thanksgiving*

January 1865   *Retiring Governor's Message*

April 1865   *Remarks on the Assassination*

Part Two

Messages, Speeches, and Remarks—1845–1860

Oration at Tecumseh, Michigan
July 4, 1845

A few years after moving to the Midwest, Blair was invited to deliver a speech on the fourth of July in the Lenawee County town of Tecumseh. Only twenty-eight years of age, he was a candidate again for the Michigan House of Representatives—having lost in his first attempt by thirty votes in 1843.[53] *His remarks were lengthy, in keeping with expectations for a main speaker, and surveyed the history of the nation's founding, an epoch that had concluded when he was a boy. Blair's central themes were liberty, self-government, and America's unique position in world history. He regarded the revolutionary era as setting in motion a world where expanding liberty was possible and Americans were working to advance it. He invoked several faith-based metaphors. He did not exhibit a balanced view of the first peoples who had inhabited North America and instead emphasized benefits from European settlement: this aspect is largely omitted here. But his words go a long way toward revealing the sentiments with which Blair approached the impending crisis of the nation, in which Michiganders of all origins would participate on behalf of the Union. He did not mince words, employing one—traitor—that would be invoked again in 1861. These remarks were much more than a ceremonial paean to the past.*

Lenawee County had become notable for its strong anti-slavery sentiment. Two famed abolitionists, Elizabeth Margaret Chandler and Laura Smith Haviland, made it their home base, where the Logan Female Anti-Slavery Society had been founded. Haviland's Raisin Institute of Learning was the first integrated and co-educational school in Michigan. The Woodstock Manual Labor Institute, founded in 1844 by Prior Foster, an African American born free in Pennsylvania, operated as one of the first

---

53. Harris, *Austin Blair*, 26.

integrated schools in the nation. The area was an underground railroad haven.[54]

For ease of understanding, headings have been added along with appropriate edits in brackets. The length is approximately 3,600 words or 35-40 spoken minutes.

[Introduction]

The day of bonfires and illuminations has returned! The birth day of American liberty ever more glorious with each returning anniversary is with us! Freedom's gala day! Jubilee of liberty! We greet thee!

Fellow Citizens, we meet here today in the very heart of our beautiful peninsula, under the face of the broad canopy of heaven, with smiling fields and whispering groves all around us, to exchange congratulations upon the great subject of American independence. We meet as Americans. Citizens of one common country. We meet too as freemen—free as the pure air we breathe. This is a national day, a day of great memories, of glorious hopes. It brings with it, no tinge of sectional jealousy or party zeal. This great national festival is the common property of us all. And the liberty it heralds is the priceless inheritance of every man.

[Birth of the American Nation]

Well may we as Americans be proud of our country, and especially may we justly indulge ourselves on this day in enthusiastic reflections upon her glorious history and rising greatness. From what small beginnings has she arisen and how has she grown and prospered. Sixty nine years ago to day, there were assembled in the city of Philadelphia representatives from thirteen colonies of Great Britain, numbering scarcely two & a half millions of people, without a government & without resources. But they had felt the weight of the tyrant[']s hand and they had met to consult with regard to the public weal. In that

---

54. Carol E. Mull, *The Underground Railroad in Michigan* (Jefferson: McFarland & Co., 2010), 41-42, 84.)

assembly upon that memorable day, there arose a bold and fearless man, who uttered these never to be forgotten words, "Mr. President I move you Sir that these colonies <u>are</u> and of right ought to be free and independent States.["] And this was no rash youth, but a man of gray hairs and tried wisdom.

He spoke to men like himself. There was no pause there, no hesitation. They had counted the cost. The resolution passed with but a single dissenting voice. And the United States sprung into existence in a <u>breath</u>. They adopted that declaration which has been read in your hearing, setting forth very briefly but with wonderful force and earnestness the grounds of their separation from the mother country and their pledging to each other their lives[,] their fortunes[,] and their sacred honor in support of this declaration, appealed to arms and the God of battles to sustain them in the position they had taken.

So sublime a spectacle as this the whole history of the world does not furnish. So august a body of men never before assembled to decide any questions. How incalculable the responsibility assumed & how dreadful the rec[k]oning if they failed. And what could they expect but failure[?]

Whence were to come the men & the money whereby their paper declaration was to become an acknowledged fact in the world. Whence all the blood that must flow before the haughty king of the most powerful and proud nation in the world would yield to a comparative handful of his despised subjects in the almost unknown wilds of North America. How were the untrained, half armed soldiers of the feeble Colonies to fight & conquer the disciplined legions of the mother Country.

And yet there was no hesitation, no faltering in that assembly. They were willing to do & to dare everything for liberty. Adams & Jefferson & Hancock & Franklin were there & they could not be <u>slaves</u>. No eye in that Congress wandered and no heart quailed. They were grave but determined.

Well they knew the fearful struggle that must follow, but they also knew that truth and justice are the offspring of God & loved of him, they stopped not to measure strength & calculate chances. It was enough for them that they were to fight for freedom and the inalienable rights of man. There was no demagogue among <u>them</u>. Patriotism, self-sacrificing and deep belonged to the iron men of '76. And their reward is fame: the fame of the great and good. They shall not be forgotten upon this day, the day they have made. Their pure renown shall be spoke & sung in every town & hamlet throughout the wide extent of this great Country, whose chief glory is that it was their Country.

The brilliant success which attended the revolutionary struggle has become matter of history. The little band under the lead of Washington met and conquered the proud armies of England.

And the youthful Eagle of Newborn America spread her wings over the prostrate Lion of England.

Let there be a sunny spot in our memories to day for the soldier of the revolution, for though he was less conspicuous he acted a not less worthy part than the signers of the declaration. The last of those signers is gone and the last soldiers of the revolutionary army are fast hastening off the stage of life, and may God grant that the closing events of their lives may be as happy for them as their youthful deeds have [sic] glorious for us.

The great results of the revolutionary struggle are before us. They cannot be magnified or calculated even now. The feeble & disunited colonies have become one great and powerful nation. The experiment of Republican government has been tried & its efficiency fully proved. Liberty in the largest sense has been secured to all. A growth & prosperity entirely unequaled has been ours. The population have increased from two & a half to nearly twenty millions & our borders have extended into regions then unknown. Our ships are traversing every sea & our flag is found by the breezes of every clime. Cities & towns have sprung up in the middle of the dense forest as if by enchantment and magnificent improvements are seen on every hand. Wealth and civilization are here, where but a few years since were poverty and barbarism. The rapidly increasing strength and fast developing genius & enterprise of the modern republic is the wonder of the whole world.

What reason have we then to celebrate this day, not only with public manifestations of joy and festivity but with devout thankfulness to Almighty God. And it is fit that thus the day should be observed by us who are the sons of the Pilgrims. The men who fled from the oppressions of the old world & sought freedom in the wilderness of the new. They who established the first republic & set up the first altars on the wild New England shore amid prayers & thanksgivings to heaven. To them scarcely less than the men of 76 do we owe our national character. In truth they may be said to have laid broad & deep the foundations of liberty on this continent in its very infancy. Of a poor & despised sect, hunted & oppressed for conscience sake, they formed the heroic project of fleeing from their oppressors & seeking peace & freedom in the Western Wilds. They came without pomp or shout [?], and without war, a "little band they moored their bark on a stern & rock bound coast." And there at Plymouth rock in an unbroken wilderness amid ferocious wild beasts & merciless Indian Savages, they formed the first American Colony upon republican principles.

Their heroic examples have not been lost upon their descendants and the fires of liberty will not have ceased to glow here until degenerate sons have forgotten the fame of their <u>Pilgrim</u> <u>fathers</u>.

[The Union and Liberty]

Fellow Citizens. The fourth of July is a favourable point of observation. Standing at this point between the past & the future we may obtain very just views of the great system of popular liberty as it presents itself in this Country, the dangers to which [it] is liable and our peculiar duties in respect to it. For duties we have many & very important duties in regard to it.

It is true we can win no laurels on the battle field of a revolutionary war, but fields of scarcely less promise and of equal concern are ours. The priceless inheritance which has descended to us cannot be preserved & rendered valuable by shouts and huzzas alone.

The noble task of preserving those rights for which our fathers fought is bequeathed to us. They have left us a great and glorious country upon which nature has been bountiful of her favours and to us is also bequeathed the great task of her improvement in everything essential to the support of a great people. Let us take care that we perform manfully & well the great duties imposed upon us, taking for our guides the light of experience & the ever glorious examples of those who first achieved our independence.

The first care of the great men of the revolution after that struggle had been brought to a successful issue was to effect a union of the then thirteen independent States under one general government, thereby to secure the common defence and the liberties of all in all time to come.[55]

The present Constitution of the United States was the final result of their endeavors. Many and very great difficulties were encountered in effecting this object. There were conflicting & jarring interests of different Sections to reconcile. There were independent States jealous of their liberties, but newly acquired, to be brought to see the necessity of surrendering some of their rights as independent Sovereignties for the common benefit. A system of Government as yet entirely new & untried was to be agreed upon, which while it left the people free, should yet have sufficient strength to maintain its rights abroad & enforce obedience to its mandates at home.

Great as these difficulties were, & greater could not be, they were all overcome by the wisdom[,] the patriotism, & the Compromising Spirit of the men of that day.

The Constitution was adopted, that instrument so wonderfully contrived to reconcile every conflicting interest and so admirably adapted to the condition of things in the country. The government

---

55. Perhaps Blair had in mind Federalist No. 1, which within its first fifty words spoke of the "New Constitution for the United States of America" as critical to "the existence of the Union." The 1838 Hallowell edition (see Bibliography) would have been available to Blair for reference and inspiration. James Madison's first entry (No. X) began by defending "a well constructed union."

went into operation under it & the union of the states was complete. That Union which was perfected with such skill & labor & cherished with such zeal & hope by the fathers of the republic. It was the first rich fruit of independence, & has brought and will continue to bring with it untold blessings to us & to all posterity unless in madness & folly we throw it away. The Constitution was the result of a compromise. The Union is a compromise, & it has been thus far sustained by that enlightened kindness & forbearance which gave it existence. The dying injunction of the father of his country was to preserve the Union.[56]

It has always been regarded as the great ark of our political safety. The severest tests have thus far left it unscathed and every friend of his country still clings to it with undiminished faith and hope. He who seeks to destroy it is a traitor & deserves the reward of a traitor.

[Union and Slavery]

I know there are those among whom it is the fashion to speak of the Constitutional Union of these States as if it were a very trifling thing, but they have not considered what they do. It is true there are exciting topics agitating the Country at the present time, and most unfortunately these topics are some of them of a purely sectional character. The sounds North & South have come to be used in many instances in opposition to each other, as if there was a great gulf between these different sections of the Country with men of different tastes & widely opposing interests on either side.

There is something there in the South which we of the North would have otherwise. Men & women wear chains there, & this we cannot see without blushing, in the land of Washington. And those men & women are beaten with stripes & that not for crimes, and against this indignity we cry out even to tears. We grow excited on this subject & taking the bible & the Declaration of Independence in our hands, we go to our Southern brethren in no very amiable mood

---

56. Referring to the first president's farewell address of Sept. 19, 1796.

& tell them that they are tyrants & robbers & we will have no part in the monstrous wrongs they are committing.

We are met upon the other side in the same spirit & informed not to intermeddle with affairs which do not concern us. That by the compromises of the Constitution they are permitted this thing & they will suffer no interference with it by any one[.]

We have the best of the argument & we know it and knowing that we urge it strenuously. The Southern Spirit is aroused & war & disunion are threatened. From words we have proceeded to acts which in some instances have been very violent & aggressive on both sides & great bitterness of feeling has been engendered. Events have occurred during the last year which if I am not mistaken have a very deep significance & which furnish matter for earnest reflection to the people of this Country. There have been men found both at the North & at the South to speak favorably of the dissolution of the Union of these States & there have been public meetings which have passed resolutions in favor of it. There have also been public presses to advocate it in case their own petty schemes could not be adopted.[57]

During the past season a citizen of Massachusetts a descendent of the men of Lexington & Bunkerhill went to the state of South Carolina with the commission of his state in his hands upon a lawful & peaceful errand and was driven away with indignities & insults by a mob the descendants of Sumpter & Marion. Another upon a like errand was driven in like manner from New Orleans the field of the glory of Andrew Jackson.

During this same year several of the great denominations of Christians in the Country have assembled & after most unchristian discussions have finally separated the Northern from the Southern church, as if they were about to worship a different God.

The effect of all this is too obvious for argument. A great breach has been created between the two Sections of the Union which has

57. For example, the *New York Daily Tribune*, Nov. 9, 1860, 4, opined: "if the Cotton States shall become satisfied that they can do better out of the Union than in it, we insist on letting them go in peace."

been widening of late with fearful rapidity. One link after another of the chain which has bound us together in feeling and interest is being sundered & there is beginning to be a fearful looking forward to the time when it shall be broken altogether.

[Solution to Sectional Division]

I do not speak of these things to excite unkind or partisan feelings. God forbid that I should do that to day. I wish only to speak of this great & dangerous subject as a national question, one concerning very nearly the peace & even the existence of the Union. I seek not to enquire upon whom the blame if any is to be cast. But people are beginning to enquire what is to be [the] result of all this. Must the Union fall between these contending powers. Will we dash down now the great fabric which our fathers erected and turn backward from the high destiny to which they have pointed us. Shall we now in the very midst of our triumphant progress to power & true glory, turn aside to fight & destroy each other, for be assured if the sun of this Union shall set at all, he will go down in blood & civil war.

No fellow citizens the Union must be preserved. [B]eyond it we must not look, horrid frightful spectres are there. We must not fight & destroy each other. Oh heaven we cannot! In the spirit of the founders of our republic, we must mutually yield something, even of that we deem to be right, rather than contend, lest we do a much greater evil than that we would remedy. It becomes us to exercise great charity towards each others['] faults. It is not to be expected that the different members of a great confederacy like this can always agree & it is not strange that difficulties & disputes occur, but it is the duty of every good citizen to use his utmost endeavors to prevent them from becoming irreconcilable.

He who does not so is not the friend of his Country, and I wish upon this 4th of July to denounce every man who can speak of the dissolution of the Union of these States as a thing at all possible or to be in any way desired. The word itself, when so applied, implies everything that is abominable & wicked.

But fellow citizens alarming as the indications of the present time certainly are, we will not permit ourselves to despair of the republic. I confess myself one of those who have an abiding faith in the final success of American institutions and the perpetuity of American independence.

The patriotism of the people will be aroused and the great Conservative power of the nation will bear down all obstacles & overwhelm every section & every faction that shall dare to touch the union with profane hands.

[Importance of the Midwest]

One great element of this power will be found in the West, the great and glorious West.[58] And we look upon her one [of] the great bulwarks of the Union with peculiar pride, for she is a new element in it. [A]t the time of the formation of the Government there was no West. She has been formed[,] absolutely discovered and made since then. Her almost boundless tracts of rich & fertile lands were one vast forest waste as unknown as the interior of Africa.

[A discussion of the relations between the British, first peoples, and Americans is here truncated.]

The pioneer has been followed by the agriculturist & the artisan. As the extreme richness of the soil the [word missing] & [s]alubrity of the climate & great advantages of position came to be understood, the tide of emigration began to pour into her lap. Her broad & fertile plains were soon teeming with industrious & worthy citizens. Cities & towns challenging a comparison with any for enterprise & beauty were soon springing up in every direction.

[A discussion of the settlement of the Midwest is omitted.]

If we could be transported to our own beautiful State as she will appear fifty years hence, we should be bewildered at the prospect. With a population doubtless of more than two millions her whole

---

58. Meaning the "Old Northwest" and then the Midwest.

face will be smiling with beauty, and yet some who hear me now will see it.[59]

It is evident that this great section is about to exercise a controlling influence in the national Councils. Already her voice in the national Congress carries a potency with it, & when she shall have gained her full strength & power her voice will be loud. From this we have everything to hope. Upon all the great questions which agitate the country she is sound. She is deeply devoted to the Union for she is the child of its paternal care, indebted alike to every portion of the old States. Her very position forbids her to be anything but the friend of the Union. Her market on the one hand is through the [Great] lakes & their outlet to the Atlantic Seaboard, & on the other by the Mississippi & her tributaries to the Gulf of Mexico in the South. What has she to do with disunion & where shall she the child of the Union go when the parents are divorced. If she will go with the North then her Southern outlet is in the hands of her enemies, & if she goes with the South her egress to the ocean on the East is in a like condition. And if she would be independent of both then she is blocked up on every hand. But she will never give up the Union, with her strong affection & power she will hold together & preserve that Union which protected her in her infancy. And in her trumpet-toned upbraiding voice she will make every traitor tremble who shall dare to seek its overthrow. It is a striking fact that thus far all the disunion meetings & projects have come from the South & that part of the North lying East of the Lakes. The West will have no part nor lot in that matter. She spurns the traitorous scheme & she will hate its authors.

[A discussion of America's destiny as a beacon of freedom to the world is omitted.]

[Conclusion]

The night of darkness & despotism will not again settle down upon the world through our fault. There is patriotism yet among the people

---

59. Accurate prediction: Michigan reached two million in population by 1890.

of the United States. They have not drunk of [the] clear fountain of liberty to permit it to be dried up at its sources now. No. We shall go on as we began. Liberty and the Union shall be our motto, triumphs not revealed even to the imagination of man shall yet be won under it. The tree of liberty shall strike her roots deeper & deeper, & spread her branches wider & wider until the whole world may repose beneath its shades.

Peace, plenty, & happiness shall reign throughout our Land and every Soul within her borders shall be free[.][60]

Blair tracked sentiments found in his denomination's recently published A Protest Against American Slavery, *by One Hundred and Seventy-three Unitarian Ministers (Boston: B.H. Greene, 1845). It harmonized with his interpretation of the Declaration of Independence.*

Possibly among Blair's listeners was Samuel Emlen Pittman, born in Tecumseh on June 25, 1831, who would receive his commission from the governor in 1861 and change the course of the war during the Maryland campaign in September 1862.[61]

Blair would win election to the Michigan House.

---

60. Blair Papers, Burton.
61. See *Michigan at Antietam.*

Report on Suffrage for Blacks
April 25, 1846

A joint resolution to amend the Constitution of 1835 was introduced during Blair's first legislative session. Section 1 of article II, "Electors," specified this qualification: "In all elections, every white male citizen above the age of twenty-one years, having resided in the state six months next preceding any election, shall be entitled to vote at such election ...." The amendatory measure was referred to the House Judiciary Committee on which Blair sat. He voted for the resolution and presented a minority view when it was reported unfavorably. The Senate Judiciary Committee unanimously opposed the measure, contending that it was "inexpedient and impolitic" to remove the racial limitation on the elective franchise; further, "Our Government is formed by, for the benefit of, and to be controlled by the descendants of European nations."

Blair's rejoinder kept faith with the Declaration of Independence. He spent 1,500 words laying out a succinct case for extending the elective franchise on a color-blind basis. Paragraph notations are inserted.

Report of A. Blair, from the committee on the judiciary, upon the subject of the extension of the right of suffrage to colored persons.

The undersigned, one of the committee on the judiciary, to whom was referred a "joint resolution proposing to amend the second article of the constitution relative to the elected franchise," together with a very large number of petitions very numerously signed by citizens of the state generally,[62] praying such amendment, respectfully reports:

That he has given the subject all the consideration which a very limited time and the various duties of the committee would allow.

---

62. From numerous counties: Branch; Calhoun; Genesee; Jackson; Lapeer; Lenawee; Macomb; Monroe; Oakland; St. Joseph; Washtenaw; and Wayne.

And though the undersigned is not able now to go into so thorough an examination of this question in this report as he would be glad to do, it is still hoped that a very long continued agitation of the question of the extension of the right of suffrage to all male citizens above the age of twenty-one years, without distinction of color, outside of this hall, and the enlightened advance of public opinion consequent upon it, have rendered lengthy argument unnecessary here. The extension is demanded more particularly in behalf of our fellow citizens of the long neglected (and I think I may safely say, long oppressed) African race.

In the consideration of this subject, I have had no difficulty in arriving at the conclusion that the prayer of the petitioners ought to be granted. Any other conclusion is deemed to be directly at war with the very spirit of our republican institutions, based as they are upon the doctrine, that a perfect equality of rights, both civil and political, is the birthright of every man of whatever name or color or nation. The constitution of Michigan, which it is now proposed to amend, in the very first line of its first article, as the fundamental proposition upon which all the rest is based, asserts, that "all political power is inherent in the people." Believing as I do, most fully in the truth of this doctrine, I am entirely at a loss for any pretext upon which a large class of the people can justly be denied the free exercise of the right of suffrage. If the word "white" was to be inserted anywhere in the constitution, surely it should have been in this first and fundamental proposition, and then it would have read, "all political power is inherent in the 'white' people'—a principle, the absurdity of which, is too palpable to escape the notice of the most obtuse intellect. There is in this country but one way by which political power is manifested by the people, and that is by the right of suffrage.

He who may not vote is as powerless practically as if he were dead or enslaved. How monstrous a wrong then do we commit, when we forbid a portion of our people the ballot box, acknowledging at the same time the inalienable right of all to the exercise of political power. Such is the wrong now done to the colored race—a wrong we venture to say without a reason—without cause or excuse, unless an unjust and wicked prejudice, which is a disgrace to those who feel it, ought to be called an excuse. Our laws require of the colored man that he shall submit to the government we have established, and be obedient to the laws of its making, and more than that, he must pay taxes and take share in the burdens incurred for the support of that government. And yet he is denied any the least voice in the choice of his rulers, or in the making of the laws. What better is this than the oppressions against which our fathers rebelled? If "all just government is instituted for the benefit of the governed," then what opinion must we form of the justice of Michigan towards her colored citizens? To these questions there can be but one answer. Michigan must make haste to repair this great wrong—her people must be free.

[¶] I would willingly leave this subject here, but feel it my duty to advert for a moment to some of the arguments by which the denial of the right of suffrage to the colored man is sometimes attempted to be sustained. It is said that the race is ignorant and degraded and therefore unfit for the exercise of so important a right as that of voting. This, like every other argument in a bad case, is untrue in point of fact: But suppose it were true, does it furnish any ground for continuing a system which has had such a result? So far from it, that it is one of the strongest reasons why our system, as it regards this race, should be changed at once. If by our unjust laws we have degraded the man and besotted his intellect, it is a refinement of cruelty to make this the pretext of further continued oppression. And that such is the case, so far as there is any shadow of truth in the charge at all, who can deny? We have by the scorn of the community and its oppressive laws driven the colored man in most instances into the most menial employments, (none other being left open to him,) and thus has he become a blacker of white man's boots, and a sweeper of white man's chimneys!

[¶] But who shall say that under a system of just and equal laws—laws which shall strengthen his hopes, protect his rights and elevate him to the right of a citizen, he will become nothing else. All experience in this country has proved that the best way to make a good and intelligent citizen, is not first to strip him of all the rights and the hopes of one. But on the contrary, whenever you extend the duties and responsibilities of the citizen additional motives are furnished him to be prepared to meet them, and he has been but a poor observer who has not been convinced by the history of our country of the full ability of man to govern himself. But there is still an easier answer to this cavil. If even ignorance and degradation are a sufficient reason for denying the right of suffrage, they should apply as well to the white as the black man, since neither of these are the necessary adjuncts of any color. If we will drive the colored citizen from the ballot box because he is less learned or less virtuous than we could wish him, then by every rule of right the unlearned and vicious white man should go with him. But we adopt no such rule when the white race is concerned. No degree of ignorance or vice excludes them, come they from whatever quarter of the globe they may.—Is it not a shame then, that in a land which boasts of liberty, a colored man may not be treated with equal fairness? Is it a crime that he <u>cannot</u> be white, that we should thus punish him?

One objection more seems to require a remark and then I have done with the question. It is said that great numbers of blacks will flock to this State as their residence, if the proposed amendment should be made. That this would be the case to any very great extent is doubted. But if it should prove true to the utmost of the fears of the most tim[o]rous, then would it indeed be an honor to Michigan, that the justice and humanity of her laws caused the oppressed of other states to seek a home within her borders. Besides, it is yet to be proven that the black man necessarily makes a bad citizen. The very effect of the law which attracted him here would be to elevate him, and the fact that he <u>came</u> would be evidence that he at least had spirit enough to love liberty and respect himself. From such a man most evidently the state has nothing to fear, but very much to hope. And shall it go for nothing that by the adoption of this amendment we take a great step towards the elevation of an oppressed race? Does their common humanity with us give them no claim to the consideration of the state?

Believing most fully that the time has come when the colored men of America should be allowed to assume their rightful position as citizens of the republic, upon an equality in all respects with their white brethren, and especially that Michigan ought not longer to permit in her constitution a word which creates an unjust distinction between her citizens, and denies that great principle which lies at the very foundation of her whole political fabric, I can come to no other conclusion than that the joint resolution ought to pass. The committee report back to the House the joint resolution referred to them and respectfully recommend its passage; but for the reasoning of this report the undersigned is alone responsible.

All which is respectfully submitted.

Austin Blair.[63]

This historic document was offered in legislative session in the first Michigan capitol at Griswold and State streets in Detroit. Within two years, the hastily constructed capitol in Lansing housed the legislature—Blair had lobbied for Jackson. He likely rode the Michigan Central Railroad to attend session; the line reached from Jackson to Detroit by January 1842. Perhaps this document was prepared in his lodgings at "No. 34, Wales' Hotel," situated on the south side of Jefferson Avenue just east of Randolph Street. The building that "formed the nucleus of that hotel" dated from 1807. It burned in 1848 and was replaced by the ornate Biddle House.[64] In 1865, it would host a reception for a then-famous general, Ulysses Simpson Grant.

63. House Doc. No. 12 in *Documents Accompanying the Journal of the House of Representatives of the State of Michigan at the Annual Session of 1846* (Detroit: Bagg & Harmon, 1846), 1-4; *Journal of the House of Representatives, 1846,* 529, 580-581.

64. *Manual, Containing the Rules of the Senate and House of Representatives, of the State of Michigan* (Detroit: Bagg & Harmon, 1846), 33; Silas Farmer, *The History of Detroit and Michigan or The Metropolis Illustrated,* 2d Ed., Vol. One (Detroit: Silas Farmer & Co., 1889), 480-481, 485, 966.

Mass Meeting
February 27, 1854

On February 18, citizens in Detroit gathered to consider the prospect that Congress might repeal the Missouri Compromise of 1820. That historic package of bills admitted Missouri into the Union as a slave state and Maine as a free state. It declared a national policy of prohibiting slavery in the area remaining from the 1803 Louisiana Purchase north of a longitudinal parallel. President James Monroe signed it into law on March 6, 1820. The measure resolved sectional tensions for several decades, allowing pro-slavery admission of Texas and Arkansas and pro-liberty admission of Iowa, Wisconsin, and Minnesota.

The repeal became a real possibility on January 23, 1854, when Senator Stephen A. Douglas of Illinois introduced legislation to supersede the Missouri Compromise in favor of "popular sovereignty," a policy under which the settlers of a territory would decide for themselves whether to authorize the institution of slavery. Nine days after the Detroit assembly, the following notice appeared in a Jackson newspaper:

SHALL THE MISSOURI COMPROMISE BE REPEALED?
A meeting of the citizens of Jackson and vicinity, without distinction of party, is requested at the court house, on Friday evening next, at seven o'clock, to consider the provision of the Nebraska bill, by which the Missouri Compromise is sought to be repealed, and to express the sentiments of the community in relation thereto.

Twenty-eight people were signatories, including Kinsley S. Bingham, Charles DeLand, and Blair. The meeting on Friday evening, March 3rd, included this development:

Austin Blair, Esq., in pursuance of a call of the meeting, addressed it at length in explanation of the principles of the Nebraska bill, exhibiting in a masterly and convincing manner the falsity and danger of the pretexts and arguments resorted to by the friends of the measure, and eliciting the frequent applause of the audience.[65]

65. *DeLand's History*, 169-170; Linda Braun-Hass, *Charles Victor DeLand: Wheelhorse of the Republican Party, 1852 to 1854* (East Lansing: Michigan State University, 1988) (Master's thesis), 46, both quoting *Jackson Citizen*.

Appeal to the People
June 21, 1854

A "mass convention" met in Kalamazoo on this Wednesday to consider responses to the Kansas-Nebraska Act that now left the issue of slavery in the hands of territorial settlers. Despite a rainy day, a large number of "Free Democrats," Whigs, and Free Soilers joined together to plan their course of action. After resolutions were approved in opposition to the act, a committee was appointed to draw up an appeal for attendance at a statewide meeting to carry on the work. Notable Free Soil men—including Hovey K. Clarke, Jabez Fox, and Blair[66]—produced the following 500-word statement.

To the People of Michigan:

A great wrong has been perpetrated. The slave power of the Country has triumphed. Liberty is trampled under foot. The Missouri compromise, a solemn compact entered into by our Fathers, has been violated, and a vast territory, dedicated to freedom, has been opened to slavery.

This Act, so unjust to the North, has been perpetrated under circumstances which deepen its perfidy. An administration, placed in power by Northern votes, has brought to bear all the resources of executive corruption in its support.

Northern Senators and Representatives, in the face of the overwhelming public sentiment of the North, expressed in the proceedings of public meetings and solemn remonstrances, without a single petition in its favor on the table, and not daring to submit this great question to the people, have yielded to the seductions of executive patronage and, Judas-like, betrayed the cause of liberty; while the

66. *Michigan Liberty Press*, Aug. 25, 1848.

South, inspired by dominant and grasping ambition, has, without distinction of party, and with a unanimity almost entire, deliberately trampled under foot a solemn compact entered into in the midst of a crisis threatening to the peace of the Union—sanctioned by the greatest names of our history—and the binding force of which has, for a period of more than 30 years, been recognized and declared by numerous acts of legislation.

Such an outrage upon liberty, such a violation of plighted faith, cannot be submitted to. This great wrong must be righted, or there is no longer a North in the councils of the nation.

The extension of slavery under the folds of the American flag is a stigma upon liberty. The indefinite increase of slave representation in Congress is destructive to that equality between free men which is essential to the permanency of the Union.

The safety of the Union—the rights of the North—the interests of free labor—the destiny of a vast territory and its untold millions for all coming time—and, finally, the high aspirations of humanity, for universal freedom, all are involved in the issue forced upon the Country by the slave power and its plastic Northern tools.

In view, therefore, of the recent action of Congress upon this subject, and the evident designs of the Slave power to attempt still further aggressions upon freedom, we invite all our fellow-citizens, without reference to former political associations, who think that the time has arrived for a union at the North to protect liberty from being overthrown and downtrodden, to assemble in

Mass Convention,

on Thursday, the 6th of July next, at 1 o'clock p.m.,

At Jackson,

there to take such measures as shall be thought best to concentrate the popular sentiment of this State against the aggression of the slave power.[67]

---

67.   Stocking, 39-40.

A new political entity, the Republican party, emerged from the July ses-
sion at Jackson. Blair energetically worked for its success. At the 1855
Republican convention in Kalamazoo, he represented his district and
spoke "in a masterly effort." He attended the state convention in Ann
Arbor on March 26, 1856, and again spoke while also serving on the
Committee on Resolutions. The Detroit Democratic paper called it "The
Negro-Worshippers' State Mass Convention." Blair went to the 1856
national convention as a delegate-at-large, and he campaigned for the
ticket under the banner of "free soil, free speech, free labor and free men."[68]
John C. Fremont was the Republican candidate for president; he lost to
Democrat James Buchanan.

---

68.   *DeLand's History*, 184; *DFP*, Mar. 28, 1856, 2; A.D.P. Van Buren, "Michigan in Her Pioneer Politics; Michigan in Our National Politics, and Michigan
in the Campaign of 1856" in *Michigan Historical Collections*, Vol. XVII, 2d Ed.
(Lansing: Wynkoop Hellenbeck Crawford Co., 1910), 257, 274; Harris, *Austin
Blair*, 77.

Speech at State Convention
May 2, 1860

Pursuant to due notice, Republican delegates appointed by county conventions "met in State Convention, at Merrill Hall," on Wednesday, May 2, 1860. The main purpose of the meeting was to appoint twelve delegates to represent the party at the national convention to be held in Chicago on May 16. Located on the east side of Woodward Avenue in downtown Detroit, Merrill Hall had just opened the preceding November (it would be demolished in 1950, replaced by what is today the Coleman A. Young Municipal Center). The facility served as a commodious space for meetings, lectures, and recitals.

Blair was elected as "Delegate at large" from the 1st Congressional District. After all delegates were chosen, a committee was formed to propose resolutions for consideration at the national convention. The convention requested a speech from Blair, who referred to the ongoing Democratic national convention meeting in Charleston, S.C.

The committee retired, and in response to a unanimous call, Hon. Austin Blair took the stand. No man, he thought, could be true to his better nature and not be a Republican. The principles of the party were those of '76. They needed no argument to establish them, they were self-evident, and were at the foundation of liberty everywhere. It was singular that any other party could maintain other opinions and exist as a party, yet there was now sitting, sweating in a hot southern clime, under coats of northern wool, a set of men who claimed to be representatives of a party, who were seeking to establish wrong. It is no wonder that they can't agree, and it is strange that the party was not sundered and destroyed years ago. The late Democratic State Convention, that appointed delegates to Charleston, was silent on national topics. Its delegates dared not venture upon such a sea of trouble, but contented itself with spitting forth slurs on the present State government. The real subject matter of such a convention was ignored.

Having left true Democracy, the Charleston delegates from the North find themselves in the hands of hard masters. They have been obliged to abandon principle after principle till now they are required to abandon the last show of adherence to right, and protect the rights of slavery as against those of freedom. [Stephen] Douglas cannot receive the nomination without subscribing to the slave code, but his Northern friends are trembling, for their instinct tells them that with thus yielding now, nothing more can remain to them. But what matters their action? Can not the Republicans sweep away, with the besom of destruction, both man and platform? Our principles are those upon which stood the fathers of this Republic, and they must prevail, whether they triumph now or not—it is merely a question of time—therefore I would have as a candidate none but a sound, and tried, and true Republican. Under one with the genuine ring, I can work with spirit. Yet I have no fears, for I believe the Convention will choose such an one. We begin the contest where we left it in '56, and carry it forward with renewed vigor and hopes, and if we are beaten now (and I believe we shall not be) we will again advance our columns in '64 and march on to victory. Our party is one of principle, and if we cannot win under a true Republican leader, then it is destined that the principles upon which were founded the Constitution, and which were embodied in it, shall not have power.

The first choice of Michigan is undoubtedly the tried and wise statesman of New York, William H. Seward. (Here the applause was overpowering, and it was sometime before silence permitted the speaker to resume.) I hope the Democrats will nominate Douglas, for he is the representative of all that is bad. I want on the other platform a man who is the exponent of all that is good in politics. Some of the Republicans are afraid of Douglas if nominated, for they think there is more fight in him than in others, but that is what I want. Fun and fight is the thing. We dont want too easy a victory, and I am sure we shall beat Douglas so badly that it will seem a wonder that any body should have thought of nominating him at all. We should be "harmless as doves but wise as serpents," and we have great work to do.

[¶] He continued his remarks for some time, concluding with saying that the Republicans of this State were all on fire with truth, they "snuffed the battle afar off," and hoped to meet the hosts of slavery in solid column, and not in broken ranks, for they wanted to overthrow them horse, foot and dragoons.

The speech was eloquent and spirited and called forth, repeatedly, the warmest applause.[69]

Despite being the front-runner, Stephen A. Douglas was not nominated for president as the Charleston convention concluded on May 3. He did win nomination when Democrats reconvened at Baltimore on June 18, but Southern Democrats met there on June 23 and nominated John C. Breckinridge of Kentucky, the incumbent vice-president.

---

69. *LSR*, May 9, 1860, 2.

Speech of the Hour
May 18, 1860

Blair led the Michigan delegation to the Republican convention in Chicago during May 16-18. He and his colleagues were fully committed to William H. Seward, the front-runner. On the third day, the nominating process commenced; Blair seconded Seward's nomination, claiming a prime position for the Michigan delegation should their man win. The successful candidate needed 234 votes. On the first ballot, Seward led all with 173.5; Abraham Lincoln was second with 102. Seward would gain with the next vote, but the tally revealed a shift in Lincoln's direction when he garnered 181 votes to Seward's 184.5. The third ballot proved conclusive: Lincoln initially received 231.5 votes while Seward plateaued at 180. Before the tally could be announced, the chairman of the Ohio delegation announced that four voters had gone over to Lincoln, putting him over the top. Other delegations followed suit, and the shift of votes into Lincoln's column put the announced tally at 364. At that point, the New York delegation moved to make the nomination unanimous, and supporting speeches were offered by Massachusetts chairman John A. Andrew and others. The Michiganders had not changed a single vote from Seward to Lincoln; Blair clung to Seward for his long record against slavery; and the question was how the delegation would now respond. Chairman Blair secured recognition for the "speech of the hour" (Hesseltine, 61).

Gentlemen of the Convention:

Like my friend who has just taken his seat, the State of Michigan, from first to last, has cast her vote for the great statesman of New York. She has nothing to take back. She has not sent me forward to worship the rising sun, but she has put me forward to say that, at your behests here to-day, she lays down her first, best loved candidate to take up yours, with some beating of the heart, with some quivering in the veins (much applause); but she does not fear that the fame of Seward will suffer, for she knows that his name is a portion of the history of the American Union; it will be written, and read, and beloved long after the temporary excitement of this day has passed away, and when presidents themselves are forgotten in the oblivion which comes over all temporal things. We stand by him still. We have followed him with a single eye and with unwavering faith in times past. We marshal now behind him in the grand column which shall go out to battle for Abraham Lincoln, of Illinois.

Mark, you, what has obtained to-day will obtain in November next. Lincoln will be elected by the people. We say of our candidate, God bless his magnanimous soul. (Tremendous applause.) I promise you that in the State of Michigan, which I have the honor to represent, where the Republican party from the days of its organization to this hour, never suffered a single defeat, but has carried this standard with an increasing triumph from that day to this, we will give you for the gallant son of Illinois, and glorious standard-bearer of the West, a round twenty-five thousand majority.[70]

Blair served on the committee who traveled to Springfield to officially inform Lincoln of his nomination. The committee consisted of the president of the convention, George Ashmun of Massachusetts, and the chairmen of the various state delegations. Blair was chair of the Michigan delegation and on the party's national committee. The group arrived at the Lincoln home at 8th and Jackson around 8:00 p.m. on Saturday, May 19, and were first greeted outside by seven-year-old Thomas "Tad" Lincoln. Then, gathered in the north parlor, they listened to the notification by Ashmun and Lincoln's reply. Ashmun began introductions until all had personally congratulated their nominee. They all paid respects to Mrs. Lincoln in the south parlor of the Lincoln home.[71]

70. *Proceedings of the First Three Republican National Conventions*, 157-158; *Proceedings of the National Republican Convention, Held at Chicago, May 16, 17 and 18, 1860* (Albany: Weed, Parsons & Co., 1860), 109, 123-124.

71. *New York Tribune*, May 25, 1860, 6; *Illinois State Journal*, May 21, 1860,

Speech Accepting Nomination for Governor
June 7, 1860

The Republican party held its state convention at the Merrill Hall in Detroit in early June to select candidates for statewide office. Fifty-two counties from both peninsulas were represented by 169 delegates. Charles DeLand of Jackson County nominated Blair for governor; James William Tillman of Detroit seconded the motion "in behalf of a large number of the delegation from Wayne County." After James M. Edmunds of Wayne County was also nominated, Blair won by a vote of 108 ½ - 65 ½. Henry Barns of Detroit then moved to make the nomination unanimous.[72] A committee brought Blair to the rostrum (he was present, though not a delegate), where Barns introduced him to the convention. His appearance "was greeted with prolonged applause," after which he offered brief remarks.

Mr. Blair then said he hardly knew what to say on such an occasion as this. If the subject referred to republicanism, he should know what to say, but when it related to himself he hardly knew what to repeat. But in behalf of the county in which he dwelt, and in behalf of the true friends who have stood by him, he had to thank the committee for the honor conferred upon him. He came now in obedience to their call to accept the trust that had been reposed in him. He would accept that trust, and would carry the republican banner with triumph to the end. When elevated to the office of Governor, as he believed he would be in November, he would discharge the duties to the best of

---

2; *Proceedings* (Chicago), 37.

72.   As editor of the *Detroit Tribune and Advertiser*, Barns obtained authority to raise a black regiment during the Civil War.

his ability. Not wishing to detain the convention from its regular business, and again thanking it for the honor done him, he would retire.[73]

Blair won the November 1860 election by a comfortable 57-43 percent margin. He carried all but six of Michigan's fifty-one counties—and those few only totaled 1,449 votes out of his 87,780 total. In the Democratic stronghold of Wayne County, he won 7,301–6,948, a feat not achieved in 1854, 1856, or 1858. The biggest margin came in the largest county to go Republican: Calhoun, 4,053 to 1,261, a 61%–39% gap.[74]

Under the headline "What Blair's Election Means," a Republican newspaper recounted that "the fight" at the state level for the top spot "was especially severe." Their party had been unjustly vilified, while "the nominees of the slaveholding locofocos" had been misrepresented. The paper predicted the results of Blair's victory:

The administration of Gov. Blair will be, without doubt, fully worthy of the confidence with which the people have honored it. It will be upright, honorable and economical; conservative, in the noble sense of that word, and just toward all citizens and all sections of the State. It will be, we are entirely assured, well worthy of the great honor of a majority of MORE THAN TWENTY THOUSAND.[75]

---

73. *DFP*, June 8, 1860, 1; *Livingstone's History of the Republican Party*, 524.

74. Michael J. Dubin, *United States Gubernatorial Elections, 1776-1860: The Official Results by State and County* (Jefferson: McFarland & Co., 2003), 124-125. His opponent tallied 67,053 votes.

75. *LSR*, Nov. 14, 1860, 1, quoting *Grand Rapids Eagle*. "Locofoco" was a derogatory reference to Democrats.

Plates

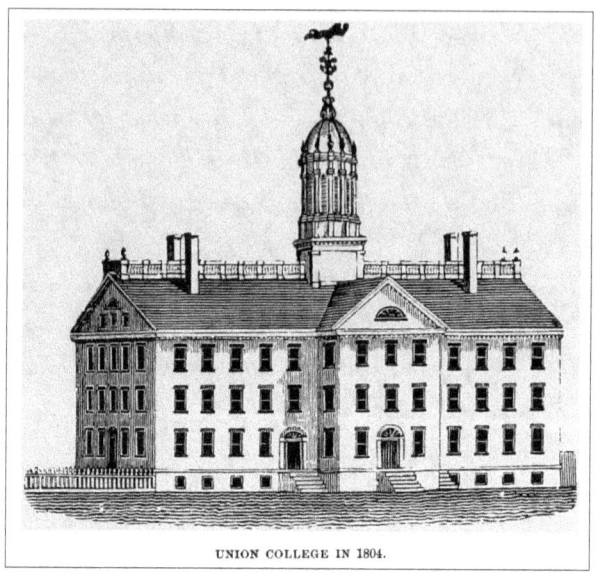

UNION COLLEGE IN 1804.

1. Union College, early 19th century. *A Record of the Commemoration, One Hundredth Anniversary*, New York: De Vinne Press, 1897.

2. Bird's eye view, Jackson, Michigan, 1860s. Library of Congress.

3. Michigan's first Capitol, Detroit.
BL 004049, Bentley Historical Library, University of Michigan.

4. Blair report on Black voting rights. *Documents Accompanying the Journal,* Detroit: Bagg & Harmon, 1846.

5. Wales Hotel, Detroit. Silas Farmer, The History of Detroit and Michigan.

6. Blair home, Jackson. Burton Historical Collection, Detroit Public Library.

7. Michigan Avenue, Jackson. John Carbutt, photographer, 1860–1870.
https://www.loc.gov/item/2023636836/

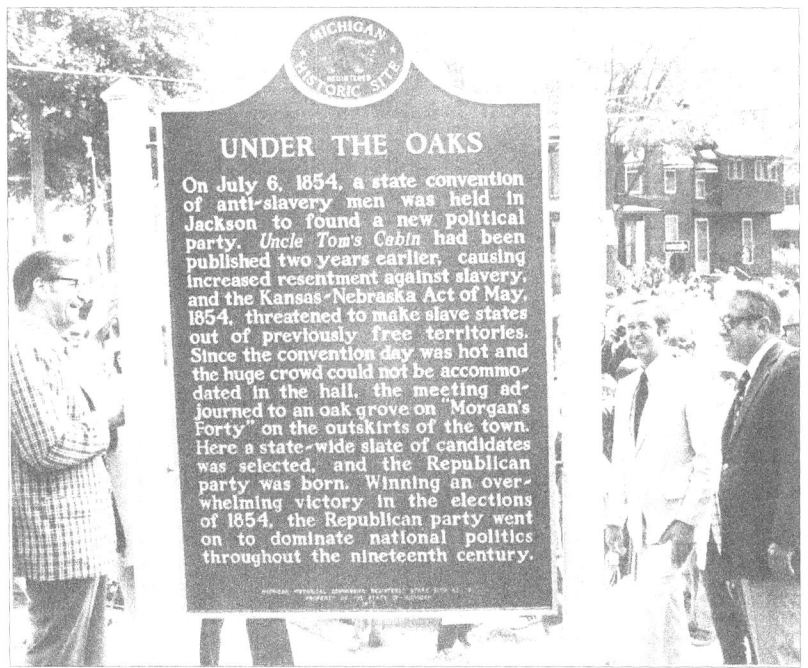

8. Under the Oaks historical marker dedication ceremony, July 1972,
including Congressman Garry E. Brown and Governor William G.
Milliken. Archives of Michigan.

9. Republican convention, "Wigwam," Chicago, May 1860. *Harper's Weekly*, May 19, 1860.

10. Old rail station building, Jackson. Ella Sharp Museum of Art and History.

11. Austin Blair, cabinet card, Edward S. Tray's Jackson studio. Burton Historical Collection, Detroit Public Library. It was not uncommon after the war for photographers to acquire studios, their contents of studios, and negative collections. Since Tray was born in 1865, it appears he acquired the negative from one of Jackson's earlier artists.

12. Rally and taking of oath of allegiance at old post office, Detroit, April 1861. Archives of Michigan.

13. Michigan's Civil War Capitol, Lansing. Archives of Michigan.

14. Presentation National battle flag of the 1st Michigan Infantry
(Three Months). Michigan Capitol Commission/Save the Flags.
Only three days after the firing upon Fort Sumter, Blair began the
organization of Michigan's first regiment and within just a few weeks'
time the 1,000-man regiment was mustered in at Detroit.

15. 2nd Michigan Infantry, Fort Wayne, likely summer 1861. Burton Historical Collection, Detroit Public Library.

16. Regimental battle flag of the 16th Michigan Infantry. Michigan Capitol Commission/Save the Flags. The regiment formed in September 1861 in Detroit and saw extensive action throughout the war as indicated by the long list of battle honors upon its folds.

17. The 5th Michigan Cavalry mustered into service on August 30, 1862. Michigan Capitol Commission/Save the Flags. In 1863, Russell A. Alger, future governor of Michigan, took command of the regiment.

18. The 20th Michigan Infantry formed in August 1862 and received its training in Blair's hometown of Jackson. Many of its battles, from the very first engagement at Fredericksburg in December 1862 to its last, are proudly recorded on this flag. So great was Blair's attachment to the regiment that in 1885 he would attend and address their reunion in Jackson. Michigan Capitol Commission/Save the Flags.

19. The 26th Michigan Infantry also formed in Jackson, mustering into service December 12, 1862. This regiment became a particular favorite of Mrs. Blair. Michigan Capitol Commission/Save the Flags.

20. Telegram to Blair from Lincoln, July 3, 1862, showing reliance on State recruiting for victory. Burton Historical Collection, Detroit Public Library.

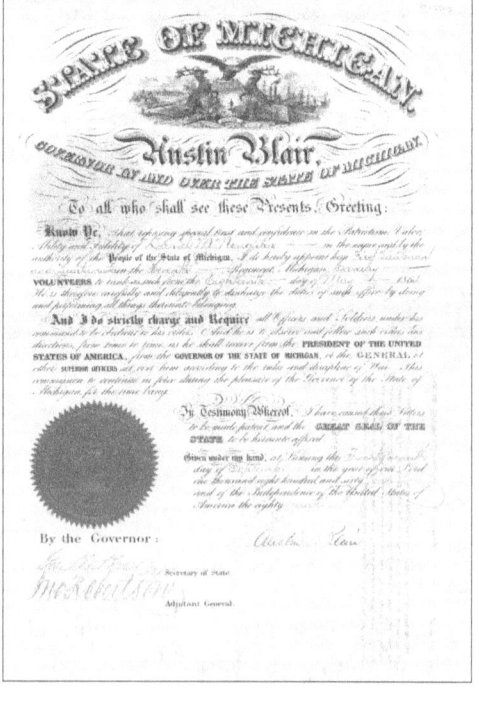

21. Austin Blair's distinctive signature. Burton Historical Collection, Detroit Public Library.

22. One of many officer commissions signed by Blair, Sept. 1864. Grand Rapids History Center, Grand Rapids Public Library, Grand Rapids, MI. Coll. 242.

23. Camp Jackson. Sketch by Spring Arbor University Associate Professor of Art Brianne Witt, courtesy Jackson County Historical Society.

24. Banner of the Austin Blair Camp of the Sons of Union Veterans of the Civil War from Jackson, Michigan. Courtesy of Michigan Capitol Commission/Save The Flags and flag donor Douglas Hinton III.

25. Blair portrait in Capitol. Michigan Capitol Commission.

DEATH OF PRESIDENT LINCOLN. MEETING ON THE CAMPUS MARTIUS, APRIL 17, 1865.

26. Memorial service for President Lincoln, Campus Martius, Detroit, April 1865. Burton Historical Collection, Detroit Public Library.

27. Austin Blair, graying, cabinet card, Edward S. Tray's Jackson studio. Burton Historical Collection, Detroit Public Library. The burdens shouldered by the "War Governor" are reflected in his appearance.

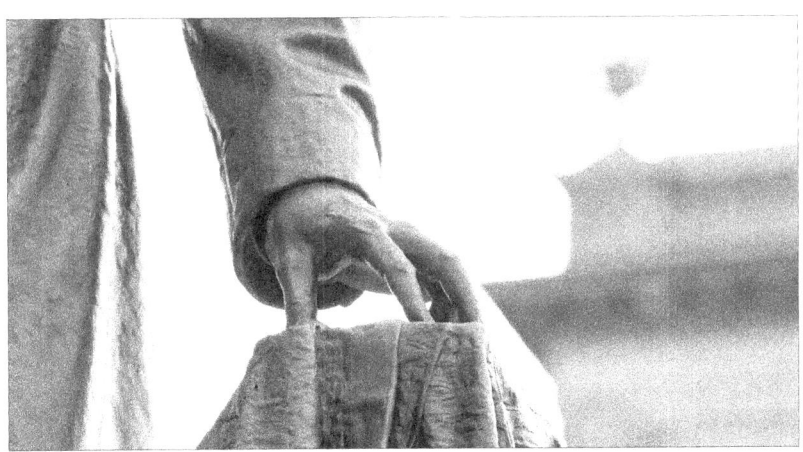

28. Left hand, Blair monument, Lansing. Courtesy of Bradley M. Egen, MotionPossible.

I do not expect the grand result immediately,
nor that it will be attained without great sacrifices,
yet I cannot doubt the final issue

Part Three:

Messages, Speeches, and Remarks—1861–1865 (April)

Inaugural Address
January 2, 1861

With the Democratic vote split between sectional candidates, Abraham Lincoln received enough electoral votes to win the presidency. The prospect of the first anti-slavery president taking office precipitated South Carolina to enact an ordinance of secession on December 20. Other states threatened to withdraw from the Union, aided by a campaign that sought the founding of a slaveholding government within America.[76]

   The Constitution of 1850 specified that the "Legislature shall meet at the seat of government on the first Wednesday in January." As the new year began, members "made their slow way by stage-coach and sledge through the snows to Lansing," the nearest rail station being at Jackson. They convened "in the church-like little wooden capitol" at Allegan and South Washington Square, which "contained legislative and supreme court chambers, an office for the governor, a few other offices and a library."[77] Opening the session in accord with tradition, the legislature invited the new governor to speak. Blair's inaugural remarks equated secession with treason and vowed loyal support to the national government. As with any "State of the State" or inaugural address, topics encompassed other aspects of public affairs, such as education, agriculture, infrastructure, and finances. For purposes of this monograph, only the Civil War-related points are included. Length of selection: approximately 3,700 words.

Fellow-citizens of the Senate and House of Representatives:
After a period of two years, during which the Legislative body has not

76.   See Charles B. Dew, *Apostles of Disunion: Southern Secession Commissioners and the Causes of the Civil War* (Charlottesville: University of Virginia Press, 2002).

77.   Charles Moore, *History of Michigan*, Vol. I (Chicago: Lewis Pub. Co., 1915), 411, 413; marker, Michigan historic site 587C.

assembled, we meet, charged with the duty of re-examining the laws and institutions of the State; to correct, so far as we may, the errors of the past in the light of experience, and to provide wisely, if we can, for the exigencies of the future. No higher trust than this can be reposed in a citizen. As the Representatives of the people, diligence and patriotism will become us. An earnest regard for their rights, interests and liberties, is a solemn obligation upon us.

I have the highest satisfaction, in being able to congratulate you upon the general good order and prosperity of the State. The past year has been one of great fruitfulness.

Bountiful harvests have put famine and distress far away from our doors. No pestilence has afflicted the people of the State; but general good health has prevailed among them. The laws have been cheerfully obeyed by the mass of the people, and their infraction, by the criminal, has been promptly punished by a wise and patriotic Judiciary. The State has advanced rapidly in wealth and population. The census of 1860, taken under the laws of the United States, shows the population of the State to be, in round numbers, seven hundred and fifty thousand.

Our soils are rich, and of great variety, producing in abundance all the crops which belong to this latitude. The State possesses immense forests of valuable timber, which are already a source of great increasing wealth. In minerals, Michigan is without a rival. Her mines of copper and iron are of the very finest quality; and, thus far seem to be measureless in extent. Coal, also, of good quality, is now proved to be abundant, while the explorations for saline waters in the Valleys of the Saginaw and Grand Rivers, have been entirely successful. Possessing a great area of territory, surrounded on three sides by the greatest chain of lakes on the Continent, furnishing a cheap and easy outlet to the ocean, and the markets of the world, Michigan has all the elements of an empire within herself. We have reason to be thankful to that "good providence" which is rapidly guiding us in the course of a great, free, and happy commonwealth.

...

The Act, approved February 14, 1859, "to provide a Military Fund, in aid of the volunteer uniformed militia," and appropriating for that object, the sum of three thousand dollars each year, has produced a most beneficial effect. Thus stimulated by the countenance and aid of the State, a considerable number of volunteer companies has been formed and well equipped, and the organization of the militia, which was almost abandoned, has been revived and placed upon a good footing. I recommend that the yearly appropriation for this object, be materially increased in amount. The United States supports but a very small standing army, and the great reliance of the government to defend itself against foreign enemies, and to put down domestic insurrection, is upon the militia of the States. It is neither safe nor wise, to allow the organization and discipline of the militia to fall into discredit or disuse. The military spirit of the people ought to be kept up, and their confidence in their ability to bear arms and defend themselves, should be fostered. In point of expense also, it is much less burdensome to the people to pay a reasonable amount to support volunteer companies, than to call out the whole body liable to bear arms, as was the old method. Besides, the volunteer organization is much more effective, and forms a nucleus for a larger force, always to be relied upon.

Gentlemen of the two Houses:—While we are citizens of the State of Michigan, and as such deeply devoted to her interests and honor, we have a still prouder title. We are also citizens of the United States of America. By this title, we are known among the nations of the earth. In remote quarters of the globe, where the names of the States are unknown, the flag of the great Republic, the banner of the stars and stripes, honors and protects the citizen. In whatever concerns the honor, the prosperity and the perpetuity of this great government, we are deeply interested. The people of Michigan are loyal to that government—faithful to its Constitution and its laws. Under it they have had peace and prosperity; and under it they mean to abide to the end.

Feeling a just pride in the glorious history of the past, they will not renounce the equally glorious hopes of the future. But whether in peace or war, they will rally around the standards of the nation and defend its integrity and its constitution with fidelity.

The existence of the government is threatened, not by enemies from without, but by traitors from within. The State of South Carolina, possessing a free white population of less than three hundred thousand, of all ages and sexes, has assumed to dissolve the national government. By a convention called under State authority, and without consulting any other State or people, and without the least discussion which seems to have been interdicted, she passed an ordinance annulling the laws and Constitution of the United States. In her own cherished phrase, she has seceded from the Union. If it could be properly done, I presume the country, generally, would be willing to let that restless, heady little nation, retire from the confederacy forever. But that cannot be, without admitting the right of secession to exist in all the States. This done, and no government remains to us; but only a voluntary association of States, dissolvable at the pleasure of any of them. If South Carolina may of right secede, then may also New York and Louisiana, thus cutting off the free right of way, of the entire North-west to the ocean, in both directions. The doctrine cannot be admitted. Self-preservation, if no other reason, would compel us to resist it. But the doctrine has no foundation in fact or reason. It is said, that a State having entered voluntarily into the Union, may also voluntarily, and of right, withdraw whenever such State may think its rights are no longer protected, or its interests secured, by the connection. And the State is itself, the sole judge in this respect. The argument is altogether fallacious—at war with every just idea of compact.

If it were admitted that the Constitution and government of the United States is a mere voluntary compact of sovereign States, still it would not follow, that the compact might be at any time dissolved by any one of the contracting parties. That would necessarily depend on the terms of the compact itself. If the compact by its terms, or by manifest implication, was intended to be perpetual, then it could not be dissolved without the consent of all the contracting parties.

The Constitution of the United States, if a compact at all, is one of government in the term of its continuance, without limit, and in its powers sovereign. It is also by its terms "the supreme law of the land, and the judges in every State are bound thereby, anything in the constitution or laws of any State to the contrary notwithstanding." If the State of South Carolina regards this Constitution as a contract or agreement between States, then she is bound in good faith to keep it according to its conditions. She is bound to submit her grievances, if she has any, to the Congress established by the Constitution, in which she has an equal voice with the other States; and to abide by the decisions and acts of that body, so long as they conform to the fundamental law, and are within its granted powers. If the Congress shall usurp powers not granted, then the injured parties must resort to the Courts for redress. But the Constitution of the United States of America is not in any sense a compact or league between independent sovereign States. On the contrary, it is a foundation of government established by the people of the United States, as a whole, perpetual in its character, and possessing all the elements of sovereign power and nationality. This is plain from the instrument itself, and is fully stated by the preamble, as follows: "We the people of the United States, in order to form a more perfect union, establish justice, insure domestic tranquility, provide for the common defense, promote the general welfare, and secure the blessings of liberty to ourselves and our posterity, do obtain and establish this Constitution, for the United States of America."

It is true, that the State organizations were availed of for the purpose of ratification; but it was only as a convenient method to ascertain the wishes of the people. By resolution of Congress on the 28th day of September, 1787, it was directed, that the report of the Convention, which included a Constitution for the United States, should be "transmitted to the several Legislatures, in order to be submitted to a Convention of delegates chosen in each State *by the people thereof*.["]

The Constitution of the Federal Government, and the laws of Congress enacted under its authority, therefore operate upon individuals, and not upon States, in the same manner and with the like effect, as if there were no States. The Constitution of the United States was formed by the people of the whole country, in the same manner, and with the same effect as the State governments were formed in their respective jurisdictions. The States are independent of each other in all respects, and they are independent of the National Government in all the powers not granted by the people to that government, and as to those they are entirely subject. There is, then, no right of secession in a State, but the State has the exclusive sovereignty over its domestic institutions and laws, and in respect to these the Federal government has no authority whatever. It results, that the purely local and domestic institution of slavery, wherever it exists in the States of this confederacy is wholly beyond the interference or control of the national government. In respect to the common Territories, however, the case is entirely different. The Constitution of the United States deals only with the people of the States, and has made no provision for the government of the Territories, unless the section authorizing Congress "to make all needful rules and regulations respecting the territory or other property belonging to the United States," should be held to be such a provision. The power to acquire and hold territory, carries with it the power to govern. From whatever source derived, therefore, the sovereignty over the Territories resides wholly in the General Government, and this is also in accordance with uniform practice. Slavery may be excluded from the Territories by law of Congress, and no State can lawfully complain of such action with any more show of reason than in case of Congressional action upon any other subject. Nor is there any power in the National Government to dismember itself. No power, but that of the people in their ultimate sovereignty, can do that. We are one nation, and our people indivisible, with a common government, and common interest. South Carolina is still a State of the Union in spite of her ordinance, and her people cannot be absolved from their obligation to obey the Constitution and laws of our common country.

If there is no right of secession, still, it is said, there is a right of revolution against unbearable oppression. Grant it—this is not the country in which to deny that; but it ought to be a revolution against, and not in favor of, oppression. It must be justified by such clear and undeniable acts of usurpation as will justify rebellion before the civilized world. Of what acts do the slaveholding States complain? In what have they been oppressed? What right has been denied to them? We have had abundance of eloquent speech from them, and endless general complaint of aggressions upon them and their rights. But the charge still lacks specification. I deny the whole indictment. There have been no such aggressions. No right of theirs has been denied or refused to them by us. Our personal liberty laws furnish an example of no such denial. They were enacted for the protection and safety of free citizens of the State against kidnappers, and with no view to defeating the reclamation of actual fugitive slaves, under the law of Congress. That law is so entirely wanting in the usual safeguards against abuse of its provisions, that there is constant danger of its being used as a cover for the most nefarious practices. Michigan is a sovereign and independent State, and her first and highest duty is to guard the rights and liberties of her people. This she has sought to do by the laws in question. It is altogether her own affair, and with all due respect to the States of the South, she does not hold herself under obligation to justify her conduct in this regard to them. If they think these laws are unconstitutional, then the Courts of the United States are open to them, to have them so declared;[78] and they may be assured that neither mob violence, nor any other power, will be resorted to prevent

---

78.   The reference was to *Prigg v. Pennsylvania*, 41 U.S. 539 (1842), which allowed state legislation to prohibit its officials from aiding the federally authorized recovery of fugitives from enslavement. Arthur T. Downey, *The Civil War Lawyers: Constitutional Questions, Courtroom Dramas, and the Men Behind Them* (Chicago: ABA Publishing, 2010), 362 n.35. See Lysander Spooner, *A Defence for Fugitive Slaves, Against the Acts of Congress of February 12, 1793 and September 18, 1850* (Boston: Bela Marsh, 1850).

the full measure of redress to which they may be entitled. As a law abiding people, we invite judicial scrutiny into the legislation of the State, and we are ready to abide its results. We ask nothing which we are not willing to grant to others. The State only seeks to maintain her rights under the constitution and laws of Congress. Less than that she cannot do.

There seems, however, no intention in the Southern States to resort to this peaceful method of trial, provided by the Constitution and laws; but we are told, we must immediately repeal these laws, or the government will be broken up, and the Constitution destroyed. I cannot advise you to listen to this appeal to your fears. I am not willing that the State should be humiliated by compliance with this demand, accompanied by threats of violence and war. For myself, I will wait until the Cotton States repeal their unjust and unconstitutional laws, which consign to imprisonment citizens of the free States visiting their parts on business, and guilty of no crime, and by which such citizens are sold into hopeless slavery. I will wait until they cease to murder and maltreat innocent citizens from the North, without even the forms of a trial; until the freedom of speech and of the press, guaranteed to us by the Constitution of the country, is restored in the Southern half of the Union, and until the reign of terror and mob violence is over.

When the madness which rules the hour is past, and treason has been rebuked and crushed; when the Southern States, now threatening rebellion shall have returned to their loyalty, to the national constitution and government, and to obedience to the laws, then no doubt the State will be willing to do towards them, not only all that is just, but also all that is generous. I know very well it is said by eminent men in the free States, that we must repeal these laws, not because the South threatens us, nor because we wish to appease their wrath, but because the laws themselves are wrong. Yet it must be admitted, that even if we were to confess the wrong, which, on the contrary we deny, our conscientiousness would seem to have been quickened at a very peculiar season. Whatever we may claim about it, if the Personal Liberty laws are now repealed, the judgment of the country will be that it is done under the smarting of the Southern lash, and that judgment will be correct. Instead of such a course tending to restore peace in the country, its effect will be exactly the contrary. It is not concession that is needed now; it is patriotic firmness and decision. All the present evils either arise from, or are greatly aggravated, by the weak and compromising policy of timid men, in the past. Treason has been abetted and encouraged by humiliating expedients, until the malcontents of the present, feel secure in the temporizing precedents of the past. Let us have an end of compromises, and appeal only for constitutional rights. Besides it is not claimed or even pretended that the Personal Liberty laws have in fact had the effect to prevent the execution of the Fugitive Slave law in a single instance. They have stood as a mere protest on the statute book. And whenever an appeal has been made to the courts to enforce that law, it has been uniformly done in good faith, though some of its provisions are extremely distasteful to the people.

It is not at the personal liberty laws that the secessionists aim. They openly scoff at the notion that their repeal will satisfy them. Their war is upon the Constitution of the United States. That instrument does not answer their purposes, and they demand its amendment or its overthrow. Its great doctrine of government by majorities stands in the way of the establishment of the great slave Empire which they have set themselves to erect, with the infamous African slave trade for one of its pillars, and one way or another it must be destroyed. Governor Pettus, of Mississippi, in his late message to the Legislature of that State, sums up his reasons for secession with this pregnant question: "Can the lives, liberty and property of the people of Mississippi be safely entrusted to the keeping of that <u>sectional majority</u> which must hereafter administer the Federal Government?" That is the real question and the only one. Shall the Government continue as our fathers made it? Shall it be administered by majorities or shall a new one be constructed to be ruled by minorities. The people have, in a constitutional and legal manner, chosen an eminent citizen of the State of Illinois, President of the United States, and the South demand that we shall repent of it.

That act has been accomplished by a wilful majority, and it is demanded that we give up the great principle of free government— the rule of the majority. We can do neither the one nor the other. We are satisfied with the Constitution of our country, and will obey the laws enacted under it, and we must demand that the people of all the other States do the same. Safety lies in this path alone. The Union must be preserved and the laws must be enforced in all parts of it at whatever cost. The President is bound to this by his oath, and no power can discharge him from it. Secession is revolution, and revolution, in the overt act, is treason, and must be treated as such. The Federal Government has the power to defend itself and I do not doubt that that power will be exercised to the utmost. It is a question of war that the seceding States have to look in the face. They who think that this powerful government can be disrupted peacefully, have read history to no purpose. The sons of the men who carried arms in the seven years' war with the most powerful nation in the world, to establish this government, will not hesitate to make equal sacrifices to maintain it. Most deeply must we deplore the unnatural contest. On the heads of the traitors who provoke it, must rest the responsibility. In such a contest the God of battles has no attribute that can take sides with the revolutionists of the Slave States.

I recommend you at an early day to make manifest to the gentlemen who represent this State in the two Houses of Congress and to the country, that Michigan is loyal to the Union, the Constitution and the Laws, and will defend them to the uttermost; and to proffer to the President of the United States, the whole military power of the State for that purpose. Oh, for the firm, steady hand of a Washington, or a Jackson, to guide the Ship of State in this perilous storm. Let us hope that we shall find him on the 4th of March. Meantime, let us

abide in the faith of our fathers—"Liberty and Union, one and insep-
arable, now and forever."

Austin Blair

Executive Office, Lansing[79]

---

79. *Joint Documents of the State of Michigan, for the Year 1860*, No. 2 (Lansing: Hosmer & Kerr, 1861), 1-24; George N. Fuller ed., *Messages of the Governors of Michigan*, Vol. II (Lansing: Michigan Historical Commission, 1926), 425-442 ("*Messages*").

Transmittal on the Peace Conference
February 14, 1861

Consistent with Blair's remarks, the legislature passed a joint resolution on the state of the Union that rejected any terms of concession or compromise in favor of tendering "the whole force and means" of the state in defense of the Constitution and the federal government.[80]

Attempts to resolve sectional differences proceeded through various avenues, including a conference of representatives from twenty-one states that convened on February 4, 1861, at the Willard Hotel in Washington, D.C. The seven states in the south that had by then adopted measures of secession were not represented, and representatives from six other states— Michigan included—absented themselves. On February 11, however, Senator Zachariah Chandler switched gears and wrote Blair "urging him to send delegates, 'stiff-backed men or none,' who would vote against compromise." The letter would cause a sensation when it was publicized because of this postscript: "Without a little blood-letting this Union will not, in my estimation, be worth a rush." Senator Kinsley Bingham wrote Blair on the 15th with a similar recommendation. Blair referred the matter to the legislature as follows.

February 14, 1861

To the House of Representatives:

I herewith transmit to the Legislature, joint resolutions of the States of New York and Indiana, for the appointment of commissioners from those States, to meet commissioners from other States in the city of Washington, on the invitation of the Legislature of Virginia.

Being aware of the previous action of the Legislature upon this

---

80. *Documents Accompanying the Journal of the House of Representatives of the State of Michigan at the Biennial Session of 1861* (Lansing: Hosmer & Kerr, 1861), 5-6.

subject, I have hesitated before further calling attention to it; but it has seemed to me that the circumstances affecting the propriety of sending the commissioners, are so far changed as to justify a further consideration of the question. It is, perhaps, also proper for me to say that I have communications from some of the delegation in Congress, indicating, that while they have entirely approved of the previous action of the Legislature, they think that Michigan might now be represented in the so-called Peace Convention, with credit to herself, and benefit to the whole country. It is also said, that if commissioners can arrive in Washington by the 20th instant, they will be in time to take part in the deliberations of the Convention.

Without any expression of my own opinion upon this delicate question, I submit the whole question to the wisdom and patriotism of the Legislature, in which my confidence is perfect.

Austin Blair

The message was referred to a special committee, and, though brought up several times, approval to send delegates did not pass.[81] *Blair's lack of enthusiasm for compromise drew the ire of a letter by "Morris" in which the governor's priority was castigated as "ultra abolitionism" at the expense of Union and peace.*[82]

---

81.   Wilmer C. Harris, *Public Life of Zachariah Chandler 1851-1875* (Lansing: Michigan Historical Commission, 1917), 53-53; *Journal of the House of Representatives of the State of Michigan, 1861* (Lansing: Hosmer & Kerr, 1861), 683-687 (showing attachments).
82.   *DFP*, Feb. 16, 1861, 1.

Transmittal on Military Readiness
February 21, 1861

Anticipating the possibility of armed conflict with secessionists, as mentioned in the inaugural address, led the Michigan Senate to inquire about the state of military affairs. The Constitution, Article V, Section 4, provided that the governor was commander-in-chief of the military and naval forces of the state and authorized to call out the militia to execute the laws, suppress insurrection, and repel invasion. Blair's reply, showing little if any background in this arena, underscored the lack of knowledge he possessed on this point—a profile not dissimilar to Lincoln.

To the Senate:

I acknowledge the receipt of the resolution of your honorable body requesting certain information in regard to the arms and military equipments of the State. In reply I herewith transmit the response of the Adjutant General to my demand for such information, which is all that is within my reach. Though the Governor is by law made Commander-in-Chief, yet practically the military department has been entirely under the control of the Adjutant General, whose office is kept at a distance. It results that my means of knowledge in respect to that department are not of the most satisfactory kind.

Very respectfully,

Austin Blair[83]

Frederick W. Curtenius, age fifty-four, had been adjutant general since 1855. Blair soon appointed John Robertson, born in 1814, to fill the post (see Appendix). The governor's other customary duties of office continued. On April 5, for example, he attended a meeting of the state board of

---

83. *Messages*, 443.

agriculture and was appointed president. The board met three days later in the governor's room, establishing professor salaries equal to his own at $1,000 per annum.[84]

During those early April days, 2nd Lieutenant Norman J. Hall of Monroe, acting commissary, reported on the dwindling supplies inside Fort Sumter. Confederate authorities had blocked resupply. On April 4, the U.S. War Department got underway an expedition to provision the garrison and enable it to hold the fort.[85]

84.   https://projects.kora.matrix.msu.edu/files/157-544-235/MINUTES 1861.pdf

85.   *The War of the Rebellion: A Compilation of the Official Records of the Union and Confederate Armies*, Series I, Vol. I (Washington: Government Printing Office, 1880), 230-231, 235 ("*OR*").

Proclamation on Formation of Volunteer Regiments
April 16, 1861

War came. The attack on Fort Sumter on April 12, and its surrender on April 13, galvanized those loyal to the Union. President Lincoln issued a call for volunteers to suppress the armed rebellion on the 15th; that evening, Blair was called to an historic public assembly in "Jackson's immense hall" (the third floor of William Jackson's grocery store) that "was packed to overflowing." The local militia company, the Jackson Grays, "pushed their way through the dense crowd and formed in front of the platform." Blair appeared, and "the cheering was again renewed." Company commander William H. Withington told the assembly that the men had unanimously tendered their services. Blair read aloud a telegram "calling upon him for one regiment of volunteers. He then addressed Captain Withington, accepting the proffer, and then addressed the Grays and the audience in a most eloquent and fervid speech."[86]

The next day, Blair arrived in Detroit "to make the arrangements rendered necessary by the present exigency" of national affairs. His quarters were at the Michigan Exchange Hotel, where a large number of excited citizens called on him. A meeting was organized with James E. Pittman acting as secretary, resulting in a commitment for raising private funds and forming a committee to aid in recruiting the infantry regiment. The committee featured men with leading military reputations: Henry L. Chipman; Pittman; John Robertson; Henry M. Whittelsey; William D. Wilkins; Orlando B. Willcox; and Alpheus S. Williams. After adjournment, Blair issued a statewide call to arms.

---

86. *DeLand's History*, 162; James M. Thomas, *Jackson City Directory and Business Advertiser for 1867 & 1868* (Jackson: Carlton & Van Antwerp, 1867), 87. The building, located at 152 West Michigan Avenue, remains in use today. A letter from Blair to Withington in November 1862 concludes "Your friend." Austin Blair Collection, Bentley Historical Library.

Proclamation

Whereas, The President of the United States has made a requisition upon the State of Michigan for military aid in enforcing the laws and upholding the constitution and the Union of the United States;

And Whereas, The laws of this State already authorize the raising of two regiments of militia for the service of the Federal government;

And Whereas, Said laws contemplate that the uniformed volunteers shall first be called in such exigencies;

Now, therefore, the Adjutant General of this State is hereby authorized to accept the service, first, of ten companies of infantry, to be mustered into the service of the United States for three months (unless sooner disbanded).

To this end, the companies of the uniformed volunteer militia that may desire to tender their services will forthwith report, through their company commanders, to the Adjutant General at Detroit, the names of company officers, and the number of the rank and file, ready for service; the number, kind, and condition of their arms; and the number of officers and men already in uniform, the kind of uniform, and the number in want of uniform. Out of the whole number of companies the Adjutant General will first select ten companies for immediate service.

The companies which may be accepted will be required to fill up according to the following schedule:

For each company, one Captain, one First Lieutenant, one Second Lieutenant, four Sergeants, four Corporals, two musicians, and sixty-five privates.

All companies formed and to be formed will be instructed and put in serviceable condition as soon as possible, and will at once begin drilling according to "Hardee's Tactics."

Those not immediately required will be formed into one or more additional regiments, as the exigencies of the service may demand.

It is confidently expected that the patriotic citizen-soldiery of Michigan will promptly come forward to enlist in the cause of the

Union, against which an extensive rebellion in arms exists, threatening the integrity and perpetuity of the government.

The Adjutant General will issue and enforce the necessary orders to carry out the objects of this proclamation.

Given at Detroit, the 16th day of April, A.D. 1861.

Austin Blair.

Governor and Commander-in-Chief.

Jno. Robertson, Adjutant General.[87]

At Lansing, "a large evening war rally" convened on April 18 inside an empty capitol, the legislature having adjourned on March 16.[88] *Blair would soon call it back into session.*

---

87.   *DFP*, Apr. 17, 1861, 1. *Hardee's Tactics* was an infantry instructional manual (actual title: *Rifle and Light Infantry Tactics; for the Exercise and Manoeuvres of Troops When Acting as Light Infantry or Riflemen* (Philadelphia: Lippincott, Grambo & Co., 1855).

88.   Matt Vanacker, *Lansing and the Civil War* (Charleston: The History Press, 2023), 17.

Official Letter to Secretary of War
April 19, 1861

Blair sent a response to the U.S. War Department confirming Michigan's acceptance of its responsibility to provide an infantry regiment. The communique went beyond a mere formal reply; Blair sought to portray the loyal response by Michiganders to the need to defend the nation. He also offered additional aid.

Executive Office,

Lansing, Mich., April 19, 1861.

Hon. Simon Cameron,

Secretary of War:

Sir: I have the honor to acknowledge the receipt of your communication of the 15th instant, calling for one regiment of militia of this State, in pursuance of the law of Congress of 1795. I have also your dispatch by telegraph to the effect that if the quota of Michigan shall be ready by the 20th of May it will suffice. I am enabled to say that the people of Michigan respond with the utmost enthusiasm to the proclamation of the President. The regiment will be ready to march by the 15th of May next, and will be at the rendezvous at Detroit at that time to be mustered into the service and pay of the United States. I can have them ready on the 1st day of May without inconvenience, if the Department desires it.

Allow me to say further that Michigan will send another regiment at the same time if the War Department at Washington desires it. In fact, the second regiment is very anxious to go.

I have the honor to be, very respectfully, your obedient servant,

Austin Blair.[89]

89.   *OR*, III, I, 88.

By contrast, several other governors rejected the president's call. Opposition in loyal slaveholding states turned violent on the same day Blair sent this letter. In Baltimore, a mob attacked a Massachusetts regiment in the city's center. Michigan's troops would follow that route to the capital. Would Maryland—and Kentucky and Missouri—remain in the Union? Virginia not only rejected Lincoln's proclamation, it soon seceded and joined the Confederacy.

Proclamation Convening Legislature
April 23, 1861

*To muster the full resources of the state, and in keeping with his dem-
ocratic principles, Blair called for a special session of the Michigan legislature authorized for "extraordinary occasions," as his words sought to
portray.*[90] *Coincidentally, his call issued the same day that the president
transmitted to the governors "an authenticated copy of a Joint Resolution
to amend the Constitution of the United States." The proposed Thirteenth
Amendment, approved by the outgoing Congress in hopes of averting war,
would deny Congress the power "to abolish or interfere, within any State,"
the institution of chattel slavery. The measure is not mentioned in the legislative journals; they would have recorded its transmittal from Blair. He
appears to have considered the matter a dead letter.*

Whereas, The States of South Carolina, Georgia, Alabama, Florida,
Mississippi, Louisiana, Texas and Virginia, unmindful of the obligations of patriotism and duty, have without cause, rebelled against the
just and lawful authorities of the United States; and by combinations
too powerful to be suppressed by the exercise of the civil power, have
violently seized and destroyed the public property, and have levied
fratricidal war against the Constitution, Government, and people of
the Republic;

And whereas, The President of the United States, in pursuance
of his constitutional duty, and for the purpose of suppressing such
unlawful combinations and insurrection, has made a requisition upon
me for a portion of the Militia of the State, for the furnishing of which
adequate provision is not made by law;

---

90.   *Journal of the Senate of the State of Michigan. 1861* (Lansing: Hosmer &
Kerr, 1861), 3, 1128, 1139; *Revised Constitution, 1850*, 12.

Now, therefore, in this extraordinary emergency, in order that the whole military power of the State may be made available, and sufficient means furnished for arming and equipping the forces, to be used in defence of the Constitutional rights and liberties of the people, and in the preservation of the Government of the United States from destruction, and that the insulted majesty of the Nation may be fitly vindicated,

I, Austin Blair, Governor of the State of Michigan, by virtue of the power in me vested by the Constitution, do hereby convene the Legislature of this State, in extra session, requiring the Senators and Representatives to assemble in their respective chambers, at the Capitol, in the city of Lansing, on Tuesday, the seventh day of May next, at twelve o'clock, noon, then and there to consider of the matters aforesaid, and to adopt such measures as the safety, dignity and honor of the country and the State demands.

In testimony whereof, I have hereunto set my hand, and caused to be affixed the great seal of the State.

Done at Lansing, this twenty-third day of April, in the year of our Lord one thousand eight hundred and sixty-one, and of the Independence of the United States the eighty-fifth.

By the Governor,

Austin Blair.[91]

Two days later, the governor left Jackson for Detroit in order "to arrange for mustering the various companies of the First Regiment into the United States service."[92]

---

91. *Journal of the House of Representatives of the State of Michigan, Extra Session of 1861* (Lansing: John Kerr & Co., 1861) May 7, 1861, 4-5.
92. *DeLand's History*, 162.

Remarks at Campus Martius
April 25, 1861

A "great meeting" of an "immense crowd of people" gathered at Campus Martius in the center of Detroit on this Thursday to take part in raising the U.S. flag over city hall. The ceremony was accompanied by an artillery salute, the ringing of church bells, cheering by the crowd, and patriotic band music. Notable leaders were called upon to speak, including former U.S. Secretary of State Lewis Cass and U.S. Judge Ross Wilkins—and the governor.

Governor Blair's Remarks

Governor Blair was called out and spoke at some length, as follows:

Fellow-Citizens—It was not my expectation to have been called upon to make any remarks. I take a high pleasure in being able to join you in the exercises of to-day. You have looked upon the sword which was here presented, I have no doubt, with swelling hearts.[93] On the sword we have yet to rely, though we say it with sorrow, for the maintenance of the [illegible]; on the sword and the patriotism of the American people. We begin now to beat the drum and to run up the American ensign. All honor to the gallant men who rally to the fame of that flag, who are coming forward by thousands. (Applause.) Forgetting all party ties they come to fight to sustain the constitution and laws. We have already four regiments—the government has called for but one,—and in a few weeks we will have more.

[¶] I am aware how long our people have forborne. So free, so good, is the government of the United States that [it] has looked on and allowed this treason to grow until its existence is threatened. Forbearance is no longer a virtue, and now the freemen rally around the flag. This is a rebellion, and it is to be crushed, though the blood

---

93.   Wilkins exhibited a sword attributed to George Washington.

of the men of the South and the North has to flow. This government is not to be overthrown. Never. (Cries of "Never.") We can look back and see the bloody track of our fathers who fought for freedom and the right, and we must do as they did. There will be returning reason with the people of the South when the real struggle comes,—when they learn that the men of Massachusetts are the same as they were in other times,—when they learn to respect us for our courage and strength. If I were to do what I thought was the best thing for the men of the South I would strike. As General Houston said, if they go on as they have been doing, instead of having King Cotton they will have King Davis.[94] Then we owe it to them, as well as to ourselves, to put down this rebellion. It is causeless, and they cannot justify it before the civilized world. It must be crushed. Then let us rally round our glorious American flag, which has always waved over our victorious columns.

[¶] I will give my poor abilities, and I ask you to stand by me. We will carry this banner at the head of our Michigan regiments, and will win glory and fame under it. I have had almost contests before me in the anxiety of men to go with us. In God's name, they say, can't a man have a chance to serve his country? Wait a little, and you can have an opportunity. As fast as we have the guns and the blankets and other means, we will send off these men, all in good time.[95]

---

94. Samuel Houston of Texas; "King Cotton," a reference to the importance of the crop and slavery to American commerce. Jefferson Davis, Confederate president.
95. *DFP*, Apr. 26, 1861, 3.

Remarks to Cleveland Crowd
May 3, 1861

At the invitation of Ohio governor Dennison, several northern governors met in Cleveland within a few weeks of the outbreak of the rebellion to co-ordinate activities and discuss the posture of the federal government. Blair attended the meeting, held at the Angier House hotel on Bank Street (now West 6th Street) at St. Clair on May 3. The unprecedented nature of the emergency meant the governors were raising, housing, feeding, and clothing regiments, "but the national government was dilatory in taking over the burden of their support." The state leaders "became disgusted with the administration's lack of coordination and its timidity" and "believed that popular enthusiasm should be harnessed immediately for victory."[96] They agreed on a communication about strategy, sent to the president on May 7 by the Wisconsin governor.[97] At the conclusion, several appeared on the hotel balcony to speak to the gathered crowd. The "fiery" remarks of the governor of Michigan were reported as follows.

The time for speaking has gone by, and the time for action has come. We are in the midst of war—a war of which we cannot stop to count the cost. Our flag has been insulted; and more—it has been torn down. But, fellow-citizens, I have reason to believe that the brave Anderson will yet head an army which shall go down to Charleston, and that his hands will again raise the stars and stripes over the walls of Fort Sumter. (Cheers)

[¶] In the name of Michigan I promise to stand by you shoulder

96. W. Scott Robison, *History of the City of Cleveland: Its Settlement, Rise and Progress* (Cleveland: Robison & Cockett, 1887), 88; William B. Hesseltine & Hazel C. Wolf, "The Cleveland Conference of 1861" in *Ohio Archaeological and Historical Quarterly*, Vol. 56, No. 3 (July 1947), 262-263.
97. *OR*, III, I, 167-170.

to shoulder, and to march beside you of Ohio, and beside them of Pennsylvania, and beside brave old Massachusetts, who has tenderly taken to her bosom her beloved dead. We bought the mouth of the Mississippi, and we will hold it. The traitors may go into the Gulf, but they shall not take the territory with them. We will stand by the old flag which has waved over so many battle fields; the flag under which we have so long lived, and under which, please God, we will die.[98]

---

98. Major Robert Anderson had defended Fort Sumter. *Cleveland Morning Leader*, May 4, 1861, 1; Fennimore III, 214; Hesseltine, 163.

Message to Special Session
May 7, 1861

When the Michigan legislature convened, Blair delivered his address in person to set forth a proposed agenda for their consideration. He emphasized the centrality of slavery to the breakup of the nation. He continued to defend the perpetual nature of the Union and attack secession as treason. Although the governor lacked military experience, he saw—more clearly than many—that the war would be no six-week affair. The message amounted to approximately 3,300 words.

Fellow-Citizens of the Senate and House of Representatives:

Under the authority vested in the Executive by the Constitution of the State, I have summoned you together in extra session upon the most extraordinary occasion which has had existence since the formation of the Federal Government.

African slavery, the great and only disturbing element in our institutions, after having ruled the country for sixty years, and during that time driven the free States from one humiliating concession to another, until they had fairly reached the wall, and from the mere instinct of self-preservation refused to go further, has dropped the mask and taken up arms. Grown overbearing from its former successes, and insolent through its long cherished pride and disregard of the rights of men, it now seeks to make its power predominant over the whole country by force. Having been beaten in an election, it deliberately nullifies the Constitution, defies the laws, confederates in a pretended form of government, raises armies, besieges and takes a fortress, marches boldly upon the National Capital to unseat the lawfully elected President of the Republic, and makes its final appeal to the arbitrament of battle. It has left us no choice but to surrender our free government or fight for its preservation. In that choice a brave and loyal people could not hesitate. The President of the United States, occupying the chair of Washington, by the same right and under the same solemn forms by which the Father of his Country held it, has accepted this issue. He has unfurled the flag under which all our history has been made, and summons the loyal sons of the heroic founders of the government in arms to defend it. He will fight to maintain the Constitution and the Union, and the whole people of the loyal States with one voice have affirmed the wisdom, the justice, and the patriotism of that determination.

In this sacred war, for it is nothing less, the people of Michigan desire to do their whole duty, and it is for us, their chosen representatives, to provide the means and lead the way.

On the evening of the 15th of April last, I received a telegram from the War Department at Washington, that a call was made upon me, as Commander-in-Chief, for one regiment of the militia of the State for immediate service. On the next day, however, I was informed from the same source, that if the quota of Michigan should be ready by the 20th of May, that would suffice. Immediately upon receiving these dispatches, I issued my proclamation to the people of the State for volunteers to form two regiments of infantry, in pursuance of the law of your late session, authorizing the organization of two regiments to meet such a call. That law had this strange omission, that while it provided for raising the regiments and paying the volunteers and officers at certain fixed prices, it did not appropriate so much as one dollar to meet the expenses to be incurred by virtue of its provisions. It, therefore, became necessary to seek outside of the statutes, means to defray the expenses of recruiting, arming, equiping and uniforming the regiments. This was done by an appeal to the patriotic people of the State to advance the money as a temporary loan, trusting to the justice of the Legislature for its prompt repayment. That resource was found amply sufficient, and I desire now, on behalf of the whole people of the State, in this public manner to thank those public-spirited gentlemen who came forward with such promptness to aid me with their money and their advice in that emergency. You, gentlemen of the two Houses, will take care that no man suffers in the smallest degree in consequence of his generosity in that respect.[99]

The people answered the call for volunteers with such enthusiasm and alacrity as will forever be an honor both to them and the government under which we live. In just nine days from the time when the call of the President was received, the ten companies, composing the first regiment, were full, and the officers commissioned; and in one day more the second regiment was in like manner organized. On the 30th day of the same month of April, both the regiments were in camp in Detroit, in good order and in fine condition.

When it is taken into account that at the time the President called for one regiment of Infantry from Michigan there was not anything like a full regiment in the State, nor even a single company with the full complement of men required by the call, and that there was no money in the Treasury, that could be used for military purposes, I am more than satisfied with the progress made.

For a more detailed account of the present condition of the military forces, I refer you to the report of the Adjutant General, John Robertson, which will be laid before you, and of whose efficiency I have occasion to speak in the highest terms.

In the choice of companies to compose the first and second regiments, some embarrassment was felt in consequence of the great competition between them, to be included therein, arising chiefly from the fact that many of our fellow citizens either did not understand the statute under which we were acting, or in their zeal refused to recognize its justice. That statute left me no discretion, but absolutely required me to select first such companies of the uniformed militia of the State as might be offered, and these were nearly sufficient to answer the entire call. The people, however, will not be satisfied with the two regiments provided for by law, and already full companies enough

99.   The list of subscribers to this loan included notables such as Lewis Cass but also included firms, banks, and women, among whom were Mary E. Armstrong, Catherine Jones, and Ann Martin of Detroit, Mrs. Parmelia Parr of Grand Haven, and Mrs. James Taylor of Kalamazoo. Robertson, 18-21.

have been formed to fill at least three more regiments, while the business of recruiting still goes on as briskly as at first. They recognize the fact that the struggle is imminent and great,—that the existence of the government is involved in its success. It had not been really believed by our countrymen of the Free States that such a government as this could be broken up by those who had grown great and rich under its benign protection; but the attack upon Fort Sumter, and the fall of that stronghold, roused them like the shock of an earthquake! All previous political differences were at once forgotten, party lines obliterated, and the whole mass of the people have seized their arms and demand to be at once led forth to battle against this most foul and unnatural rebellion. They are not satisfied with an army of 75,000 men, and they mean to quadruple it. They call upon the President of the United States to abandon at once and forever the policy of mere defense of the national forts and property, and immediately to take the field to punish the traitors, who are in arms against their country, and reduce rebellious States to unconditional obedience. A dishonored flag and gallant little band driven forth with fire and sword from a national fortress, call for speedy redress, and the people of the country declare that they shall get it.

It has been thought best in all respects, that the troops to go from Michigan into the service of the United States, should be fully armed, equipped and uniformed before they leave the State. So far, this has been, I believe, well and economically done, and the two regiments are prepared to march to the assistance of the National Government, in a condition immediately to take the field, and if need be, to fight a battle. They are under the command of the most intelligent and thoroughly educated officers, several of whom have seen previous and honorable service in the army of the United States. Both officers and men are rapidly perfecting themselves in military drill and warlike science. They are gallant citizens from all the walks of life, who go forth to fight, not for conquest, but for liberty, security and peace. I look to see them return, bearing the laurel wreath of victory.

Though the President has thus far, called for but one regiment from this State, there can be little doubt that he will finally ask for several more, and it will be your duty to provide amply in all respects, for meeting promptly and efficiently such a demand. I recommend, therefore, that the law of your late session, authorizing the raising of two regiments be so amended as to authorize calling immediately into the field for drill and placing on a war footing, four more regiments, making in all six, with power, in case of emergency, to raise the number to ten. It would seem proper also, to pay the volunteers while in the service of the State, preparatory to being called into the service of the United States, at the same rate that they will be entitled to after being mustered into that service.

The great addition to the duties of the offices of Adjutant and Quarter-Master General, occasioned by calling into active service so large a body of the militia, has rendered it necessary for these officers to devote the whole of their time to the business of their respective offices. The salaries allowed them by the present law are wholly inadequate as a compensation, having been provided solely in view of their duties during the time of peace. I recommend, therefore, such an increase of the salaries of these officers as will be a fair compensation; such increase to continue during the present national troubles. I also recommend that all subsequent enlistments be for the term of three years, or until discharged from service by the Government of the United States; and that authority be given to order the volunteers so enlisted to any point out of this State, in aid of the General Government, or of any loyal State that may be invaded by the armies of the Confederate States, or any other mob. This seems necessary for the present, and until Congress shall confer upon the President sufficient authority to call volunteers into service for a much longer term than three months.

In many instances, the companies of the volunteer uniformed militia have been mustered into the service of the United States; and other cases will occur, while these companies still desire to retain their position in the ordinary volunteer force of the State. I recommend that these companies be authorized to organize reserve corps of their companies, which may be officered temporarily, in order that they may continue their practice and drill. I recommend also that the companies of the uniformed militia now limited to forty, be allowed to be increased to sixty.

Considerable expenses have already been incurred and paid from the voluntary loan of citizens to the State, and large expenses have been incurred in recruiting, by individuals, which there is now no authority of law for paying, while very heavy outlays will become necessary in the future, in putting the State into a condition to meet such calls as may hereafter be made by the government of the United States for troops. I recommend the raising of the necessary amount to meet every exigency, by a loan. As to what may be the best manner of effecting such a loan must be left entirely to your discretion. I think, however, it will be wise to consider that the suddenness with which this war has been thrust upon the country, has taken nearly every loyal State of the Union by surprise, and they are all, like ourselves, borrowers in the market. It will, therefore, be found essential that the loan be issued in such form as to enable our own people to take it, to a very great extent, and thereby avoid going abroad into markets where we shall meet the active competition of other States. For this purpose it seems evident that to issue a large portion of it in bonds or other securities, moderate in amount, with interest at seven per cent, payable annually at some point within the State, will be most likely to effect the object. If this course is taken, I have reason to believe that by far the greater portion of the loan will be taken in Michigan, and thus we should have the satisfaction of knowing that the patriotism of our own people was found a sufficient resource in the very greatest emergency. The whole amount to be raised, I think, should not be less than one million of dollars, to be issued and used as the necessities of the State may require.

Of the power of the Legislature to authorize such a loan, I entertain no doubt whatever, and therefore do not stop to discuss it. We are in the midst of war. The very existence of the government is imperilled and we cannot stop to levy and collect taxes before forces are raised, nor would it be wise, if we could, to add to the calamities of war those of heavy taxation. That belongs properly to the times of peace and business prosperity.

It is only the dictate of humanity and justice to make provision for the support of the families of such as volunteer to fight the battles of the country in case any occasion should arise for such support. I therefore recommend that you enact a law authorizing the towns and cities of the State to levy taxes for that purpose.

Gentlemen of the two Houses: We are just entering upon a war, the exact result of which no man can foresee. The sudden and splendid outburst of popular enthusiasm which has illumined its commencement will shortly, in a great measure, disappear, and must be replaced by calm determination and resolute vigor. There will be calamities and disasters which have not been looked for. He who went forth joyously singing the national anthem, will sometime be brought back in a bloody shroud. The national resources will be rapidly consumed, business will suffer and ordinary avocations be sadly broken up. This is to be no six week's campaign. I do not under-estimate the gallantry of Southern men, and they will find it a grave error that they have underestimated ours. The sectional pride and bitter remembrance of previous taunts, which enter into this contest will make its battles fierce and bloody. We are all sprung from a race in which cowardice is almost unknown. Although we have been mainly at peace for thirty-five years past, yet ours is naturally a martial people. It will, therefore, be wise for us to proceed very calmly and deliberately to our preparations to meet a very great occasion. Mere outbursts of patriotic fervor will not avail. Now, that we have entered upon the war, we must patriotically accept its inevitable conditions. To whatever of calamity and disaster it may bring us, we must cheerfully submit; and whatever of self-sacrifice it may require, must be cheerfully borne. The war is just and righteous, because it is waged in behalf of the laws and the constituted authorities of our country; a country which has never, in the smallest particular, oppressed those who are in arms against it. It is our plain duty, therefore, to support and uphold, to the utmost of our ability, the National Administration at Washington. It is for the time being the government, and necessarily has entire charge of the conduct of hostilities. That they will be wisely conducted for the common interest and glory of the nation, we may safely believe. All captiousness of fault-finding should be discouraged. It is not possible for all to know at once the reasons for every act or even the act itself. Results are the only true tests of administration and for these we must patiently wait. Time is essential to create great armies and to conquer States, as it is to accomplish any other grand result.

It is only two months since Abraham Lincoln was inaugurated President of the United States, and during that time events have been so precipitated upon each other that it has seemed well nigh impossible to avoid some confusion. And yet, I do believe there is not much to complain of, and abundance to approve.

The power of the National Government begins to show itself unmistakably, and I take it for granted, that the time has now arrived when that government means to take the offensive and will follow the traitors to their strong holds and severely punish them. It cannot longer confine itself to mere defence of the national domain and property—it must strike treason wherever it is to be found—all the delusive pretences of the rebels about coercion and the invasion of States must be thrown to the winds, and the full right of the troops of the Federal Government to march at pleasure over every inch of the territory of the United States must be put beyond question. There can be no neutrals in this contest. That State which refuses to aid on the lawful call of the President is as much guilty of treason as the one which, like South Carolina, makes actual war upon the Federal armies and must be treated in the same manner.

To aid in the accomplishment [of] this great task, let us put Michigan in a situation to be able promptly and vigorously to answer any call the President may make upon us; and in doing this we must remember that one trained soldier is worth more than two untrained ones. To second the National Administration is our whole province; and to do it effectually must be our great endeavor. And while I do not expect the grand result immediately, nor that it will be attained without great sacrifices, yet I cannot doubt the final issue. It cannot be that this wicked rebellion will succeed. Utterly without cause, based upon unchastened ambition and lust of power alone, it can have neither the sympathies of mankind nor the favor of God. In point of material power the odds are very greatly with the Government; and these must finally prevail in a just cause, which enlists in its behalf the enthusiasm of all loyal citizens, and the sympathies of the just and good everywhere. I look confidently, then, to see the complete triumph of the Constitution and Government of the United States in this great contest, and the final and firm establishment in the country of the doctrines of the Declaration of Independence. They who have taken the sword will perish by the sword, and this war, inaugurated to establish slave-holding despotism forever on this continent, will result in its total and speedy destruction.

Our free and ever to be revered form of government, tried in this fierce furnace of revolution, will prove itself equal to every occasion. It will be doubly strengthened and secured in the hearts of our own people, while its power and respectability abroad will be immensely enhanced. The fame of Washington and his compatriots will glow with a brighter lustre, and the hopes of men everywhere will be cheered and strengthened. Liberty, the great aim of mankind, will, in the triumph of the Great Republic, secure a home upon earth forever.

That God, by His mighty power, will overrule all to this great end, let us devoutly trust.

Austin Blair.

May 7, 1861.[100]

The Union War effort faltered more than once. Notwithstanding, consistent with this initial call, Blair remained "confident of the success of the Union cause, never lost heart or faltered, and kept up the spirits of the people at home and of the soldiers in the field."[101]

---

100. *Journal of the House*, Extra Session of 1861, May 7, 1861, 9-18.
101. Bingham, 106.

Communications on Recruitment
May and June 1861

The War Department initially limited the number of regiments that Michigan could supply even though its response to Lincoln's call had been immediate. The 1st Michigan Infantry arrived in Washington late on May 16 and marched up Pennsylvania Avenue accompanied by an enthusiastic crowd. Two days later, the president greeted the regiment at the White House and remarked how it was "the first installment from Michigan and the great Northwest." The New York Tribune *reported it to be "the first Western regiment that had arrived at the capital."*[102]

A progress report to Washington showed how this initial speediness had been matched with more recruits.

Adjutant-General's Office,
Detroit, Mich., May 11, 1861.
General Simon Cameron,
Secretary of War:

Sir: I am authorized by the Governor of this State to say that four regiments (a brigade) are ready for U.S. service, to be mustered for three years, unless sooner discharged. The Governor desires that they may be accepted as a brigade and move together, if the interests of the service will permit. The regiments are fully equipped, except arms and accouterments for two regiments.

Very respectfully, your obedient servant,

Jno. Robertson, Adjutant-General Michigan,

P. S.—Men enough are enrolled for seven regiments.

---

102.   Frank B. Woodford, *Father Abraham's Children: Michigan Episodes in the Civil War* (Detroit: Wayne State University Press, 1961), 34-35, 260.

Other leaders joined Blair in believing more troops would be necessary. Former congressman and Democrat Hiram Walbridge of New York pressed Lincoln to allow more recruiting, and he wrote to the Northern governors to urge support. In reply, Blair sent this letter, which became public after several years.

Michigan
Executive Office,
Lansing, June 3d, 1861.
Hon. Hiram Walbridge:

Dear Sir: — I have this moment received your letter of May 27th, having been absent from the Capital at the time it arrived. I hasten now to say, that your views meet my hearty approbation, and nothing will give me greater pleasure than to cooperate in any effort to procure their adoption at Washington.

The Government, after persistent teasing, have allowed me to furnish from Michigan, four regiments, and no more. These are now all ready to march, and in good order. Four more quite as good are claiming to be received, and refuse to be satisfied when I tell them they are not desired. I think it safe to say, that at least nine-tenths of our people think the force called for entirely too small, and persist in maintaining that more troops will be received. I cannot stop their recruiting. Companies are all the time forming now, and they fairly weary me with their incessant demand to be organized and instructed. The truth is simply—the people feel that they have the power to crush this rebellion at a blow, and they cannot see why they should not be allowed at once to do it. As to expense, I believe in the long run it will cost less, and the saving of blood would be immense. It is also of great consequence to demonstrate the power of the Government to quell rebellion quickly. Every way it seems better to me, that the force should be made overwhelming as soon as possible.

Hoping you may have entire success in your efforts,
I remain, your obedient servant,
(Signed) Austin Blair.[103]

---

103. *Correspondence between His Excellency, President Abraham Lincoln, with General Hiram Walbridge, of New York, in 1861* (New York: John F. Trow, 1865), 13-14.

Reply to Serenade
July 25, 1861

The governor traveled outside the state on a number of occasions, both to Washington and to camps where Michigan soldiers were stationed. On July 25, 1861, on the heels of the Union defeat at the Battle of First Bull Run, he received special acknowledgment while in the national capital.

Serenade to Gov. Blair, Of Michigan
Washington, July 25.
Governor Blair, of Michigan, was complimented with a serenade to-night by one of the regimental bands of that State. He addressed the large and enthusiastic crowd. He said that

"although our forces were checked, not defeated, at the late battle, they will soon be prepared for a renewal of the fight, in defence of all that is dear to American freemen—the preservation of the Constitution and liberty. We have now a young man, a soldier of the West, General McClellan, under whose lead our army cannot fail of victory. (This allusion elicited vociferous cheers.)

Till now it was supposed that rebellion would be soon suppressed, but facts show that a more extended effort is necessary for the restoration of peace. The slogan is sounding throughout the North and West, and stout hearts are burning to enter into the service of their country. The war must be vigorously prosecuted, and the end cannot fail to give us victory.

We have to-day obtained from the Government authority to send five additional regiments into the field, and they will be here within the next four weeks."

The Governor retired amid cheers from the delighted multitude.[104]

Having met George McClellan in early May, Blair held high hopes for his leadership.

---

104. *Philadelphia Inquirer*, July 26, 1861, 1; Washington *Evening Star*, July 25, 1861, 3.

Proclamation: Day of Humiliation, Prayer, and Fasting
September 20, 1861

Amid some successes, the Union war effort experienced embarrassing defeats. On August 12, 1861, Lincoln issued a proclamation in response to a congressional request for a national day of prayer. The president designated the last Thursday in September to be devoted to this purpose.[105] *Blair did not need to take action in response, but he issued a companion proclamation.*

The President of the United States having recommended that the last Thursday in September, instant, be observed as a day of public humiliation, prayer and fasting, by the people, with religious solemnities and the offering of fervent supplications to Almighty God for the safety and welfare of these States, his blessings on their arms, and a speedy restoration of peace, I, Austin Blair, Governor of the State of Michigan, in conformity with the Proclamation of the President, and more fully to impress upon the people of this State the duty of respecting the same, do earnestly unite in recommending the people of this State to observe and solemnly keep the said day.

It becomes us as a Christian people, in this time of peril to our country, to remember the blessings of peace and liberty which have been so bountifully conferred upon us by Divine Providence in the past, and to humiliate ourselves in view of the ingratitude with which such blessings have been received. Now when the hand of the assassin and the traitor is raised to smite and destroy our country, and turn into mockery all the holy utterances of our fathers in the founding of the Republic, let Almighty God be implored to inspire our public men with the pure spirit of patriotism, turn away the hearts of our

---

105. *CW*, Vol. IV, 482-483.

leaders from all selfish scheming, and guide our brave and loyal troops to victory, and our country to peace and security.

And I do further recommend that, so far as may be, all public offices and places of business be closed, and that ordinary avocations cease throughout said day.

In Witness Whereof, I have hereunto caused to be affixed the great seal of this State, at Lansing, this 20th day of September, in the year of our Lord one thousand eight hundred and sixty-one.

Austin Blair.

James B. Porter, Secretary of State.[106]

After the Union defeat in the Battle of Ball's Bluff on October 21, 1861, the governor made a frontline trip. "Gov. Blair and suite" paid Brigadier-General Alpheus S. Williams a visit near Muddy Branch, Maryland. They dined together, thanks to volunteer William Dollarson.[107] A letter home by a soldier in the 2nd Michigan Infantry, dated October 27, recorded "The Gov. of Mich. is here to day" in Fairfax County, Virginia.[108]

106.   *LSR*, Sept. 25, 1861, 2.

107.   Milo M. Quaife ed., *From the Cannon's Mouth: The Civil War Letters of General Alpheus S. Williams* (Lincoln: University of Nebraska Press, 1995), 29.

108.   Letter of Alphonso Crane, Archives of Michigan. Location "Eagle Mountain" referred to the Mount Eagle plantation near Alexandria.

Proclamation of Thanksgiving
November 11, 1861

The first proclamation of a national day of thanksgiving issued forth from the Continental Congress in 1777. Ironically, the action was taken in the Congress's temporary location in York, Pennsylvania, while the British occupied the national capital at Philadelphia. The antecedents to this formal action hearkened back to the early 17th century. Lincoln's proclamation of November 27 called for the closing of government offices.[109] Not until 1863 would the president set aside the last Thursday of November as a national day of thanksgiving and praise. Blair's call anticipated that decree.

In accordance with a custom long established and deeply cherished by the people since the earliest settlement of our country, and with reverent thankfulness towards the Supreme Ruler over man and nations for his great bounties and mercies to us, I do hereby appoint and set apart Thursday, the twenty-eighth day of November instant, as a day of Thanksgiving and Praise. Our liberties, civil and religious, still remain to us. The rude shock of war has not so much as touched our borders, but peace and plenty yet surround our dwellings. The free republican government, founded by our fathers after heroic sacrifices and struggles, still bears aloft the national flag, and grows daily stronger in the hearts of the great body of the people. I therefore earnestly urge all people of this State that, refraining from their usual employments, they fitly and devoutly keep that day; and that in their houses of public worship, and in their own homes, they remember the language of Thanksgiving and Praise to Almighty God, beseeching Him that He may continue His great mercies to us as individuals

---

109. *CW*, Vol. V, 32.

and as a nation; that He may give a speedy triumph to the national arms over the malignant horde who now seek the destruction of the Republic; and that, chastened by adversity, we may be led to put away every injustice, oppression and wrong, and transmit to our posterity a nation undivided, loving liberty, obedient to law, and cherishing the institutions of peace and religion.

(L.S.) ["Locus Sigilli," Latin for "place of the seal"]

In testimony whereof, I have hereunto set my hand and caused to be affixed the great seal of the State of Michigan, this eleventh day of November in the year of our Lord one thousand eight hundred and sixty-one.

Austin Blair.

By the Governor:

James B. Porter, Secretary of State[110]

It was all quiet along the Potomac late that month. Brigadier-General Williams and staff enjoyed a holiday meal of turkeys and chickens prepared by citizen-liberator Dollarson.[111]

---

110.   *DFP,* Nov. 23, 1861, 3.

111.   Michigan Civil War Association, *Warriors for Liberty: William Dollarson & Michigan's Civil War African Americans* (Traverse City: Mission Point Press, 2024), 61.

Proclamation Convening Legislature
December 9, 1861

Blair called the legislature into a January session for the specific purpose of responding to a tax measure by the federal government. The constitution empowered the legislature, once it convened, to take up all appropriate matters. The governor delivered a special message on January 9th (infra) pertaining to the war and the state. It took but one day for the Legislature to approve and Blair to sign into law a measure to accept the tax burden levied by the U.S. government for both 1862 and 1863. The sine die adjournment occurred on January 20th after enactment of another twenty-five bills and sixteen resolutions.[112]

Whereas, Since the last session of the Legislature, by section eight of "An act entitled an act to provide increased revenue from imports, to pay interest on the public debt, and for other purposes," enacted by the Congress of the United States, a direct tax has been laid annually upon the State of Michigan of five hundred and one thousand seven hundred and sixty-three and one-third dollars;

And Whereas, It is also provided by section fifty-three of the said act of Congress, "That any State may lawfully assume, assess, collect and pay into the Treasury of the United States, the direct tax, in its own way and manner, by and through its own officers, collectors," &c., and that in such case the State shall be entitled to a "deduction of fifteen per cent. on the quota apportioned to such State," thereby creating, in my judgment, such an extraordinary occasion as is contemplated by the Constitution;

Therefore, I, Austin Blair, Governor of the State of Michigan,

---

112. *Acts of the Legislature of the State of Michigan Passed at the Extra Session of 1862* (Lansing: John A. Kerr & Co., 1862), 1-2.

in virtue of the power vested in me by the Constitution, do convene the Legislature of this State, hereby requiring the Senators and Representatives to assemble in their respective chambers, at the Capitol, in Lansing, on Thursday, the second day of January next, at twelve o'clock noon, then and there to consider and determine upon the measures proper to be adopted in regard to the collection of the said direct tax, and all such other subjects as may be brought before the Legislature in pursuance of the Constitution.

In Testimony whereof, I have hereunto set my hand, and caused to be affixed the Great Seal of the State, at Lansing, this 9th day of December, in the year of our Lord, one thousand eight hundred and sixty-one. By the Governor:

Austin Blair.

James B. Porter, Sec'y of State.[113]

At year's end, Michigan had furnished sixteen regiments of infantry and cavalry and five artillery batteries, totaling over 16,000 men in uniform.[114]

113. *Journal of the Senate of the State of Michigan, Extra Session of 1862* (John A. Kerr & Co., 1862), 1-2.

114. Robertson, 24.

Message to Special Session
January 2, 1862

Blair spoke to the legislature at the commencement of session, touching heavily on his view of the underlying reasons for and conduct of the war. He dutifully reported on the offer by the University of Michigan to launch a military school if the legislature would assist in paying for it. Blair also staked out a leading position on the question of liberating the enslaved. In August 1861, the "Act to confiscate Property used for Insurrectionary Purposes" went into effect, specifying that enslaved persons required "to take up arms against the United States" or to work in supporting the Confederate military would no longer be subject to a claim for service by their owners (Pub. L. 37-60, 12 Stat. 319). The President revoked a proclamation of emancipation from Union military commander John C. Fremont to avoid driving the border slaveholding states into the Confederacy. The governor called on federal authorities, civil and military, to harbor escapees instead of acting to "protect and sustain the accursed system." He advocated for confiscation of all persons enslaved. One historian judged that Blair "showed an attitude somewhat more advanced on the emancipation issue, as he was probably the most radically loyal person of interest of influence in the state at this time. He declared that by the laws of war, emancipation was entirely justifiable."[115] The message is approximately 3,700 words.

Fellow-citizens of the Senate and House of Representatives:

At the time of the adjournment of the Extra Session, in May last, it was hardly contemplated that it would be found indispensable to call the Legislature together again within the year. The Southern

---

115.   Harriette M. Dilla, *The Politics of Michigan, 1865-1878* (New York: Columbia University, 1912), 31.

Rebellion, just then initiated by the formal secession of several States, and the seizure of Fort Sumter by military power, had not yet assumed the gigantic proportions which it now wears. It found the loyal States in profound repose, diligently engaged in the cultivation of the arts and humanities which belong to peace, but wholly unused to war. They had long accustomed themselves to believe that under our form of government every dispute that could arise would be peacefully settled by the verdict of the ballot box, and when they perceived that a considerable number of States preferred the barbarism of war, and had deliberately appealed to the sword, they were very illy prepared to meet that appeal. Of men, loyal, hardy, patriotic men, there were enough, and much more than enough; but of the knowledge of war, and of supplies of arms and munitions, there was a sad lack everywhere. Michigan, with more than a hundred thousand fighting men, had arms for hardly more than a thousand, and for military organization, she had next to none at all. The ordinary courses of trade and business had been rudely and almost instantaneously broken up, and new ones had to be sought out. Doubt and distrust were everywhere.

[¶] In the midst of these conditions we started out to explore the new paths which were to be trodden hereafter. We were now to learn war; to create armies; arm and equip them for the field and send them forth to fight those against whom they had done no wrong and had never intended any, and who were bound by obligations the most solemn to keep peace towards them. The ordinary machinery of government has been found inadequate to meet the exigencies of our present rapidly changing affairs, and a frequent resort to the legislative power is rendered imperative. Nor ought this to be regarded as at all strange. It is only in the light of events themselves that their logic is clear, and human forecast cannot always be relied upon to meet the demands of the future. Especially is this true of times like the present. Our good Ship of State is driven before a furious gale, and the best navigator can hardly tell what of disaster the next wave may bring. It is the duty of every one on board, wisely, prudently, and bravely to stand always at his post. Michigan has endeavored to meet this responsibility faithfully—even enthusiastically. Whatever sacrifice has been required of her, she has at once prepared herself to make. Both by her gallant soldiers in the field and her patriotic citizens at home, she has promptly obeyed every call made by the Federal Government upon her, and I dare promise that she will not fail in this respect hereafter.

The Congress of the United States, in consequence of the unusual magnitude of the demand upon the Treasury, caused by the war, has been compelled to resort to heavy loans, and is rapidly creating a large public debt, for the payment of the interest upon which it was necessary that new sources of revenue should be found. For this purpose an act was passed on the 5th day of August last, entitled "An act to provide increased revenue from imports, to pay interest on the public debt, and for other purposes." By section 8 of that act it is provided "that a direct tax of twenty millions be and is hereby annually laid upon the United States, and the same shall be and is hereby apportioned to the States respectively, in manner following: 'To the State of Michigan, five hundred and one thousand seven hundred and sixty-three and one-third dollars.'" The act then goes on to authorize the President of the United States to divide the States and Territories into convenient collection districts, and to appoint an assessor and collector for each district, and that each assessor may divide his district and appoint assistants. In section 13 of this act, it is further enacted, "that the said direct tax shall be assessed and laid on the value of all lands and lots of ground, with their improvements and dwelling houses," with certain unimportant exemptions.

[¶] It will be observed that this law introduces to us the United States assessor and tax-gatherer, individuals hitherto unknown to us, and whose acquaintance I think we are not desirous of making. The collector comes, also, with a new rule of taxation. He is to assess only the value of all lands and lots of ground, with their improvements and dwelling houses. The personal property is to escape altogether, if this rule is followed, and it seems that the constitution of the United States will permit no other rule to be adopted in case the tax is assessed and collected by the Federal Government. Section 53, however, enacts "that any State or Territory may lawfully assume to assess, collect and pay into the Treasury of the United States the direct tax, or its quota thereof, in its own way and manner, and by and through its own officers, assessors and collectors." And in case of such assumption and payment, or assessment and collection, a deduction of fifteen per centum will be made from the quota of direct tax apportioned to the State or Territory, notice of the same being given to the Secretary of the Treasury on or before the second Tuesday of February next. The same section (53) contains a proviso to the effect that "the amount of direct tax apportioned to any State shall be liable to be paid and satisfied, in whole or in part, by the release of such State, duly executed to the United States, of any liquidated and determined claim of such State of equal amount against the United States." And in that case the same deduction is allowed as in case of actual payment into the Treasury. In order to secure such a deduction it is also required that payment into the treasury be made on or before the last day of June in the year to which such payment relates.

The advantages to be derived to the State from the assumption and payment of the direct tax, according to the provisions of the law of Congress, are so manifest and so great that I cannot doubt that you will adopt that course without hesitation. In that event it will be found that the State will be able to pay the entire amount of the tax due in June next, by its release to the United States, and without any resort to collections from the people, unless the tax should be increased by the present Congress, of which there is some probability.

The gross amount of the advances which the State has made on account of the General Government in the raising of troops, is about five hundred and thirty-nine thousand dollars, which is likely to be increased in finishing what remains to be completed to about six hundred thousand dollars. Of this sum, ninety-two thousand dollars only has been refunded to the State from the appropriations made by Congress for that purpose. For exact amounts I refer you to the reports of the Auditor General and State Treasurer. And for the precise details of the manner of the expenditure, and for what it was made, I refer you to the report of the Quarter Master General, and the vouchers and accounts of that office, and the State Paymaster on file in the Auditor General's office in pursuance of law.

Accompanying this message I submit for the consideration of the Legislature, a circular transmitted by the Department of State at Washington, in October last, to the Governors of the loyal States, upon the subject of the fortifications of our sea and lake coasts. With this circular the public are already familiar. At the time of its issue it was difficult to perceive any adequate reason for it. In fact it seemed more likely to create ill-blood and furnish the occasion for trouble with our immediate neighbors than to assure the continuance of peace. The circular is, however, altogether temperate in tone and without offence to any. Subsequent events have put an entirely new face upon the whole subject.

[¶] The British people, both American and transatlantic, seem suddenly, and to us mysteriously, to have become possessed of the passion for war. Turning their backs upon all their history for the last half century, they are anxious to assist the assassins of liberty in the South to establish a slave oligarchy there upon the ruins of the American Union. It is patent to all the world that we seek nothing but peace with them. Involved in a trying domestic struggle, war with England, at any time a great misfortune, would be now an evil of incalculable magnitude. This the British government cannot fail to know. With our immediate neighbors of Canada we have been on terms of the most perfect amity for many years. Notwithstanding their strange excitement of late, our people still entertain the most friendly spirit towards them. We have not mounted a gun upon one of our dismantled forts, nor committed any act to disturb our friendly relations with them. All our business interests have become so interlocked that in our material progress, we have became [sic] almost as one nation. Our railroads and theirs are only parts of the same great lines, and our currency and business intermingles throughout the entire regions lying near the boundary. Nor have our relations with the mother country been much less intimate. British capital has been largely employed in the improvement of our country, and we have been, in turn, a valuable customer to them. And all this has been mutually beneficial. Can these people have thought what it will cost them to destroy it? And do they see clearly what they will gain in its place by war?

The apparent cause of the excitement was the seizure of Mason and Slidell, on board the British steamer *Trent*, but I cannot bring myself to believe that to be the real cause. It seems to be wholly insufficient to be made the ground of such a prodigious tempest, and I think it will before long be made clear, that the British Government has concealed designs, and only seeks a pretext for a rupture. Mason and Slidell, after being given a very mischievous importance by their detention, have now been given up to the English Government.[116] Whether that course was wise or not, it does not become me to judge; at least, it does not change my purpose of recommending to you to put the State in a posture of defence as soon as may be, and for this purpose I think we need not so much fortifications as a full supply of arms for the people, and a powerful war marine upon the great lakes. Michigan is to be defended, if it comes to that, not upon her own ground, but upon the soil of Canada. Give us arms for the people, and the undoubted control of the lakes, and fortification may be safely left to the most convenient season. Not that fortifications would be useless, but that our main dependence cannot safely be rested upon them, for reasons too obvious to require a statement here.

[¶] I recommend, therefore, that provision be made for the reorganization of the uniform volunteer militia of the State to constitute an active force, and the speedy enrollment of the entire body to be subject to draft at any time. This may be done under our present laws with some amendments, or by the adoption of a new system similar to that in force in the State of Massachusetts. It will not be

116.   On Nov. 8, 1861, Confederate envoys James Murray Mason and John Slidell were taken from a British vessel by a U.S. Navy frigate and held in custody; England protested; on Dec. 26, Lincoln and his Cabinet approved their release.

necessary to incur very heavy expenses in effecting the organization until the force should be actually required for service, and for such an event adequate provision would require to be made. In addition to the organization of our own forces, I think it would be advisable for the Legislature to urge upon the attention of Congress the great and immediate necessity of establishing at some safe and convenient point in the North-West, a great arsenal and manufactory of arms and munitions of war, and also a naval station, to be located in some safe, spacious and convenient harbor of the State of Michigan, as being by all means the most advantageous, both from the extent of her coast and her unrivaled resources in all the materials for ship-building. As to the particular locality, you, gentlemen, are the better judges.

I also submit herewith a preamble and resolutions of the Board of Regents of the University of Michigan, which the President of that body has requested me to lay before you. By the resolutions the Board propose to establish a military school at the University, whenever the State will add to the fund $100,000, securing a permanent additional income of $7,000 yearly. That such a department as the Board proposes to establish, would be exceedingly advantageous to us as a State, I presume no one will doubt. The war in which we are now engaged has proved that we cannot safely neglect the military education of our people. Whether the present is a fitting occasion for the establishment of the proposed school, all things considered, I must leave entirely to the better judgment of the Legislature.

By the act of the extra session, approved May 10, 1861, the Governor was authorized to muster into the service of the State the volunteer militia, in number not to exceed one hundred companies, the Coldwater Light Artillery, and a corps of sappers and miners, not to exceed one hundred in number. At the time of the passage of the act it was supposed that this was as large a force as Michigan would be called upon to furnish, in any event. Such, however, was not the case. The whole force authorized by the law has been put into the field, and the State has raised, and is now raising, eleven regiments more, the United States government paying the expenses, making twenty-one in all; besides six batteries of light artillery, a squadron of cavalry, and a number of organized companies of infantry, which have joined regiments in other States, making a total of troops furnished by the State of Michigan of about 24,000 men. For details in regard to these forces, I refer you to the full and complete report of the Adjutant General.

[¶] The aggregate cost to the State, of organizing, uniforming, paying, transporting and subsisting the troops authorized by the law, including the First Regiment, which was mustered out at the end of its three months term of service, and was re-organized, has been thus far, as heretofore stated, $539,428 91; and I am confident that when the whole is closed, which will now be very soon, the entire cost will not exceed $600,000. When it is taken into account that a very large amount of the contracts were necessarily made payable in the war loan bonds at par, which were regarded as worth but ninety cents on the dollar, in the market, and that a very considerable portion of the expenses have been incurred for recruits to fill up regiments already in the field, which had become reduced by sickness or otherwise, I believe it will be found that nowhere in the Union has the like service been performed at a less expense. I think it may also be safely affirmed that no troops have taken the field better provided in all respects, (with the single exception of transportation trains,) than those from Michigan.

[¶] Of the troops themselves, both officers and privates, I can speak in terms of unreserved commendation. They have honored the State from which they went forth. Never, since Michigan became a State of the Union, did she occupy so high a position among her sister States, as now. This I attribute to her firm, consistent and loyal course throughout the whole controversy. While it was a question of politics the voice of Michigan was never doubtful. Her principles were plainly set forth and in all constitutional ways she maintained them firmly. When it became a question of war, with equal alacrity her people flocked to the standard of the Union to defend their constitutional liberties with their lives. In these straight paths I believe they will continue to the end.

Some differences of opinion have arisen in regard to the proper construction of the law assigning the duties of the Military Contract Board and the State Military Board. It does not seem entirely clear as to which of these is the proper Auditing Board. I recommend that the doubt be removed by amendment.

I recommend, also, a careful revision of the act "for the relief of the families of volunteers by counties." As the law now stands it seems to offer a premium to the volunteer to retain the entire amount of his wages received from the United States, and leave the support of his family entirely to the county. The burden upon the counties is becoming very heavy, and the relief does not seem always to be wisely applied. Perhaps the law might be so changed as to make the relief to the families depend upon the volunteer first securing to his family by allotment some reasonable proportion of his wages. Great favoritism, also, is said to be used by some Supervisors, in the dispensation of the fund. For the purpose of correcting this, it is worth considering whether some system of proofs, to be submitted to the Supervisor, might not be adopted, which should be uniform in all cases. It has also been made a question whether troops raised not under the State laws, but by authority from the War Department, were entitled to the benefits of the law at all. It would gratify the Independent Regiments, so called, if all distinctions between Michigan troops were now removed. The whole subject is submitted to, and I think requires the earnest attention of the Legislature.

. . .

Gentlemen of the two Houses: I cannot close this brief address without an allusion to the great subject that occupies all men's minds. The Southern rebellion still maintains a bold front against the Union armies. That is the cause of all our complications abroad, and our troubles at home. To deal wisely with it, is to find a short and easy deliverance from them all. The people of Michigan are no idle spectators of this great contest. They have furnished all the troops required of them, and are preparing to pay the taxes and to submit to the most onerous burdens without a murmur. They are ready to increase their sacrifices, if need be, to require impossibilities of no man, but to be patient and wait. But to see the vast armies of the Republic, and all its pecuniary resources, used to protect and sustain the accursed system which has been a perpetual and tyrranical [sic] disturber, and which now makes sanguinary war upon the Union and the Constitution, is precisely what they will never submit to tamely. The loyal States having furnished adequate means, both of men and money, to crush the rebellion, have a right to expect those men to be used with the utmost vigor to accomplish the object, and that without any mawkish sympathy for the interest of traitors in arms. Upon those who caused the war and now maintain it, its chief burdens ought to fall. No property of a rebel ought to be free from confiscation—not even the sacred slave.

[¶] The object of war is to destroy the power of the enemy, and whatever measures are calculated to accomplish that object, and are in accordance with the usages of civilized nations, ought to be employed. To undertake to put down a powerful rebellion and at the same time to save and protect all the chief sources of the power of that rebellion, seems, to common minds, but a short remove from simple folly. He who is not for the Union unconditionally in this mortal struggle, is against it. The highest dictates of patriotism, justice and humanity combine to demand that the war should be conducted to a speedy close upon principles of the most heroic energy and retributive power. The time for gentle dalliance has long since passed away. We meet an enemy, vindictive, bloodthirsty and cruel, profoundly in earnest, inspired with an energy and self-sacrifice which would honor a good cause, respecting neither laws, constitutions nor historic memories, fanatically devoted only to his one wicked purpose to destroy the government and establish his slaveholding oligarchy in its stead. To treat this enemy gently is to excite his derision. To protect his slave property, is to help him to butcher our people and burn our houses. No. He must be met with an activity and a purpose equal to his own.

[¶] Hurl the Union forces, which outnumber him two to one, upon his whole line like a thunderbolt; pay them out of his property, feed them from his granaries, mount them upon his horses, and carry them in his wagons, if he has any, and let him feel the full force of the storm of war which he has raised. I would apologize neither to Kentucky nor anybody else, for these measures, but quickly range all neutrals either on the one side or the other. Just a little of the courage and ability which carried Napoleon over the Alps, dragging his cannon through the snow, would quickly settle this contest, and settle it right. If our soldiers must die, do not let it be of the inactivity and diseases of camps, but let them at least have the satisfaction of falling like soldiers, amid the roar of battle, and hearing the shouts of victory, then will they welcome it as the tired laborer welcomes sleep. Let us hope that we have not much longer to wait.

Austin Blair.

Lansing, January 2, 1862.[117]

General McClellan had built up the formidable Army of the Potomac during the fall in camps around Washington but had not led it into battle. In March, it would begin to move south.

---

117. *Messages*, 446-453. As before, Blair personally delivered the message. *Journal of the House of Representatives of the State of Michigan, Extra Session of 1862* (John A. Kerr & Co., 1862), 8.

Transmittal of Legislative Items
January 9, 1862

Blair customarily sent messages to the legislature regarding referrals, sign-ing of bills, and other matters. Following is a transmittal involving two military matters.

To the Senate and House of Representatives:

I respectfully recommend to the attention of your honorable bodies the following subjects:

...

5th. A company of infantry was formed in the county of Van Buren, during the last summer, with a view to joining a State regiment, and was assigned to the 6th regiment, but being doubtful whether that regiment would go early into service, they declined to muster into the State service, and subsequently joined a New York regiment in Sickles' Brigade. Under existing laws there is no authority to pay the expenses of raising and subsisting this company. Whether it will be proper to authorize such payment by law now to be enacted, I submit it entirely to the Legislature. I presume there are other cases similar in some respects.

6th. Mrs. I.W. Ingersoll, of Detroit, lately visited Charleston, for the purpose of relieving, as far as possible, the Michigan prisoners confined there, and she has, I believe, to a considerable extent, supplied them with clothing and other things, freely given by their friends, and of which they were in great need. She has necessarily incurred considerable expenses in freight bills and her own traveling expenses, all which I felt myself, without legal authority, in duty, bound to pay. I recommend the Legislature to authorize the auditing and payment of these expenses.

....

Austin Blair.

January 9, 1862.[118]

Lydia B. Ingersoll had traveled to Castle Pinckney in Charleston harbor to attend to her son Joseph, a private in Company A of the 1st Michigan Infantry regiment, captured at First Bull Run.[119]

---

118. *Messages*, 454-456.
119. Joseph enlisted five days after Fort Sumter surrendered; he mustered out on May 20, 1862, far beyond his ninety-day term of service. *Record of Service of Michigan Volunteers in the Civil War 1861-1865* (Kalamazoo: Ihling Bros. & Everard, 1903), Vol. 1, 69 ("*Record of Service*"); Robertson, 438, 857. Born in 1811, Lydia died in 1899 having outlived all but one of her children and husband Isaac W. Ingersoll, captain in the 24th Michigan Infantry. Findagrave # 78274878.

Messages on Approval of Legislation
January 17 & 18, 1862

Blair signed bills into law during the final days of the special legislative session. The legislature adjourned sine die on January 20; while in session, its journals recorded messages from the governor regarding bills signed or vetoed. Those provided here relate to Civil War matters and demonstrate Blair's concurrence.

Executive Office,

Lansing, January 17, 1862.

To the House of Representatives:

I have approved and filed in the office of the Secretary of State, the following acts passed at the present session.

…

An act to amend an act entitled an act to provide for the relief, by counties, of the families of volunteers, mustered from this State into the military service of the United States, or of this State, approved May 10th, 1861, and to add certain sections thereto.

Also,

Joint resolution relative to the volunteer force enlisted into the service of the United States or of this State, …

Austin Blair.[120]

Executive Office,

Lansing, January 18, 1862.

To the Senate:

I have approved and filed in the office of the Secretary of State the following acts:

---

120.   *Journal of the House*, Extra Session of 1862, 255-256.

...

An act for the reorganization of the military forces of the State of Michigan;

...

Joint resolution in reference to the rebellion;

Also,

An act to amend an act entitled an act authorizing a war loan, approved May 10th, 1861;

...

Austin Blair.[121]

The action on the 1861 soldier relief act amended section 1 to read as follows:

It shall be the duty of the boards of supervisors of each organized county, at their sessions to be held in the month of June, in the year eighteen hundred and sixty-one, and at each subsequent session, whenever necessary, to make adequate provision for all requisite relief and support of the families of the non-commissioned officers, musicians and privates enlisted from their counties, and mustered into the military service of the United States, or of this State; and for such purposes the said boards of supervisors are severally authorized to borrow money, at a rate of interest not exceeding ten per centum per annum, and to issue bonds, or other securities, for the sums borrowed, payable at some time therein to be mentioned, not exceeding three years from the date thereof, and to assess, levy and collect taxes upon all the real and personal property of said counties, not exempt from taxation, sufficient to pay such moneys borrowed, and to provide the relief hereby authorized.[122]

---

121. *Journal of the Senate*, Extra Session of 1862, 178-179.
122. *Acts of the Legislature*, Extra Session of 1862, 14-15.

The "Joint resolution relative to the volunteer force" dealt with the need to keep track of the tens of thousands of soldiers who had volunteered to defend the Union—and of casualties. It directed the adjutant general to:

transmit to the county clerk of each county in this State, a correct list of the persons mustered into the service of the United States, or of this State, from such county, giving, so far as practicable, the name, date of enlistment, company, regiment, whether married or unmarried, also the number that have died in battle, or from sickness or wounds in battle, and the names of those that have been discharged or have deserted, and that additional lists shall annually, at the time aforesaid, be transmitted, giving the mustering of the current year, together with deaths, discharges, or desertions, as the case may be.[123]

The military reorganization act was a multi-page bill of ninety-six sections that formalized details for the militia and matters brought into real focus by the manpower necessary to fight the war.[124] *The "Joint resolution in reference to the rebellion" (see Appendix) had been passed by the legislature on the 17th.*[125] *The final text included this statement, in which the governor concurred: "slavery should be swept from the land." At the end of January, Michael Shoemaker of Jackson was commissioned colonel of the 13th Michigan Infantry. In one way, his appointment was surprising. See Appendix.*

A two-day battle in west Tennessee on April 6-7 inflicted nearly 24,000 casualties, proving this war would be America's bloodiest. Blair traveled to the Shiloh battleground to "bring aid when he visited his troops" (emphasis added).[126] *He left home toward the end of April and remained at least until May 19.*[127] *He returned with $35,000 of the $40,000 in*

123.   Id. 64-65.

124.   Id. 20-48.

125.   *Journal of the Senate*, Extra Session of 1862, 131, 173.

126.   Harris, *Lincoln and the Union Governors*, 40. The battle occurred on April 6–7, 1862, involving three of "his" units: 12th Infantry, 15th Infantry, and 1st Artillery Battery "B."

127.   *LSR*, Apr. 30, 1862, 3; *OR*, III, II, 45.

pay received by the men of the 13th Michigan Infantry, entrusted to him for delivery on the homefront. He also brought back letters for personal delivery.[128] *The governor was "quite unwell, owing, no doubt, to the hardships and fatigue of the journey"*[129] *and, no doubt, to the plight of those wounded or lost in battle.*

---

128.   Letter from Jacob Houseman, 9th Michigan Infantry, to Sally Wheeler, Apr. 30, 1862, Archives of Michigan.
129.   *LSR*, June 4, 1862, 2.

Official Letter to Secretary of War
June 10, 1862

Blair wrote the U.S. War Department about recruiting of the 4th Cavalry regiment. Its volunteers were ordered to Detroit for mustering in, which took place on August 29.[130] *The regiment's heroic story, among the best in the Union cavalry, are found in two histories.*[131]

State of Michigan, Executive Office,

Jackson, June 10, 1862.

Hon. E.M. Stanton,

Secretary of War:

Sir: I have the honor to acknowledge the receipt of the order of the Department authorizing me to raise one regiment of cavalry. In the order the hope is expressed that the regiment may be ready by the 4th of July next. I will cheerfully undertake to raise the regiment, but it will be impossible to do it by the time indicated. I cannot promise that it can be ready before the 1st of August, or near that time. If for any reason that length of time cannot be allowed, I should hope to be informed of it. It is the worst season of the year to recruit in the West, and the drain has already been considerable.

Very respectfully, your obedient servant,

Austin Blair,

Governor of Michigan.[132]

The 1st Michigan Cavalry regiment had mustered into service on September 13, 1861, and saw active duty in the Shenandoah Valley

---

130.   Robertson, 639.

131.   Joseph G. Vale, *Minty and the Cavalry: A History of Cavalry Campaigns in the Western Armies* (Harrisburg: Edwin K. Meyers, 1886); Rand K. Bitter, *Minty and His Cavalry: A History of the Saber Brigade and Its Commander* (2006).

132.   *OR*, III, II, 142-143. The authorization had come on May 31. Id. 101.

during spring 1862. The 2nd and 3rd Michigan Cavalry regiments also mustered in during late 1861.[133] *Michigan would contribute a total of twelve mounted regiments to the Union war effort. The Michigan Cavalry Brigade, consisting entirely of Michigan troopers, went on to earn numerous accolades beginning with the Battle of Gettysburg, and it "played a prominent part" in the Appomattox campaign of 1865. The 1st, 5th, 6th, and 7th Michigan Cavalry regiments made up its complement. Its most famous commander: George Armstrong Custer of Monroe.*

---

133.   The experiences of the 2nd would become known thanks to a detailed account written by one of its officers: Marshall P. Thatcher, *A Hundred Battles in the West, St. Louis to Atlanta, 1861-65, The Second Michigan Cavalry* (Detroit: L.F. Kilroy, 1884).

Recruiting Communiques
June-August 1862

On June 28, Lincoln and Seward devised a plan to raise more troops to supply losses incurred after the War Department had closed recruiting in April. Seward took a letter from the president to a meeting in New York City and drafted a communique from northern governors requesting a new requisition of manpower. The result: on July 2, newspapers including The New York Times *published the governors' letter along with Lincoln's response calling for 300,000 new volunteers. Not all loyal governors immediately signed onto the letter, but Blair did.*

The President:

The undersigned, Governors of States of the Union, impressed with the belief that the citizens of the States which they respectively represent are of one accord in the hearty desire that the recent successes of the Federal arms may be followed up by measures which must insure the speedy restoration of the Union; and believing that in view of the present state of the important military movements now in progress and the reduced condition of our effective forces in the field, resulting from the usual and unavoidable casualties of the service, that the time has arrived for prompt and vigorous measures to be adopted by the people in support of the great interests committed to your charge, we respectfully request, if it meets with your entire approval, that you at once call upon the several States for such number of men as may be required to fill up all military organizations now in the field, and add to the armies heretofore organized such additional number of men as may in your judgment be necessary to garrison and hold all of the numerous cities and military positions that have been captured by our armies, and to speedily crush the rebellion that still exists in several of the Southern States, thus practically restoring to the civilized world our great and good Government. All believe that the decisive moment is near at hand, and to that end the people of the United States are desirous to aid promptly in furnishing all re-enforcements that you may deem needful to sustain our Government.

Austin Blair,

Governor of Michigan[134]

On July 3, Lincoln sent a private, confidential message to loyal governors, including Blair, asking them to send new troops quickly: "Time is everything." On July 5, a special assistant to Stanton reported having met Blair and other governors: "All feel right and will do their duty." On July 7, the War Department specified Michigan's quota as six infantry regiments; on the 10th, it authorized Michigan, Kentucky, Ohio, and Wisconsin certain expenditures to encourage recruiting. On the 28th, Lincoln asked for progress reports. On July 29, Blair sent this reply:

Detroit, Mich., July 29, 1862.

A. Lincoln,

President of the United States:

Very little can be done in recruiting old regiments until the new regiments are filled up, although every exertion is being made to do so. The new regiments will commence to take the field about the 1st of August, or sooner if possible, and will all be in service in the field during that month.

Austin Blair,

Governor of Michigan.[135]

To aid recruiting, Blair appeared at events and spoke at meetings. He

134. Walter Stahr, *Seward: Lincoln's Indispensable Man* (New York: Simon & Schuster, 2012), 332-333; Lincoln's letter was dated June 28, *OR*, III, II, 180-181, as was Seward's invitation to the meeting, id. 181. The governors' letter was backdated to June 28. Id. 180, 187. Seward importuned Stanton for a bounty to aid enlistment. Id. 181-187.

135. *OR*, III, II, 200-201, 205, 208, 213, 265, 283-284.

led a fourth of July procession of cavalry in Grand Rapids.[136] *His oratory included an event in Jackson on July 19:*

We attended a very large and enthusiastic war meeting at Jackson on Saturday evening last. The meeting was held at Jackson's Hall, and was addressed by Hon. Fidus Livermore, Hon. O.W. Bennett, His Excellency Gov. Blair, and Major [blank] of the army. The speeches were able, stirring and patriotic, and were responded to with hearty applause.

Eight regiments (17th-24th) were "fitted ready for the field" in "an example of recruiting not equaled in the State during the entire war.[137]

---

136.   Richard L. Hamilton, *"Oh! Hast Thou Forgotten." Michigan Cavalry in the Civil War: The Gettysburg Campaign* (2008), 4.

137.   *LSR*, Jul. 23, 1862, 2; Robertson, 31.

Welcoming Address on Return of POW
Orlando B. Willcox
August 27, 1862

On January 13, 1862, Blair approved a joint legislative resolution peti-
tioning Michigan's congressional delegation to influence the exchange of
prisoners of war. The request singled out the plight of Colonel Orlando B.
Willcox, imprisoned since his wounding and capture on July 21, 1861,
at the Battle of First Bull Run. The resolution lamented his being "held
in close confinement as a hostage in a southern dungeon."[138] *Willcox was*
exchanged on August 16, 1862. He was promoted to brigadier-general;
years after the war, he was awarded the Medal of Honor for heroism at
First Bull Run. On August 27, a large throng gathered in downtown
Detroit to welcome him home. Blair was requested to deliver an official
address of welcome, and his words (approximately 1,400) follow. They
contain no hint of blame or shame; rather, Blair accorded the ex-POW
honor and praise. His words reflect commitment to a vigorous war not-
withstanding Union defeats during recent weeks and foreshadow the sac-
rifices yet to be made during the forthcoming Maryland campaign.

General Willcox—The committee of arrangements have assigned to
me the grateful duty of speaking to you this welcome.

This vast concourse of people have assembled to attest the sincer-
ity with which the greeting is offered. They desire at the same time to
do honor to a brave and patriotic soldier, and to prove thereby their
devotion to an imperiled country.

The people of Michigan have not ceased to watch your career as a
soldier of the Union from the commencement, somewhat more than
a year ago, to the present time.

---

138. *Acts of the Legislature,* Extra Session of 1862, 61. Congressional resolutions were introduced by Sen. Howard on Jan. 23, Rep. Trowbridge on Jan. 27.

It was my duty and pleasure, as their Commander-in-Chief, to send you forth to the field in command of the First Michigan Regiment, which hastened to the defence of the national capital.

From that time, whether as a victorious soldier leading the advance into Alexandria, a captive on the most disastrous field of the war, an inmate of a rebel prison in the worst of all the rebel cities, or as a returning friend and General, we have not for a moment lost sight of you, nor failed to extend to you our heartiest sympathies.

We have been proud of your successes, deeply lamented your captivity, and greatly rejoice in your safe return.

As one of the most loyal and one of the youngest States of the Union, Michigan has a character to maintain and illustrate in this great contest. That her reputation for determined loyalty and bravery has been steadily on the increase since the war began, is very much to be attributed to the soldierly good conduct of the First Regiment, under your command.

Their bright example has stimulated all those that followed, and the record of the achievements of our troops on all the principal battlefields of the war will form the most brilliant pages in the history of the State.

For this we owe you a deep debt of gratitude, which I know you think fully repaid by the generous confidence of a gallant people. Honor is the guiding star of the true soldier. It raises him above mercenary considerations, and has always made him the ideal of his countrymen.

We have not much time, General, for congratulations. In times like these our words must be brief and our actions prompt. You return, not to lay down your arms in peace, but to reenter the contest in a larger field. You find us engaged, as when you left us at the beginning of the war, recruiting, mustering, organizing and sending forth troops in great numbers to defend and protect the government.

For near a year and a half this has gone on with increasing energy. Our State has already raised for this war fully 35,000 men. She has fulfilled every obligation, and more than met every call upon her. As to the character of the troops, you can testify.

The patriotism and fidelity of our people is without stain. They are ready to do all this over again, and more, if need be, so precious do they hold the inheritance of good government given to us by heroic fathers.

It is not strange, I think, that they begin to look for results. We have raised immense armies, armed and equipped them in the best style known to modern times, furnished them with the most perfect munitions, and sent them with bright banners and high hopes against the enemy, and have seen them pass away, we hardly know whither, leaving no very encouraging results.

Our gallant regiments, sadly reduced in numbers by the casualities [sic] of war and disease, occupy nearly the same ground they stood upon one year ago. We seem to have marched in a circle, and just now to have arrived near the point of starting. The ranks again are being rapidly filled by the unquenchable enthusiasm of the people. New campaigns are about to commence—campaigns on which I believe the fate of the country rests.

It is a very proper time to consider our mistakes, if any have been made, and to look dispassionately for the remedies, if any such are within our reach.

I am not here to-day to complain, or to utter the language of despondency, for I feel the spirit of neither one nor the other. I wish simply to express my settled convictions. I believe that the grand mistake of the war has been, that it has not been treated altogether as war. Instead of bringing all our power to bear at once, to crush with wholesome punishment and severity a gigantic rebellion, we have rather sought by gentle violence to bring back our erring fellow-citizens, forgetting the lesson of history, that when blood flows between brothers, it can never cease until one is master.

The conspirators of the South were no erring brethren, but highhanded, desperate criminals, whose schemes of treason and blood had been long and carefully prepared. With great ingenuity and reckless audacity, their plots had been so openly laid in sight of all men, that none believed in them. Their apparent hopelessness was their greatest security, and when the first blow was struck at the Union it was the blow of an assassin who knew well the desperate character of his work, and his means of success!

The guns that battered the walls of Sumpter [sic] silenced discussion, and transferred the contest from the forum to the battle field. After that an accommodation was impossible. The government could not decently offer it, and the rebels would not.

From that moment both parties prepared for war—the South with the desperate energy inspired by a desperate undertaking from which there could be no retreat, and the government with an easy confidence inspired by its superior power and great advantages in all material particulars. In this confidence it felt able, with a surpassing benevolence, to put down the rebellion and not harm the rebels. It was a natural mistake. Their country we felt was our country, to be brought back under the flag of the Union, and to devastate it seemed like burning our own houses. And thus we played at war while they consolidated a hostile government, crushed out opposition to it, created armies, arms and munitions, and made the power which defeated us at Bull Run, and turned back the army from Richmond. Is there any longer a doubt that this was a fatally mistaken policy? I think not.

What, then, is the remedy? Simply to reverse all this. Let us make war—actual, positive, annihilating war. And why should we not? Rebellion is a crime, the most far reaching and terrible in its consequences of all crimes. Let the thousands of our brave soldiers, slain in battle and dead of disease contracted in camp, testify how great a crime rebellion is. Let our millions upon millions of wasted treasure, to be wrung from the people hereafter, answer it; and let the families who mourn the brave who fell say whether there should be forbearance any longer. Mercy towards rebels in arms is cruelty towards loyal men.

I hope and believe that the government of the United States now holds substantially this view, and will act in accordance with it. It is in this belief that the people of Michigan have joined the army of volunteers with unparalleled enthusiasm since the last call of the President. They feel an exulting confidence of victory, now that the war is to be made in earnest.

You sir, I trust, will march to the field with them in some important command. They now number thirty-three regiments, a large army of themselves. To command them is honor enough to satisfy the highest ambition.

They go now to victory in the best of causes—victory which is to bring peace again to our distracted land.

May you and they soon return again to us with your work accomplished, our government re-established in all its territories, and the liberties of the people secured forever.

Then, again, may we all once for all, bid you, as I now do, welcome home.[139]

Willcox stayed only a few days and returned to Washington in time for the Maryland campaign, where his contributions were significant. He led the 1st Division of the IX Corps of the Army of the Potomac, which included the 8th and 17th Michigan Infantry, in victory at the Battle of South Mountain on September 14 and to the very town limits of Sharpsburg in the Battle of Antietam three days later.

Was it coincidence, or had Blair traveled to Washington to greet the exchanged hero? Willcox telegraphed his wife on August 16 from Fort Monroe, Virginia, that he was starting for Washington after release. On the 18th, Blair was in Washington to meet the president and discuss "Michigan appointments" in the Treasury Department with senator Chandler and secretary Salmon P. Chase. That evening, Willcox dined

---

139. *DFP*, Aug. 28, 1862, 1. Slight changes reflect the partial manuscript in the Burton Collection.

with Lincoln and several other guests including secretary of war Edwin M. Stanton and major-general Henry W. Halleck. Blair's presence at the Soldiers' Home meal is not recorded.[140]

---

140. Robert G. Scott, *Forgotten Valor: The Memoirs, Journals, & Civil War Letters of Orlando B. Willcox* (Kent: Kent State University Press, 1999), 345-348, with an image of the scene at 352; David H. Donald, *Inside Lincoln's Cabinet: The Civil War Diaries of Salmon P. Chase* (New York: Longmans, Green & Co., 1954), 114; Earl Schenck Miers ed., *Lincoln Day by Day: A Chronology, 1809-1865*, Vol. III (Washington: Lincoln Sesquicentennial Commission, 1960), 134.

Address of the Loyal Governors to the President
September 22, 1862

On September 24-25, 1862, thirteen governors of Union states met at the Logan House Hotel, a three-story structure built by the Pennsylvania Railroad in Altoona, Pennsylvania. Blair arrived on the 25th and joined eleven others in signing onto an address to be presented to the president. The twelve took the train to Washington, D.C., and met with Lincoln on the 26th.

Although the words are not solely Blair's, his signature on the address makes it one of the public messages he subscribed to during the war. The text follows—within it is a full-throated endorsement of the preliminary Emancipation Proclamation issued by the president on the same date of this "address" (seemingly, a deliberate backdating). Blair later authored an account of the matter (see Appendix).

Adopted at a meeting of Governors of loyal States, held to take measures for the more active support of the Government, at Altoona, Pennsylvania, on the 22d day of September, 1862.

After nearly one year and a half spent in contest with an armed and gigantic rebellion against the national Government of the United States, the duty and purpose of the loyal States and people continue, and must always remain as they were at its origin—namely, to restore and perpetuate the authority of this Government and the life of the nation. No matter what consequences are involved in our fidelity, this work of restoring the Republic, preserving the institutions of democratic liberty, and justifying the hopes and toils of our fathers shall not fail to be performed.

And we pledge without hesitation, to the President of the United States, the most loyal and cordial support, hereafter as heretofore, in the exercise of the functions of his great office. We recognize in him the Chief Executive Magistrate of the nation, the Commander-in-Chief of the Army and Navy of the United States, their responsible and constitutional head, whose rightful authority and power, as well as the constitutional powers of Congress, must be rigorously and religiously guarded and preserved, as the condition on which alone our form of Government and the constitutional rights and liberties of the people themselves can be saved from the wreck of anarchy or from the gulf of despotism.

In submission to the laws which may have been or which may be duly enacted, and to the lawful orders of the President, co-operating always in our own spheres with the national Government, we mean to continue in the most vigorous exercise of all our lawful and proper powers, contending against treason, rebellion, and the public enemies, and, whether in public life or in private station, supporting the arms of the Union, until its cause shall conquer, until final victory shall perch upon its standard, or the rebel foe shall yield a dutiful, rightful, and unconditional submission.

And, impressed with the conviction that an army of reserve ought, until the war shall end, to be constantly kept on foot, to be raised, armed, equipped, and trained at home, and ready for emergencies, we respectfully ask the President to call for such a force of volunteers for one year's service, of not less than one hundred thousand in the aggregate, the quota of each State to be raised after it shall have filled its quota of the requisitions already made, both for volunteers and militia. We believe that this would be a measure of military prudence, while it would greatly promote the military education of the people.

We hail with heartfelt gratitude and encouraged hope the proclamation of the President, issued on the 22d instant, declaring emancipated from their bondage all persons held to service or labor as slaves in the rebel States, whose rebellion shall last until the first day of January now next ensuing. The right of any person to retain authority to compel any portion of the subjects of the national Government to rebel against it, or to maintain its enemies, implies in those who are allowed possession of such authority the right to rebel themselves; and therefore the right to establish martial law or military government in a State or Territory in rebellion implies the right and the duty of the Government to liberate the minds of all men living therein by appropriate proclamations and assurances of protection, in order that all who are capable, intellectually and morally, of loyalty and obedience, may not be forced into treason as the unwilling tools of rebellious traitors. To have continued indefinitely the most efficient cause, support, and stay of the rebellion, would have been, in our judgment, unjust to the loyal people whose treasure and lives are made a willing sacrifice on the altar of patriotism—would have discriminated against the wife who is compelled to surrender her husband, against the parent who is to surrender his child to the hardships of the camp and the perils of battle, in favor of rebel masters permitted to retain their slaves. It would have been a final decision alike against humanity, justice, the rights and dignity of the Government, and against sound and wise national policy. The decision of the President to strike at the root of the rebellion will lend new vigor to the efforts and new life and hope to the hearts of the people. Cordially tendering to the President our respectful assurances of personal and official confidence, we trust and believe that the policy now inaugurated will be crowned with success, will give speedy and triumphant victories over our enemies, and secure to this nation and this people the blessing and favor of Almighty God. We believe that the blood of the heroes who have already fallen, and those who may yet give their lives to their country, will not have been shed in vain.

The splendid valor of our soldiers, their patient endurance, their manly patriotism, and their devotion to duty, demand from us and from all their countrymen the homage of the sincerest gratitude and the pledge of our constant reinforcement and support. A just regard for these brave men, whom we have contributed to place in the field, and for the importance of the duties which may lawfully pertain to us hereafter, has called us into friendly conference. And now, presenting to our national Chief Magistrate this conclusion of our deliberations, we devote ourselves to our country's service, and we will surround the

President with our constant support, trusting that the fidelity and zeal of the loyal States and people will always assure him that he will be constantly maintained in pursuing with the utmost vigor this war for the preservation of the national life and the hope of humanity.

A.G. Curtin

John A. Andrew

Richard Yates

Israel Washburne, Jr.

Edward Salomon

Samuel J. Kirkwood

O.P. Morton,

  By D.G. Rose, his representative

Wm. Sprague

F.H. Pierpont

David Tod

N.S. Berry

Austin Blair.[141]

In Detroit, the Democratic newspaper condemned the proclamation of emancipation as "the beginning of a revolution" while the Republican newspaper praised it. The Free Press *predicted "it will be barren of consequences against the rebels, because it is impracticable, unconstitutional, and beyond the power of the government to enforce."*[142]

As the history of the war came to be written, the Altoona meeting and its resolution receded into obscurity. To some, it was evidence that the governors had been outwitted by the president: their insurgency was nipped in the bud by the proclamation. To Lincoln's closest confidants inside the White House, it was none of this:

Coming as it did immediately after the announcement of his new policy, President Lincoln could not but be gratified at the public

---

141.   Edward McPherson, *The Political History of the United States of America, During the Great Rebellion* (Washington: Philp & Solomons, 1864), 232-233; *OR*, III, Vol. II, 582-584.

142.   *DFP*, Sept. 24, 1862, 1.

declaration emanating from the Altoona meeting. On his military policy it assured him of the continuation of unanimous official support. On his emancipation policy it gave him a public approval from the official power of seventeen States, as against the dissent of only five States of the border, where indeed he had no reason to expect, for the present at least, any more favorable official sentiment.[143]

Convened to discuss and take measures for more active support of the Administration, the conference was thoroughly loyal and—as Nicolay and Hay recalled—a bracing tonic during a very low point for the Union side. Victory in the Battle of Antietam, together with the governors' attestation of support, enabled emancipation to become an official war aim. Blair's account of the Altoona proceedings, coming decades later after a newspaper sketch in 1883, sought to foster a proper understanding of the circumstances, purpose, and results of the governors' efforts. The account did not obtain circulation—until now.

---

143.   John G. Nicolay & John Hay, *Abraham Lincoln: A History*, Vol. Six (New York: The Century Co., 1890), 167.

Speech on Renomination
September 24, 1862

The state Republican convention met in Detroit on Wednesday, September 24, 1862, to consider party business and to nominate candidates for the November election. Blair received 186 votes for a second term; the second-place candidate received 12, after which the renomination was made unanimous. The governor made an appearance, was "received with loud applause," and delivered these 1,200-word remarks.

Gentlemen of the Convention—My first duty under the present circumstances would be to thank you, not so much for the office which you propose to confer upon me, as for the good feeling with which it has been done, and the confidence with which the people of Michigan—or, rather, the republicans of Michigan—have honored me. I feel, gentlemen, that this position now is not one to be sought after. When I received it, two years ago, at the hands of the republican convention, I thought it was about half nominal. The country was at peace; neither you nor I supposed that this office was to have any additional duties or labors thrown upon it than in years past. However, all this is changed. From an office almost without labor, and without responsibility, it has become one very grievous to be borne. From a state of peace we have suddenly been engaged in a sanguinary civil war, in which the life of the nation has been taxed. In communicating with the Federal government, the executive has been compelled to act as the representative of the State.

I found that it was with the utmost difficulty that I could satisfy myself with regard to the manner in which my work has been done, and I heartily hoped I should be able to satisfy the people of the State, and again I have to thank you that you have deemed my intentions honest. I suppose I have issued about 2,000 commissions since the war began, and in issuing them I presume there have been 10,000 applicants for them. It was hardly possible that I could have granted them so as to satisfy everybody, or without doing somebody injustice. All I could do was to use my best judgment, and leave it to the people of the State, and all I have to say is that I look to the Michigan troops for my vindication. (Applause.) I think I can leave it there safely, to the gallant men, and the courageous—and I think I may say skill-ful—officers. I am willing to leave the question to them as to whether I have done well. (Applause.)

A word or two in regard to the cause—the great cause in which we are engaged—the great cause of human liberty. I remember well the time the republican party was born. It was a party of an idea—not a party for giving office to this man and that. We had looked forward for many years previous to that time; we had seen a great—I had almost said an infernal—power in the South, growing till it was almost ready to crush out liberty in [this] broad and beautiful land. It had grown to be the most exacting tyrant the world had ever seen. Freedom of speech south of Mason and Dixon's line, and freedom of the press, had almost fallen before it. It became necessary that there should be a power in the land to keep back this tyrannical power. The repub-lican party was born to put it down. It quickly spread all over this State, and it continued to grow until [it] has spread over the nation. It is that power which drives the tyrant back and lashes him into his den again. This war has sprung, more or less, in consequence of this opposition—I should not say <u>by</u> the opposition, but <u>out</u> of it. It is the same power which we have met in a different form; when beaten at the polls it resorted to force. We have been compelled to meet it. We are in the midst of a great struggle. There is nothing before us but to win a victory or suffer a defeat,—if a victory our country is safe; if a defeat, our country is lost. It is essential to follow the great landmarks of liberty. It is not the time to run after strange gods. Let us turn back to the fountains of liberty from which our fathers drew inspiration. We should never desert them, and, above all, not in such times as these. If there was ever a time when truth was essential it is now. The question has lately been asked of us, Do you think more of your party than of your country. I answer, No; but I love my party because I love my country, and it has proved itself true on all occasions. (Applause.)

It is as essential that we put down traitors and half-hearted men at home as to meet armed traitors in the field.

Who shall sustain the administration but the party who put them in power? We welcome, heartily, others who will join us, but we will not go over to any other party. We will meet others half way, and more than half way, who will help to fight our battles. We cannot disband our party without deserting the platform upon which we stand, and the administration which we have put into power; and I can urge upon you this afternoon, with more force than I ever could before, to support the administration. (Applause.) Abraham Lincoln! God bless him! (Applause.) He has removed a great load from our hearts, and we say now, Father Abraham, we are wholly with you. (Applause.)

[¶] More than ever this war is becoming a war of ideas. Now we have got upon the platform where our fathers fought for liberty (applause) —liberty for *all* men. (Applause.) I was about to ask, is there anybody who wishes to leave his party now, when we are almost within reach of the goal of all our hopes. Will anybody waver now— will anybody tell me that now is a good time to break up and scatter? I do believe that, in great numbers, the honest republicans of the country will flock to the standard and make it victorious. (Applause.) Not for the party alone, but for the great idea that lies at its bottom—the idea which I love above all others—the idea of universal emancipation. (Applause.) I looked forward to this with bright anticipations. We go forward now, to sure and certain victory. Those armies that have been turned back will be turned back no more. Now, let men who fight for ideas take command of the armies, and we shall, in the language once used by General McClellan, "have no more Bull Runs; we have seen our last defeat; we have made our last retreat." Then we will take up the language of Pope: "We need not be careful about our lines of retreat, but press close upon the enemy until we drive him all through the South, and into the Gulf." By one grand rally we will fill those ranks that have been decimated in the face of the enemy, and we will keep them full. We will tell our soldiers to go ahead—that the people will stand back of them. I have no doubt any longer. You will soon see what a happy effect it will have upon the whole country.

Abraham Lincoln, President of the United States, republican of the republicans—true, honest, faithful—God bless you! The country will bless you to the latest day of your existence! (Immense applause and cheering.)[144]

---

144. *LSR*, Oct. 1, 1862, 1; *DFP*, Sept. 25, 1862, 1. Detroit's Republican paper recorded Blair as saying: "I can now, with my whole heart, support the administration and the President of the United States." Harris, *Austin Blair*, 141, quoting *Detroit Advertiser & Tribune*, Sept. 25, 1862.

Speech in Washington
September 27, 1862

Blair's first major activity after renomination was a trip to Washington. He visited the 24th Michigan Infantry in their quarters at Camp Shearer near Fort Baker in the southwest part of the city. He witnessed a "sham battle," and his presence inspired the soldiers, who were confident that "he will manage some way to get us into active service."[145] The regiment saw its first action in December at the Battle of Fredericksburg but gained immortal fame on the first day of the Battle of Gettysburg in July 1863. Blair later appeared at a rally in front of the house of James S. Wadsworth to congratulate the brigadier-general for his nomination as New York's governor on the Republican ticket. After the candidate spoke, Blair was called upon.

Although we are mostly strangers to each other, we are yet citizens of a common country. We have a common interest and a common feeling. We have a common inheritance in the history and past glories of our country, and a common interest in its future hopes and aspirations. I therefore feel privileged to mingle with you on the present occasion, and express my heartfelt concurrence in the principles that animate you.

[¶] We are in the midst of exciting and dangerous times, that call for all the patriotism, fidelity, and strength of character which the American people possess. We are standing in the midst of hospitals that contain the men of every loyal State, that have come here from the great lakes, from the prairies, from the farms, from the workshops, and I do not lay any blame on any one when I say that the country

145.   O.B. Curtis, *History of the Twenty-Fourth Michigan of the Iron Brigade* (Detroit: Winn & Hammond, 1891), 56; Letter of Asa Ward Brindle, Sept. 28, 1862, Ward Family Papers, Burton Historical Collection.

needs leaders that will lead this gallant army to victory. Do we lack anything? Are there not numbers enough? Is there not money enough? Are not our men brave enough to carry this war forward to a triumphant success? You all know, fellow citizens, that these are provided in abundance. For my own part, if I were to give my opinion, the best thing we could do would be to import a guillotine from France, and chop off the heads of the incompetent or cowardly men that shall presume to take the place of leaders. What we now require is that this battle be fought out, and fought out immediately; that we fight the rebels to-day and to-morrow, and all the time; that we give them rest neither day or night; that our blows fall thick and fast; and that there be no intermission in them. I want the blows should be aimed at the most vital parts of their systems. I want to see these traitors crushed and destroyed.

[¶] Let me congratulate you that the President, God bless him—(hearty cheering)—has given us a principle upon which this battle can be fought to a successful termination. We have struck at the heart of the monster—that infernal devil, slavery—that has sought to destroy us: but the grip is at his throat, and when that is completed the country will be free from danger forever. I feel as if the victory were nearly won already, for we have the most inspiring idea that ever elevated the thoughts of man—the idea of liberty. Hereafter no man so poor, no man so weak, no man so low, that he may say to himself—the government of the United States extends to me as well as the highest, the rights and privileges of humanity. This idea will fight for us with our soldiers. The element that has hitherto been the strength of the war in the South will immediately become its weakness, and instead of invading and making a wilderness of Pennsylvania, the slaveholders will require to return to protection of their own homes. Our time to strike is now, and I look forward to the most complete and perfect success.

[¶] In conclusion, the speaker paid a high eulogium to the gallant men fighting our battles in the field, and returned, on behalf of his

State, his sincere and hearty thanks for the kindness and sympathy manifested towards the sick and wounded in the hospitals around this city.[146]

---

146. *New York Herald*, Sept. 28, 1862, 5. *DFP*, Oct. 2nd, 2, blasted the remarks under the headline "The Guillotine."

Proclamation of Thanksgiving
November 15, 1862

Blair's reelection victory just days before issuing this call provided a personal aspect to his call for public appreciation to Providence. He had won in the face of—or perhaps because of—the Democratic opposition that tarred him as a "Black Republican." The Free Press *articulated this criticism in its pre-election assessment that Blair was running on "The Congo Platform," and that whoever favored emancipation, i.e., "negro voters, negro office-holders, negro scholars, and negro school-masters, negro jurors and negro judges," would cast their tally for the incumbent.*[147]

Another year has passed away into history. It has been a year of great events; a year of civil war and all the bloody sacrifices, harassing doubts and alternating triumphs and defeats which surely follow in its track. Vast armies raised from the midst of the people have gone forth to fight our country's battles, with a courage and constancy which will brighten the history of the Republic forever. They have beaten back the hosts of rebellion and despotism from the loyal States, and saved our homes from the horrors of invasion. Our liberties and laws are still preserved to us, and the power of the Government is gradually but surely being re-established over all the territory of the Union. Rebellion is being punished, and upon the wicked authors of this unseemly strife is falling the sure reward of their unparalleled sin. The war is carried into the midst of their country, and the victorious armies of the Union hasten on to strike them a final blow in the strongholds of the far South. There are solid grounds of hope for speedy victory and permanent peace.

While many of our homes are made desolate by the inevitable

---

147. *DFP*, Nov. 2, 1862, 2.

casualties of war, and we mourn the heroic dead, there is consolation in the faith that the blood of the true patriot is never shed in vain.

Our people under all their trials still cling with unflinching firmness and fidelity to the institutions and Government of our country. Trusting in God and the righteousness of our cause, they are ready to incur greater sacrifices and bear heavier burdens in the confidence and hope that the future will more than compensate for the past, and that the blessings of liberty will be permanently secured and greatly increased to our posterity.

The destinies of nations and individuals are in the hand of God. For bountiful harvests, for general health among the people, for civil and religious liberty and the diffusion of knowledge and education, for the continued existence of the Republic and the triumphs of its arms, and for all the great and good gifts of a benign Providence, our acknowledgments and praise are due to Him alone. That we may suitably acknowledge our dependence upon Almighty God, and with reverent thankfulness give glory to Him,

I do hereby set apart, and appoint Thursday, the 27th instant, as a day of public thanksgiving and praise.

I request that upon that day the people may assemble in their places of public worship and in their homes, and keep this day in the spirit in which our Fathers kept it, with pure, religious and patriotic hearts, full of faith and hope.

Given under my hand and the great seal of the State, at the capitol, in this city of Lansing, on the 15th day of November, in the year of Our Lord one thousand eight hundred and sixty-two.

Austin Blair

James B. Porter,

Secretary of State.[148]

---

148.   *DFP*, Nov. 18, 1862, 1.

Address to the People on the Federal Draft
November 29, 1862

Although the Confederacy was the first government on the American mainland to institute conscription, the launching of a U.S. draft proved no less contentious. Civil insurrection broke out in several northern cities. The bloody toll of the war necessitated recruitment into the U.S. military of those who had not yet volunteered. Blair had a difficult task: to attempt to assuage the anger and fear in the hearts of those who opposed a draft while remaining loyal and true to the Union cause. His special address on the topic proved a kind of tonic: no riots broke out, and Michigan met its quotas.

To the People of the State of Michigan:

It is essential to the maintenance of the honor of the State, by meeting its obligations to the Federal Government, that the quota of the troops required of Michigan under the call for 600,000 men should be speedily furnished. I have felt great confidence that this might be done without resort to a draft, but it will be impossible at the rate enlistments have been making for the last month and more. The number required of each town and ward in the State has been assigned upon the principle of giving credit for all recruits furnished since the first of July last. Substantial justice in this respect has been done toward all. To be exact was impossible, and to go back of the first of July was impracticable, both because the order of the Secretary of War did not authorize it, and because there was no reliable record by which such credit could be made up with any chance of fairness.

It is, therefore, indispensable that the several towns and wards of cities should furnish the number of recruits assigned to them, and I take this occasion to assure the people that unless the men are furnished by voluntary enlistment they will be taken by the draft.

For the purpose of still giving abundant opportunity to fill the quota of the State by voluntary enlistment, recruiting will be continued as follows:

1st. Recruits will be received for new regiments now forming in the State, and for all the old regiments now in the field, until and including the 29th day of December next. These must be enlisted for the term of three years or during the war.

2d. From the 1st to the 16th day of December next volunteer recruits will be received for the old regiments only, to serve for nine months, in pursuance of the act of Congress.

3d. On the 30th day of December next the draft will commence and proceed until the requisite number is obtained in all those towns and wards which shall then be found delinquent.

Less than four thousand men are now required to fill the entire quota of the State, and I earnestly hope that they will be found to come forward cheerfully and enlist for the war, as all our troops thus far have done. And I desire this not so much because there is anything discreditable in a draft, as because it is exceedingly desirable that all the troops from Michigan should stand on the same footing in the army. Let the people of Michigan make one more loyal and vigorous effort, and the entire number required can be obtained, and the high reputation of the State for patriotism and promptness will be maintained.

Austin Blair.

Dated Jackson, November 29, 1862.[149]

---

149. Robertson, 38.

Second Inaugural Message
January 1, 1863

Reelection, though by a slimmer margin than in 1860, brought continuity to Michigan's war effort. It was an especially sweet victory given how Democrats made gains in Illinois, Indiana, and Ohio. Opponents of the conduct of the war complained of "mistakes, delays, and defeats, of burdensome taxation, and of the dreaded draft."[150] Blair insisted that progress was being made. His message also revealed growth in military sagacity by, e.g., outlining the basis for "the pride of the soldier in his corps." He had seen that esprit manifested firsthand. This "State of the State" address surveyed more than war-related matters. The portion of his address included here ran (ellipses show excisions) to approximately 6,000 words; it also was supplemented before publication.

Fellow Citizens of the Senate and House of Representatives:

The People of Michigan have committed to us the responsibilities of the State Government for the coming two years. We assemble to enter upon our duties in a time of great seriousness and public trial. It will become us to pause at the threshold of our term and survey the work before us, acknowledging our entire dependence upon that Divine Providence which is constantly over us alike in war as in peace. The state of the country and the temper of the times demand a cautious wisdom and patriotic energy in every department of government. Our first duty is naturally and properly with the internal affairs of our own fast growing Commonwealth. And here we are not without many causes for congratulation. After some years of difficulty, the State finances are free from embarrassment, all the avocations of business flourish, harvests are abundant, general health prevails, and

---

150. Moore, 423.

the diffusion of education is almost universal. The public order has been maintained, and all the institutions of civil government hold undisturbed sway to the general happiness and security of the people. Our one great need is national peace, and the only route to that leads through the gate of victory.

...

Under the "act authorizing a war loan," bonds have been issued and sold to the amount of six hundred and seven thousand three hundred dollars, and the money has been expended in pursuance of the law. The principal portion of this sum has been expended in raising and equipping troops for the General Government, and for which the State has a claim for reimbursement. The accounts and vouchers have been forwarded to Washington for allowance, and no doubt will be adjusted in due season. When so adjusted the amount will be due to the State less the direct tax due from the State to the National Government, amounting to $426,484.

...

Military.

The military department, which before the war was regarded as of a slight importance, and was generally dismissed in the messages of Governors with a paragraph, now demands the principal place. To it nearly all my time and attention have been given for the past two years, and to it they must still be given. We are yet engaged as actively as at the beginning, in raising troops. The total number raised, and organized in the State since the beginning of the war, is 45,569. Of these, 24,281 were sent to the field before July last; 987 (the Lancers), were disbanded before leaving the State. The quota of the State under the calls of July last, was 23,312

Of which there have been raised as follows:

Thirteen Regiments and a Battery, sent to the field, 13,759

Recruits for old Regiments since July 2d, 2,162

Provost Guard, at Detroit Barracks, 101

Estimated strength of Regiments yet recruiting, 4,400

– 20,402

Remaining to be raised to fill the call, 2,970

The State has now in the field twenty-six regiments of Infantry, one regiment of Mechanics and Engineers, six regiments of Cavalry, and eight Batteries. There are recruiting in the State, two regiments of Infantry, one regiment of Sharp Shooters, three regiments of Cavalry, and two Batteries. The returns of the late Military Census show an aggregate, subject to draft, of ninety-five thousand, in round numbers. Many of the older regiments have become greatly depleted in numbers, and their efficiency correspondingly impaired. To reinforce these, and bring them up again to the maximum standard of strength, is at present the most imperative demand of the service. It is certainly much easier to keep up the quota of the State by raising new regiments, than by filling the old ones, but both justice and sound policy forbid such a course. To abandon the old regiments, which have fought with marked distinction through all the campaigns of the war, would be to disregard the first principle of military success, the pride of the soldier in his corps. It would also be in disregard of the importance of military skill and discipline. New recruits put into old organizations, under trained and competent officers, are of much greater value to the service than if organized into new bodies, with officers unused to war. They quickly catch the spirit, and acquire the skill of old soldiers. It is far better for the soldier himself, because by contact with men of experience he is led to avoid the bad habits so ruinous to the new soldier, and to adopt those which tend to preserve his health and life. There is nothing from which the new regiments have suffered so fatally as a causeless disregard of the rules of health as applied to camp life.

Notwithstanding the obvious advantages of enlistment in old regiments, it has been found impossible to fill up their ranks while new ones are raising in the State. The superior activity of new officers on the ground working for their commissions, with the ambition of the soldier for the non-commissioned offices of the company, have swept the great body of recruits into the new organizations, and so it will continue while new regiments are raising. To get clear of this difficulty it is proposed to organize no more new regiments after the present are completed. The recruiting will then be confined wholly to the regiments in the field. When this shall have occurred I anticipate but one remaining difficulty, and that grows out of the vicious but well intended system of citizens' bounties. As soon as the draft is over no doubt those bounties will entirely cease. They have been the cause of endless trouble. Being of various amounts in different localities, those seeking to enlist have been induced to offer themselves wherever the highest bounty was offered. The result has been a very injurious bidding between different places, and very much higher bounties have been paid than reason would dictate. Appeals have been constantly made to the cupidity instead of patriotism of the citizen to enlist, to that extent degrading the service. Inconsequence some have enlisted merely to obtain the bounties, and have then deserted disgracefully. The evil has grown not out of the fact that a bounty is offered, but out of the want of uniformity in amount. When the citizens' bounties cease I think we must have a substitute for them, or the enlistments will also cease. What shall that substitute be? I can think of nothing but a uniform State bounty, moderate in amount, to be paid only to those who enlist in the regiments and batteries now organized and organizing, on their being mustered into the service of the United States. The amount of the bounty I think should be fifty dollars, and it might be paid from the war loan of which there remains a balance unexpended, of near $400,000. Perhaps it would be well to give a discretion to increase that loan by two hundred and fifty thousand dollars in case the money should be required, which I do not anticipate. If this plan should be adopted there is no reason to doubt that the Michigan regiments can be kept in efficient force.

One of the principal sources of encouragement to enlistments is the law for the relief of the families of the volunteers, when in destitute circumstances. In the main the law is well administered and is productive of great good. In a few localities, however, there are hard, unsympathising supervisors, who exercise their discretion, not only without humanity, but with positive cruelty, if my information is correct. I do not know as it is possible to remedy this. A discretion must be left somewhere, and any change might result in an increase of the evil. I recommend you to consider whether an appeal might not be allowed from the supervisor to some county officer, in such cases, with authority to review his action, and thus increase the probabilities of justice being done.

Such an appeal may now be made to the board of supervisors, but it is an inconvenient tribunal to reach, consisting of a considerable number and assembling but seldom.

The duty of the State to its soldiers does not cease with their enlistment. It should follow them to the field and the hospital, and make its active sympathy and aid manifest in all their trials and sufferings. The Government of the United States does all it can. It furnishes abundant supplies of every kind, and, to the soldier in health, all that is necessary. It furnishes good and sufficient hospitals for the sick and wounded, and nurses and attendants in number enough; but it cannot make sure that they will all do their duty kindly and well. It is in the hospital that the soldier needs sympathy and help. He who is bravest in the active duties of the field, grows a child when languishing of disease in the hospital. Far away from friends, the tedious hours drag heavily, and he sighs for home and the attendance he was accustomed to there. He is one of a thousand, and the physician comes on his hurried round once a day, looks sharply at him, makes a hurried prescription, and passes on. So it goes on for weeks, and perhaps months. The physician ceases even to call, and says truly he can do nothing for him—the nurses neglect him and he steadily declines. It is not medicine he wants. Send him home, and the bracing air of his native clime, and the cheerful voices of sympathizing friends, will restore him to manhood again like magic. Leave him there in that hospital and he will die.

That, he knows well himself. He begs for a discharge, and is told that there is not much the matter with him, and he will soon be well. Meantime, through the carelessness of his officers, he has no descriptive list, and cannot get his pay; he is therefore soon without money. That soldier needs somebody to go from Michigan to help him, and his case is that of a thousand. As a last resort, he writes to me, or gets a friend to do so; but I have no contingent fund at my control; no money appropriated for such a purpose. The State needs at least two active agents, to travel all the time among the hospitals, with a small amount of money at their command, to be used in the way of loans to sick and discharged soldiers, until they can receive their pay, for the purpose of sending them home. A contingent fund of ten thousand dollars would be ample for this purpose, and I earnestly recommend you to provide it.

The "Act for the re-organization of the military forces of the State of Michigan," approved January 18, 1862, by some ill-considered provisions, has created confusion in the laws in regard to the military service during the war. That act was intended for the better organisation of the militia of the State, and to create a State military fund for the purpose of maintaining that organization, but not to supercede the war loan act, or any of the laws providing for the raising of troops for the war. The fund provided has none of it yet come into the treasury, and when it does, will be totally inadequate in time of war to pay the necessary expenses. Yet the act provides, in section 94, that "all expenses incurred for the maintenance of the military forces of the State, by virtue of any of the provisions of this act, shall be paid by the State Treasurer from and out of the State military fund.["] The provisions of the act contain the law for a draft and the recruiting service. The repeal of section 94, and an amendment of section 96, so as to save from repeal the "act to provide a military force, approved March 10, 1861," and the act amendatory thereof, approved May 10th, 1861, would remedy the difficulty. This, or something equivalent to it, I recommend.

For full details of the military operations of the State, I refer you to the truly excellent report of the Adjutant General, to whose assiduity and efficiency the State owes a great obligation.

Gentlemen, I commend the Michigan troops to your active

sympathy and support. By their heroic endurance of the hardships of war, and by their splendid bravery in battle, they have crowned the State with glory. Their battle cry is "Michigan, remember Michigan," and Michigan must remember them. We have already a long list of immortal heroes dead in battle. I hope you will in some appropriate way place upon the enduring records of the State your appreciation of the valor and patriotic devotion of these brave men. Let us hand down their names to posterity upon an illuminated page, that they may be revered as examples for all time to come. They belong to history now. We must take care that it is rightly written. Your hearty thanks are also due to the gallant men who still uphold the flag of our country in the field, and have lately borne it on to victory over bloody ground. Let us send them warm words of cheer from home. May God give them other and greater victories, and bring them speedily back in peace and triumph. Then, indeed, shall Heaven's arches ring with glad shouts of welcome.

Ex. Governor Wisner.

Since writing the foregoing, intelligence has been received of another of the great sacrifice we make to save our country. My predecessor, Ex-Governor Moses Wisner, Colonel Commanding the 22d Regiment of Infantry, died at his post of duty, in Kentucky, on the 4th day of January, instant. His conduct is his best eulogy. A man of great intellectual, as well as physical power, in the meridian of life, surrounded by all the comforts of family, home and friends, he obeyed the call of his country, and took the field. Deeply imbued with a love of those free institutions which had done so much for his country and himself, he put away from him everything but this service, and went forth at the head of his regiment, to peril all, in defense of the Union. As a commanding officer of patriotic volunteers, he was successful in an eminent degree, as he had been in all the walks of life. He died of the diseases of the camp, in the midst of his command, in the doing of his duty. More than this need not be said. For him the pomp and circumstance, and the battle, are no more. To his family and friends, he leaves the rich remembrance of an honorable fame, and to the State he loved, the pride that she had so noble a citizen. To you, gentlemen, the Representatives of the People, is committed the duty of fitly commemorating his services.

Fellow Citizens—Having thus disposed of the subjects which concern us more particularly as a State, I should disappoint your expectations if I did not invite your attention to the affairs of the nation. Whatever concerns the national government, concerns us. In its great struggle for existence, we have the most momentous stake. Every blow aimed at its life, strikes at us. The best and bravest of our people fight in the ranks of its armies. Scarce a battle-field of the war but has drunk of Michigan blood, and the graves of our men mark the camping-ground of every army of the Union. Not many households but have some stern grief to charge to the account of the Southern rebellion, and nearly every heart is bruised by its cruel blows. And still the bloody struggle goes on, growing more fierce and deadly, day by day.

It avails little to look back and inquire for the cause of the war. The time for that argument has long since passed away. They alone are to blame who first resorted to arms, and made the war. There were no causes of dispute between the sections which required such a resort, taking any view of them. When the Southern traitors commenced this bloody contest they did it wholly without excuse; and upon their guilty heads must rest forever the responsibility of that enormous crime. Not a groan escapes from a dying Union soldier on the field or in the hospital, that is not a cry to God for vengeance against them.

Every despairing wail wrung from the hearts of the countless widows and orphans they have made, appeals to the same high throne against them. The liberty-loving and just men of all lands will condemn them, and history will doom them to its impartial bar and write them down among the scourges of the world. The Government is wholly blameless in this affair. With a long suffering and forbearance bordering upon weakness, it hesitated to take up arms and resort to war measures for its own preservation and defence.

We have now to deal only with existing facts. The single choice is left us between abject submission to such terms of peace as the rebels may choose to offer on the one hand, and a vigorous and determined prosecution of the war, in spite of every obstacle, to final victory, on the other. Between these a people fit for self-government could not hesitate. The people of Michigan, brave and manly, both in the field and at the ballot-dox, have not hesitated. They simply inquire for the surest means to secure a speedy triumph and lasting peace. It is undeniable that the rebellion had its origin, not in any danger, either fancied or real, menacing the institution of slavery in the Southern States—for all parties were agreed to let it alone there—but it had reference entirely to its growth and spread in the future over territory now possessed, and hereafter to be acquired. Visions of a great despotic empire, the foundation stone of which should be slavery, had taken strong hold of the imaginations of the bold, bad men who lead the Southern mind. In a community already corrupted by the idleness, ignorance and servility which necessarily comes of such a social system, these leaders found it easy to impress the great mass of the people with their own designs. So long as any fair prospect remained that the Union might be made subservient to their grand purpose, none clamored so loudly for it as they. All such as warmly supported the system of free government based upon the principles of the Declaration of Independence, were fiercely denounced as disunionists. But the moment it appeared that the Union could no longer be used for such a purpose they proceeded at once to break it up, and to lay carefully the foundations of their new system.

That this was done with consummate tact is now evident. Knowing well that no great revolution can be effected without some great leading idea as its foundation, they boldly proclaimed the only one left to them and resolutely planted themselves upon it. That the system of slave labor is the best and most beneficent which man can devise, was now, for the first time, I believe, declared as a fundamental principle of government. It was even pronounced to be the divine system of the economy of labor. It has, therefore, from the first, been relied upon as the principal source of strength to the rebellion, and such it has undoubtedly proved to be. Its first effect was to unite substantially the Southern people, who are mainly composed of two classes, to-wit:

1st. The aristocracy who own the slaves, and have the deepest interest in the establishment of the new order of things; and

2nd. The ignorant and debased non-slaveholding whites of the South, who are too proud to work, and too poor to buy laborers; but, nevertheless, still live in hope that, by some means or other, at some time they may attain to the high felicity of owning a slave.

The leading traitors, therefore, have been able to appeal powerfully to all the worst passions of every class. To the aristocratic slaveholder they have promised, not only security for his present position, but greatly increased wealth, dominion and power. The result of the rebellion, if successful, we easily understand is to be a strong military government, in which himself and his associates will be the only ruling class; and in the not far distance he beholds principalities and powers, stars and garters, and all the paraphernalia of despotic empire. Shall we wonder that men taught in the school of the plantation, the ideas of absolute power, and scorn of control, fight desperately for the accomplishment of these magnificent objects. While such ideas prevail with the men of wealth and position, they promise the ignorant class that when the hated Yankees are once put down, and the old government destroyed, there will be nothing left to prevent them from rising to the class of masters; then the slave trade shall be re-opened, and negroes plenty and cheap shall reward their valor, and secure their position in the ruling class.

Stimulated by these ideas, combined with the always popular notion of independence, the Southern people have endured privations and hardships, and put forth exertions, which would be admirable if done in a good cause. Nor can it be controverted successfully, that thus far their system has been a tower of strength to them. It has not been necessary for them to withdraw their laborers from the field, to any considerable extent, to aid them in carrying on the operations of war. The slave has continued, as heretofore, to till the soil, and by his unpaid labor to produce the means to enable his master to take up the sword in behalf of the rebellion. He really feeds and clothes the soldier, buys the arms and munitions of war, and supplies the fuel to the tremendous flame that is consuming our country. And yet the rebellion offers nothing to him. It does not even allow him to hope that at some time away in the far off future, the sweat and the toil and the bondage may cease. On the contrary, the very foundation of the Confederate system is that his degradation shall never end, but grow deeper and more unbearable from generation to generation, and forever.

Here, then, lies the incurable weakness of the South, and our own invincible strength. Their despotism we must fight with liberty. This servile class, composing almost the entire body of the producers of the revolted States, must necessarily be our friends, loyal in feeling and anxious to become loyal in action, whenever we will allow them the smallest rights of men. The only price they ask is freedom; a price which we can easily pay, but which the rebel government cannot offer without destroying its entire fabric.

Remove these millions of workers from the plantations and workshops of the South, and it is plain that rebellion cannot last a year. One chief difficulty thus far has been, not in repossessing the Southern country, but in holding it afterwards. Our armies have passed over and taken formal possession of extensive regions of the Southern territory, driving out the organized forces of the Confederacy, but leaving the property of the people untouched, and existing institutions undisturbed. Upon this system it has been found necessary to keep as large a force in such regions to hold them, as it did to take them in the first instance. If the army passes on, these people immediately rise in its rear, cut off its communications, destroy its munitions and supplies, seize its reinforcements in small detachments, and thus become more dangerous than before. It follows that the further we progress, the more difficult our task becomes. The army is constantly reduced by detachments for garrison duty and keeping open communications, until it becomes too weak for offensive operations. At the same time our occupation does not harm the rebel government materially; its people adhere firmly to that cause, and their means of warfare remain much the same. Unless this condition of things can be changed our cause is plainly hopeless, without long years of war, accompanied by sacrifices appalling to contemplate, and which we can hardly expect our people to make.

Seeing this clearly, and after a year and a half of effort to subdue the Rebellion without disturbing existing laws and institutions in the insurgent States, the government of the United States has adopted the two great remedies of emancipation and confiscation. We are about to strike hands with the entire loyal population of the South, whether white or black; We shall no longer respect the claim of a white traitor to compel a black loyalist to aid him in destroying the government; neither shall we any further admit his title to use his property of any sort for the same purpose. By the proclamations of September 22d, 1862, and January 1st, 1863, the President, by virtue of the power vested in him as Commander-in-Chief of the armies and navies of the United States, has by a single blow struck the shackles from near 3,000,000 of slaves, and added them to the loyal free people of the Republic. This act will be memorable as long as history endures. It has been done for the strengthening of the country against its enemies and under the war power; but it is not forbidden to the philanthropist and the good everywhere to rejoice in the redemption of a race. With it fades away the one great and humiliating stain upon our National escutcheon. From this point our country starts upon a new course; and the experiment of Republican liberty may be fairly tried. Of the necessity and legality of this great measure, there is little room for doubt. And it is hardly worth while to stop to answer the feeble croaking of that class of people who always find in the Constitution an insurmountable bar to everything that justice and truth require to be done. Their wicked pretences and aimless logic are only a thin disguise of real disloyalty.

The President has now not only to execute the ordinary powers of government conferred upon him by the Constitution, but he has also to protect and defend the Constitution itself from destruction. By virtue of that instrument he is Commander-in-Chief, and as such, in conjunction with Congress, he possesses all the war powers possessed by the most despotic government on earth, and for the exercise of those vast powers he is responsible only to the Congress elected by the people. The Constitution itself has not undertaken to prescribe the manner of the exercise of those powers, but has left that to be determined by the exigencies of the case. But that it would be exercised arbitrarily and contrary to the usual forms in many cases is clearly contemplated, by the 2d sub-division of Section 9, which permits the suspension of the writ of habeas corpus in cases of rebellion or invasion, if the public safety requires it. That is the only limit. Whatever the public safety requires, is not only within the power of the President to do, but it is his solemn duty to do it. The slow processes of the law, which are sufficient in time of peace, fail altogether in the presence of war. The schemes of the public enemies must be met with decision and promptness, and put down summarily and by whatever means may for the time being be most effectual. If the presence of a spy of the enemy is known in the army in Tennessee, and upon undertaking to arrest him he should escape into Michigan, would there be any doubt of the power and duty of the Commander-in-Chief to pursue and take him in defiance of the habeas corpus, or the power of any civil magistrate, and return him to be dealt with according to the military code? And under that code he might be summarily tried, condemned and executed, or he might be closely confined so long as the public exigency required it, without trial at all. If this be true in the case supposed, would it be any the less true if the spy in question resided in Michigan, and carried on his operations by secret correspondence with the enemy, with the assistance of others like himself, reaching the same object by a more circuitous method? In times of great public danger like these, very much must be entrusted to the enlightened discretion of those who have the chief direction of affairs. While acting with patriotic motives they are entitled to a charitable judgment, and a spirit of unjust fault finding and clamor is little less than criminal. That the National administration is entirely patriotic there are few indeed to doubt; that it is deeply in earnest in its efforts to put down the rebellion and save the Union, is also manifest. That its measures have been in the main wise, I believe, and if the great body of the people are likely to find any fault with its action thus far, it will not be that it has stretched its power too far or expressed them with too much energy and promptness.

We are a very impatient people, and prone to believe that the rebellion ought to have been suppressed in a campaign of ninety days. We are upon the pinnacle of hope when our armies win a victory, and the voice of the complainer is scarcely heard in whispers; but when they meet a repulse we sink immediately into the very slough of despond, and the rebel sympathizer goes brawling through the land with all the assurance of a patriot, while very likely neither the victory nor the defeat was of much account as affecting the final result.

Great undertakings require time, and it is not by a view of the operations of a single month, or even a year, that results are to be correctly measured. Though we have not made such rapid progress in subduing the rebellion as many, perhaps a majority, hoped, yet, upon a survey of the whole field, it will be apparent that a steady and powerful progress has been made. At the commencement of the war, the State of Maryland, lying in the track of the armies hastening to the defence of the Capitol, was thoroughly disloyal and more troublesome than any other; now she is entirely obedient to the laws, and not even the presence of a victorious rebel army could shake her fixed purpose to abide in the Union. The great and powerful State of Missouri, the battleground of the West at the beginning of the war, has been cleared of the public enemies and ranged herself upon the loyal side. The late emancipation triumph in the election in that State conveys the cheering intelligence that she is forevermore steadfast for the Union. Kentucky has been prevented from falling into the rebel grasp. The new State of Western Virginia has been entirely won, and nearly half of old Virginia is firmly held by the Union armies. We possess large portions of Tennessee, Mississippi and Louisiana, with nearly the entire valley of the Father of Waters. We hold several of the principal ports of the Confederacy in the Gulf and on the Atlantic seaboard, while the remainder of them are closely blockaded. Our armies are larger and better disciplined than at any former period. All this in a little more than a year and a half. A like success for the same length of time to come, and the power of the rebellion will be entirely broken.

Our sacrifices have indeed been great, but compared with those of our enemies, they are as nothing; our States have been entirely free from invasion, while theirs have been the scene of all the great battles of the war, and literally trampled under the feet of both armies. Our business avocations have been uninterrupted, while theirs are nearly destroyed. The whole Southern coast is either held by us, or blockaded by an invincible fleet, and their commerce mainly cut off. Is there any cause for discouragement in all this? Shall we listen to the sensation croakers, forget our manhood, and bow before these rebels? We have assaulted the enemy's intrenched position at Fredericksburg, and failed to take it. So Napoleon lost the battle of Marengo, and won it again before sun down. If we cannot bear a disaster or two without crying out for parly [sic], then indeed do we need the stern education of war. The only way to be secure of peace is to be able to conquor [sic] in war. Military prowess is essential to the stability and perpetuity of a nation. The true glory of the Republic must consist not only in the beneficence and freedom of our institutions, but also in our ability and courage to defend and protect them. It cannot be too often repeated that it cost seven years of war to found this Republic, and if it was worth the struggle then, much more is it worth it now, after the experiment of free government has proved so grandly successful. Neither were they without their defeats in those days, nor without their croakers to gloat over them with sad faces and inward jollity, predicting that utter failure must attend such a mad attempt, recommending that it were better at once to have done with such headlong abstractionists as the Washingtons, the Jeffersons, the Franklins, and the Adams', and to make terms with the old government of King and Parliament as it was.

They had also their do-nothing generals, their Benedict Arnolds, and the sad and sickening rivalries of men in high position, whose ambition far exceeded their patriotism. But they had virtue enough and valor enough to overcome all, and after years of bloody toil, through many defeats and some victories, steadfast and heroic still, they finally reached their victorious Yorktown, and gave a nation of freemen to the world. Where are their grumblers and faint hearted counsellors of submission, now? History has embalmed their very names for infamy, while it strings its never-fading garlands for the brows of the heroes of independence. In the history of the past, read that of the future. We have a proud name among the nations of the earth. Gallant ancestors left us pure escutcheons and bright names. Shall we add a glorious page to an already renowned history? Then there must be no peace with a dismembered country—no yielding to the demands of arrant traitors—Peace is indeed most desirable, but it must be enduring peace. Only one thing stands between it and us, and that is slavery. One enemy only sundered the Union, and now prevents its restoration; that enemy is slavery. All the blood and carnage of this terrible war, all the heart-rending casualties of battle, and the sad bereavements occasioned by them, have the same cause—slavery. The greatest, vilest criminal of the world, it must perish. In the smoke and flame of battle, it must perish, for so it chose; struck dead by the resistless arm of its conquering antagonist, <u>Emancipation</u>. Let us rally round the Government. The last great blow is striking. The victory once won, is won forever. The peace which follows is the peace of the conqueror, whose cause is merciful and just, bringing good will to men.

Austin Blair.
Executive Office,
Lansing, January 1, 1863.[151]

*The two sentences beginning "We are about to strike ..." were quotable
enough for other papers, including those in the nation's capital.*[152]

---

151.   *Messages*, 457-477.
152.   *Daily National Intelligencer & Washington Express*, Jan. 14, 1863, 3.

Transmittal to Legislature on Desertion
February 25, 1863

As Commander-in-Chief of Michigan's military forces, Blair faced issues common to such leaders. Desertion was a problem that befell both sides in the war. Early in 1863, as the conflict dragged on with no real end in sight, some soldiers abandoned their posts. The governor received a message from a general commanding troops in the Western Theater on the subject. The text of the telegram follows Blair's transmittal.

To The Legislature:

I herewith transmit a telegram received from Major General W.S. Rosecrans, commanding Department of the Cumberland. The subject of the dispatch is worthy of serious attention. Desertion has become an offence of almost daily occurrence, and calls loudly for a remedy. The court martial, in an organized and disciplined army, is adequate for this purpose; but in a State far away from the field of operations, it in a great measure fails. There is substantially within this State now no punishment for desertion. Unprincipled villains, with intent never to serve, but to injure the country, enlist, take a solemn oath to serve faithfully, receive large bounties, and then immediately desert. Many of them repeat the crime at different points, traveling from State to State for this purpose. In what does such a man differ from any thief or robber? And why should he not be treated as a felon by the civil law, and punished accordingly?

The army in the field has at last commenced to apply the utmost rigor of military law to the crime of desertion. A soldier in the Army of the Potomac has lately been convicted and sentenced to death for this offense, and the President has approved the sentence. It is our duty here in the State, to aid effectively in this direction. I therefore recommend the Legislature to take such action as in its judgment may be most likely to effect the object.

Austin Blair.

February 25, 1863

[Attachment]

Detroit, February 22, 1863.

By Telegraph from Murfreesboro, Tenn., Feb. 22, 1863.

To Governor Blair:

I think it due to those who suffer in the field as well as those who foot the bills at home, and run the risk of being called out to defend home and national life, that all deserters should be returned to duty. All citizens are interested in this. Those who oppose it, favor perjury and rascality, because a man who agrees to serve his country, takes wages and even bounty money, and violates his oath of service by deserting, is a perjurer and rascal, and probably a coward. Why should not the Legislature pass a law disfranchising and disqualifying from giving evidence all deserters, as for other infamous crimes?

W. S. Rosecrans, Major General.[153]

A bill "to punish desertion, to prevent improper interference with the military, and to promote discipline therein" passed the legislature on March 11, and Blair signed it into law on March 18.[154] It imposed state criminal penalties for desertion, as well as for those inciting it, and for draft resistance.[155]

153. *Messages*, 478.
154. *Journal of the House of Representatives of the State of Michigan, 1863*, Part II (Lansing: John A. Kerr & Co., 1863), 1217-1218.
155. *Acts of the Legislature of the State of Michigan, Passed at the Regular Session of 1863* (Lansing: John A. Kerr & Co., 1863), 187-189.

Messages on Approval of Legislation
March 6 & 14, 1863

During a busy legislative session, Blair signed and communicated to the legislature the fact of his signature on other war-related items.

Executive Office,
Lansing, March 6, 1863.
To the Senate:
I have this day approved, signed and deposited in the office, of the Secretary of State, the following:

…

An act to provide for paying or funding the bounty fund raised by the citizens of Detroit;

…

An act to authorize the payment of a State bounty to volunteers mustered from this State into the military service of the United States;

…

Austin Blair.[156]

Executive Office,
Lansing, March 14, 1863.
To the Senate:
I have this day approved, signed and deposited in the office of the Secretary of State, the following, to-wit:

…

An act to amend an act entitled an act to authorize a war loan, approved May 10, 1861;

---

156.   *Journal of the Senate of the State of Michigan, 1863* (Lansing: John A. Kerr & Co., 1863), 567-568.

...

Joint resolution of thanks to the Michigan soldiers in the field; ....
Austin Blair.[157]

Executive Office,
Lansing, March 18, 1863.
To the Senate:
I have this day approved, signed, and deposited in the office of the
Secretary of State, the following, to-wit:

...

Joint resolution on the state of the Union;[158]

...

Joint resolution to provide for a roll of honor to perpetuate the
memory and noble deeds of Michigan soldiers who have fallen in
defense of our country; ....
Austin Blair.[159]

Executive Office,
Lansing, March 19, 1863.
To the Senate:

I have this day approved, signed and deposited in the office of the
Secretary of State, the following, to-wit:

...

An act to amend an act entitled an act to amend an act entitled an
act to provide for the relief, by counties, of the families of volunteers,
mustered from this State into the military service of the United States,
or of this State, approved May 4, 1861, and to add certain sections
thereto, approved January 17, 1862; ....
Austin Blair.[160]

---

157. Id. 718-720.
158. See Appendix.
159. *Journal of the Senate of the State of Michigan, 1863*, 828-831.
160. Id. 858-860.

The two Houses met in joint convention on March 18 "to receive any communication" that the governor "may desire to make" before adjournment. Blair responded with a written message, delivered "by the hands of his Private Secretary," making three nominations:

- *for adjutant-general, John Robertson*
- *for quartermaster-general, William Hammond*
- *for inspector-general, James E. Pittman*

Robertson was approved with only seven no votes between the Houses. Hammond received six no's. Pittman, the elder brother of captain Samuel E. Pittman, aide to brigadier-general Alpheus S. Williams, was unanimously approved.[161] *The legislature adjourned on March 23.*

---

161. *Journal of the House*, 1863, Part II, 1499-1504. For more about the Blair-Robertson partnership, see Kerry Chartkoff, "Austin Blair & His Adjutant General" in *Michigan History Magazine*, Vol. 95, No. 2, Mar.-Apr. 2011, 47-53.

Speeches to the Soldiers
May 22-29, 1863

Blair traveled to Washington and was reported "in the city" on May 22nd.[162] *He went across the Potomac to visit Michigan soldiers and delivered remarks at several points. His trip took him close to Fredericksburg and not far from the enemy perched on the south bank of the Rappahannock. He experienced the reality of war in a disturbing way.*

Governor Blair Among the Soldiers.
Correspondence of the New York Herald.
Fairfax Court House, May 22.
Arrival of Governor Blair and Suite.
This day has been one of festivity, at least to a chosen few, in Fairfax. Agreeably to an intimation conveyed in a dispatch by telegraph to General Copeland yesterday, Governor Blair and suite, consisting of sixteen ladies and gentlemen, arrived today at Fairfax Station. … Dinner was then announced, the band striking a favorite air, and dispensing delicious strains of harmony throughout the meal. The table was set under the protecting shade of the trees, entirely excluding any stray ray of Old Sol which might have the impudence to intrude uninvitedly.

There is a climax in all things; so there was to the dinner, and the culminating point was reached when General Copeland arose and proposed the health of Governor Blair, and expressed sentiments of cordial welcome, which was drank with approbation by all present.

To this the Governor responded to this effect; That he was agreeably surprised at the pleasant situation of the troops. He had often remarked at home that the life of the soldier was not devoid of its

---

162. *DFP*, May 22, 1863, 1.

charms; but now he realized it, and that the people of Michigan, at the back of the officers and men, were a unit in their determination to crush the rebellion; that the eyes of the world were upon us, and that deeds of heroism were recorded, and the name of every man who distinguished himself would be handed down to posterity as a hero. He then said that he knew that the men of the army were not destitute of ambition, and in a jocular way alluded to the proof in the applications to him for promotion. He said this spirit was commendable and should be encouraged. He then touched upon the attitude of political differences, and was pleased to call all politics outside of the main issue—the Union—as being at this time foolish. He then concluded by stating that the people of the State of Michigan would never be satisfied with a result short of the entire Union, the star-spangled banner waving over every portion of the territory of the whole area of the United States, and no matter howsoever great the sacrifice, this end must be achieved. He sat down amid the loud and earnest plaudits of his audience, who seemed to echo his sentiments, and his words to have touched a chord of common sympathy.[163]

Correspondence of the New York Herald.
Fairfax Court House, May 23.
A Visit to Bull Run Battle Field.

This morning, at about five o'clock, Gov. Blair and suite, accompanied by Major General Stabel and Brigadier-General Copeland and their respective staffs, paid a visit to the battle-ground of Bull Run. An escort, composed of detachments of the Eighteenth Pennsylvania Cavalry, Sixteenth Michigan Cavalry, and the body guard of Gen. Stahl, the whole force under the command of Major Van Vorhis, accompanied the party. They first paid a visit to the outpost reserve, under the command of Colonel George Gray, Sixth Michigan Cavalry, thereby making a detour from the direct route. Colonel Gray had a portion of his command drawn up to receive them, when the

---

163. *DFP*, June 2, 1863, 1.

Governor addressed a few remarks to the troops, the substance and purport being that the war should be prosecuted until the Union should be restored, and that, although we were not so fortunate as to have achieved a success at Fredericksburg, yet this disaster was counterbalanced by the triumph of our arms in the West. The cavalcade then took up the line of march for the battle ground, the precaution first being taken of dispatching a portion of the cavalry as an advance guard, the party being outside of our lines, and therefore liable, although not likely, to be attacked. Nothing of interest transpired on the route, which was traveled principally through the woods, the foliage of the trees affording a desirable protection from the intense heat of the sun's rays.

The Battle-Field—An Alarm.

At about half a mile distant from Bull Run the party alighted and partook of a very slight luncheon, which being disposed of they proceeded towards the battle-ground, when a messenger came in from the vanguard with information of a body of cavalry observed a short distance in the advance, and supposed to be the enemy. At this notice all put spurs to their steeds and hastened on the double quick to have a share in the brush, but were not altogether disagreeably disappointed to discover the suspicious horsemen in question to be Brigadier General Hays, his staff and body guard, who had appeared on the ground to do honor to the distinguished visitors. The whole party, together with the fresh annexations, then visited the different points of interest on the field, traversing an area of several miles.

Appearance of the Battle Field.

The ground is covered with the debris of battle, unexploded shell, solid shot, burnt caissons, broken muskets and small arms, skeletons of horses, and, to add to the mournful vividness of the scene, skeletons of humanity lying about loose in all directions—hands, legs and limbs, in dreadful profusion. Bull Run battle ground bears unmistakable traces of the scenes of carnage enacted on its face, offering inducements to visit alike to the tourist, the artist, the historian, the moralist and the humanitarian. All can reap lessons of instruction from the picture presented. All leave a sufficiency of food for future reflection, and impressions never to be effaced. These mutilated, hideously repulsive objects were once things of life—men in the full prime and vigor of manhood, fathers, husbands, brothers and sons—clothed with comely forms, possessed of brave hearts and noble and generous impulses. Now how changed; scarce left a vestige of the semblance of man, a loathsome, offensive, repulsive mass of corruption and putrefaction—things to be pointed at, but not touched; remembered and treasured in thought by the mourning, weeping living, but not to be pressed by the lips of love. What a moral on the evanescence of life, what a dissertation on the vanity of ambition, and what a warning to those who need it. But I have no space to moralize, and must proceed with my narrative.

A Relic.

The Chaplain of the Sixth Michigan Cavalry, in the course of his search after relics and mementoes, discovered a beautifully chased pearl-hilted sword, evidently a Surgeon's, and of English manufacture. It bore the date of 1776, and no doubt was originally in the possession of a deceased Virginia patriot, who used it during the Revolution, since desecrated by an unworthy scion. The Chaplain gracefully presented it to the Governor, with the remark: "Sir, I have had the honor of receiving my commission from you, and have the honor, before all these high dignitaries assembled, to present you with this sword." The Governor accepted eagerly this trophy of the Chaplain, and, smiling, responded with the remark, "You shall have any commission you want."[164]

The Road of Pope's Retreat towards Chantilly was next followed. The way was strewn with large quantities of debris of all descriptions, but particularly heavy shot and shell. After spending some two hours on the ground, exposed to excessive heat, the party commenced its return route, during which no incident of note transpired until within

---

164. Stephen Sewell Norton Greely of Grand Rapids was appointed regimental chaplain on Oct. 15, 1862, age 42. He served until June 21, 1865. *Record of Service*, Vol. 36, 61. Findagrave # 117610917

about a mile and a half of Centreville, where they were halted by the videttes, who refused to let them pass, alleging that their orders were peremptory and explicit. After finding all parleying was useless, compliance was feigned by necessity, until the arrival of Gen. Stahl, who was some distance to the rear, when his word was the sesame.

Arrival Home.

The party arrived without further adventure safely at Fairfax Court House, much fatigued and jaded, man and horse, having traversed a distance in all scarcely short of forty miles, on a very hot day; and a great portion of the way exposed to the direct rays of the sun.

Review.

Shortly after returning, the First Michigan Cavalry, under Colonel Town, was drawn up for a review, the usual formula of which was gone through with, and followed by the regiment charging by squadrons, which terminated the proceedings of the day. The Governor is a gentleman in the prime of life, and must have a strong constitution and wiry frame, or he never could have endured the fatigue consequent on such exertion. Even old cavalry men acknowledge themselves worn out. The Governor told me when I inquired how he bore the fatigue, that he got along first rate; but I imagined by his looks he was considerably fagged, and will not feel much in the humor for visiting the Falls of the Potomac, as he proposes to-morrow.[165]

May 27, 1863

During the sojourn at Difficult Creek Governor Blair visited the camp. He rode over in the morning on horseback and made an odd-looking appearance in his citizen's suit and well-worn silk hat. He remained all day, made a speech to the soldiers and after supper took an ambulance and was escorted by Colonel Alger and myself back to Washington, fourteen miles away. It was a very enjoyable and memorable ride. The war governor was full of anecdote and a good

---

165. *DFP*, May 29, 1863, 3. According to an item on this same page, Union pickets were attacked on May 28 "in the vicinity of Bull run, and one killed."

talker and his companions listened with the liveliest interest to what he had to say about Michigan, her people and her soldiers. He was very solicitous about the welfare of the troops, and impressed one as an able, patriotic man, who was doing all he possibly could to hold up the hands of the government and to provide for the Michigan men in the field. We left him at the National hotel and early the next morning returned to our posts of duty.[166]

May 28
After the Battle of Chancellorsville, the 24th Michigan Infantry established their bivouac at Camp Way on the grounds of the Fitzhugh estate, near White Oak church, south of Belle Plain, Virginia. The property was famous as the purported site of George Washington cutting down the cherry tree as a boy. The regimental historian reported on events later in May.

Upon arrival in camp they found several visitors from Detroit. The following evening, May 27th, the regiment listened to speeches from several of them—from John J. Speed, brother of Captain Speed, Rev. F.A. Blades, Henry Barns, and a "rouser" from private Jones of the Sixth Wisconsin. The regiment was this day furnished with the "Black Hats" peculiar to the Iron Brigade, no other troops wearing them, making their appearance like their name, quite unique. On May 28, Governor Blair and his wife, also [banker] David Preston, of Detroit, visited the camp, the former making a speech on dress parade.[167]

Movements of the Rebels.

Washington, May 30.—[Associated Press Dispatch.] Gentlemen who arrived here to-night from the Rappahannock, say that large columns of the enemy are in motion, and were traced yesterday by the

166.   J.H. Kidd, *Personal Recollections of a Cavalryman with Custer's Michigan Cavalry Brigade in the Civil War* (Ionia: Sentinel Printing Co., 1908), 105.
167.   Curtis, 137–142.

lines of dust on the rear of their river front, where one considerable body was moving southward. The preponderance of masses appeared to be going in the direction of Kelly's Ford and Culpepper. The Rebel infantry guard at Banks, United States and Kelly's Fords has been considerably increased within the past day or two, which is construed in some quarters as a ruse to cover the movement of a raid by Stuart via Culpepper [sic].

Gov. Blair of Michigan paid a visit to Gen. Hooker yesterday accompanied by several ladies and gentlemen. They were courteously and warmly received by the General.

It is believed that the enemy are preparing to demonstrate somewhere on our line. The movement upon the other side may be only a ruse to draw attention from some other point.[168]

On July 14, 1863, Blair was in Detroit. He consulted with the provost-marshal's office on how to respond to any attempt to resist the forthcoming draft. He arranged for a complement of Michigan's sharpshooters to be brought home, ostensibly for recruiting purposes. They were posted to the Dearborn Arsenal and at Fort Wayne. No draft riot occurred.[169]

On May 3rd, the first Anishinaabe volunteer joined Company K of the 1st Michigan Sharpshooters regiment.[170] Comprised of some 150 enlisted Native Americans and one officer, the unit would fight in 1864 at the Battle of the Wilderness, the Battle of Spotsylvania Court House, and in the monthslong efforts to capture Petersburg including the Battle of the Crater, the Battle of Reams Station, the Battle of Peebles' Farm, and the Battle of Hatcher's Run. They were the first to raise the U.S. flag over the abandoned city of Petersburg on April 3, 1865. Despite this sterling

---

168. Washington *Evening Star*, June 1, 1863, 2. In fact, these movements were the inception of the Gettysburg Campaign. Blair was on the ground as it commenced.

169. *OR*, III, III, 488-489, 551-552. For a detailed account of a racially motivated riot in Detroit in March, see *Warriors for Liberty*.

170. Michelle K. Cassidy, *Michigan's Company K: Anishinaabe Soldiers, Citizenship, and the Civil War* (East Lansing: Michigan State University, 2023), 71.

record, Blair does not seem to have factored such valor into his views on Indians.

Blair made at least three frontline trips in both theaters of war during the summer of 1863. At the end of May, he was in Virginia to see A.S. Williams, and they "rode all day … to visit the Michigan regiments."[171] *On May 27, Blair visited the 16th Michigan Infantry among other Army of the Potomac units.*[172] *On the fourth of July, he was with the 13th Michigan Infantry south of Nashville.*[173]

171. *From the Cannon's Mouth*, 204.
172. Kim Crawford, *The 16th Michigan Infantry* (Dayton: Morningside, 2002), 165.
173. William J. Carroll letter, July 5, 1863, Blair Collection, Bentley; Robertson, 339. Carroll enlisted at Kalamazoo on Oct. 15, 1861, age 19, and reported Blair as saying "you would hardly know thair was any gon from Kalamazoo for the streets was as full as ever." He survived the war. *Record of Service*, Vol. 13, 31.

Proclamation of Thanksgiving
November 3, 1863

Blair's third annual thanksgiving message contained typical sentiments, but it also asked the people to remember those far from home who were "gallantly defending our heritage of Liberty." No doubt he had in mind the Union victories at Gettysburg and Vicksburg. A defeat at the Battle of Chickamauga in late September after the capture of Chattanooga, Tennessee, was a setback, which caused a change in command from Rosecrans to Ulysses S. Grant. The former Detroiter would lead his troops to victory within the month at the Battle of Chattanooga. The kind of war strategy that Blair had sought from its commencement—blows that would "fall thick and fast" with no respite, aimed at every major Confederate army—would soon unfold under "Unconditional Surrender" Grant.

In accordance with established usage, and because it is eminently fit that an enlightened and Christian people should make frequent and public acknowledgement of their humble dependence upon Almighty God for all the blessings of life, I do hereby appoint Thursday, the 26th day of November instant, as a day of Praise, Thanksgiving and Prayer, and recommend that, suspending all ordinary business, the people of this State do assemble in their places of public worship, in their houses and by the family firesides, and keep this day as becomes them, with reverence and gratitude towards our Heavenly Father, and with sincere and hearty good will towards our fellow-men. Let the kindly affections which unite the families together receive a new and stronger impulse from the good cheer of this day; and in the midst of our abundance let us not forget the broken-hearted and the poor. Many of our people will be absent from the religious and social gatherings of this Thanksgiving; dwelling in tents and in the open field, in gallantly defending our heritage of Liberty, our homes and property.

Let the united prayers of this whole people arise to the God of battles for them, that He will give them victory and the Nation re-established unity and peace. That He will shield from want and sorrow the families of these heroic soldiers, and that He will comfort those who mourn for the heroic dead in the camp, the hospital, and on the battle-field.

The people of Michigan have been prospered in business during the year that is past beyond all previous example. Let them be thankful; but put away pride and the inordinate love of gain, which leads us too often to make merchandize of the most sacred causes. Let us observe this day with humility, thankfulness and honesty towards ourselves, our fellows and our Creator.

In testimony whereof, I have hereunto set my hand, and caused to be affixed the great Seal of the State, at the city of Lansing, this 3d day of November, in the year of our Lord one thousand eight hundred and sixty three.

Austin Blair.[174]

The same day, the Governor officially wrote Secretary of War Stanton to urge the establishment of a soldiers' hospital in Michigan. It was a follow-up to his message in January that extolled the beneficial effects for recovery to the wounded or ill soldier.[175]

---

174.   *LSR*, Nov. 11, 1863, 2.
175.   Frank B. Woodford & Philip P. Mason, *Harper of Detroit: The Origin and Growth of a Great Metropolitan Hospital* (Detroit: Wayne State University Press, 1964), 72-75. See *His Sword a Scalpel*, 148.

Proclamation for Volunteers
November 9, 1863

Responding to the president's national call on October 17 for an additional 300,000 men, Blair issued a proclamation that called upon Michiganders to volunteer and forestall the impact of a draft that would make up any consequent shortages.

The proclamation of the President of the United States, of the date of the 17th day of October last, "calling upon the Governors of the different States to raise and have enlisted into the United States service for the various Companies and Regiments in the field from their respective States their quotas of three hundred thousand men," has made it my duty again to address the people of Michigan. For the purpose of allowing the State to fill its quota with volunteers, and in its own way, the President has authorized recruiting for the companies and regiments in the field until the third day of January next, and credit will be given for such recruits by sub-districts as immediately previous to the draft just concluded.

To encourage such recruiting, largely increased bounties are offered by the Government. To Volunteers in regiments whose term of service will expire in 1864 or 1865, there will be paid a bounty of three hundred and two dollars, and to Veterans who shall re-enlist in such regiments a bounty of four hundred and two dollars. If the State shall fail to furnish its quota by volunteering, then a draft will be made for the deficiency, commencing on the fifth day of January, 1864.

The quota of this State has been assigned by the War Department, and is eleven thousand two hundred and ninety-eight (11,298) men.

This call is for <u>soldiers</u> to fill the ranks of the regiments in the field,—those regiments which by long and gallant service have wasted their numbers in the same proportion that they have made a distinguished name, both for themselves and the State. The people of Michigan will recognize this as a duty already too long delayed. Our young men, I trust, will hasten to stand beside the heroes of Antietam, Gettysburg, Vicksburg, Stones River and Chicamauga [sic].

The hopes of the rebellion are steadily perishing. The Armies of the Republic are in the midst of their country, and they have not the power to expel them.

Fill up the ranks once more, and the next blast of the bugle for an advance will sound the knell of revolution and herald in the return of peace.

Fellow citizens, let us do it <u>willingly, gallantly, joyously</u>. The people of Michigan have heretofore earned the gratitude of the country by their promptness and energy in the support of the Government.

The terms of enlistment of the old regiments, many of them, will expire early next year. They must not be allowed to perish by such expiration. The quotas of the districts and sub-districts will be published accompanying this proclamation.

I earnestly request the Counties, Cities and Towns to move immediately and actively in this work. Volunteers can choose their regiments among those named in the accompanying Orders. The men of townships and neighborhoods can enlist and go together into such companies and regiments as they may prefer, and I do assure them that it is abundantly better both for them and the country to take service in old and well drilled regiments than in new ones.

Recruiting officers will be appointed wherever the people desire it to aid in the filling up the quotas.

Patriotic men of Michigan, OBEY YOUR COUNTRY'S CALL!

Given under my hand at the capital in Lansing this 9th day of November, A.D. 1863.

Austin Blair.[176]

---

176.   *DFP*, Nov. 14, 1862, 4.

Speech to 1st Michigan Colored Regiment
December 9, 1863

Blair's remarks to the men of Michigan's African American regiment were reported in full, along with all the attendant circumstances, in the supportive Detroit newspaper.

THE COLORED REGIMENT.
Review at Jackson—Speech of Gov. Blair.
From Our Own Correspondent.
Jackson, Dec. 9, 1863.

The first battalion of the 1st Michigan colored regiment arrived here at 12 o'clock last night. Properly, they should have been here at 9 o'clock, but owing to the through freight train being very heavily loaded, they were obliged to remain at Ann Arbor till a late hour. Quartermas[ter] McLaughlin preceeded [sic] the train, and through the extraordinary efforts of Judge Bennett and Mr. Eugene Pringle, the Governor's private Secretary, every arrangement had been made to provide a bountiful supper, and the proprietor of the Marion House was engaged to cook the victuals and serve them out. As the train was greatly delayed, however, it was thought best not to have the meal cold, but to defer it till this morning. This was agreed to, but when the men arrived, the proprietor of the above house cooly informed the Quartermaster, that he should have to be excused from furnishing the eatables at all. It was then about 1 o'clock at night, and the men had had nothing to eat since leaving Ann Arbor. No time was to be lost. By the aid of a colored employee of the hotel, the Quartermaster and your correspondent were shown to a place where we could probably make the desired arrangements. Calling the man and his family out of bed, by dint of hard coaxing, and after detailing several men from the regiment to help in the culinary departments, everything was at once put under way, and by 5 o'clock the first company sat down to a good breakfast. Had proper arrangements been made and the citizens assured of the precise time when the battalion would arrive, everything would have been in readiness to receive them. Through the generous liberality of Mr. Jackson, his large hall was gratuitously offered and accepted for the use of the men, as a sleeping apartments. All except the band were abundantly supplied with blankets, and the latter were provided with everything to make them comfortable, by Capt. Barry, the Provost Marshal here, to whom sincere thanks are due.

After partaking of breakfast the men formed into line preparatory to being reviewed by Governor Blair. About 9 1/2 o'clock they took up a line of march to his residence, the streets along the entire way being densely packed with human beings, by whom the boys were greeted with loud and prolonged cheering. In fact it was a perfect oration. The men, for their soldierly bearing, neat and clean appearance, were highly complimented. I did not hear a single reproachful or disparaging remark made in reference to them. Arriving at the Governor's residence, the battalion was marched into an open lot near by, where they were put through a series of military movements, in presence of Gov. Blair, Col. Loomis, Capt. Barry, the Provost Marshal, Dr. Blaker, of the 21st Infantry, and a large concourse of people, a great proportion of whom were ladies. After performing various evolutions, the battalion was formed into a hollow square, when they were introduced to the Governor by Lieut. Col. Bennett, in a few appropriate remarks. The Governor briefly spoke as follows:

Officers and Soldiers: I find my position in your square somewhat new. It is the first time that I ever saw a battalion of colored soldiers together, and I, together with the vast concourse you see surrounding you, feel proud of your general bearing. The people of this country are beginning to feel interested in you. They are proud to see colored soldiers banded together to fight for a country that has heretofore promised much, but never accomplished a great deal for the colored race. It has done much for everybody but you. That feeling is fast being dispelled, and the time will come when the world shall recognize that the

Constitution of our country means what it says, that every man shall enjoy life, liberty and pursuit of happiness. (Prolonged applause.)

[¶] I hope you will be able to fight so as to put the country under an obligation to you. Your colored brethren in arms in South Carolina have borne a conspicuous part in re-establishing the banner of our glorious country upon the ramparts of Fort Wagner, have helped to plant the Stars and Stripes where they would never again be removed by the hand of treason. (Cheers.) Take courage then; do your duty nobly. Your noble dusky brethren have indeed won for themselves the richest laurels on many a battle field. By these deeds you will secure the good will of all, and a prominent place in the country. Already there are thousands of colored men rushing to arms in their country's cause, and in a few months, I verily believe, there will be upwards of 100,000 colored men in the ranks. Imagine, if you can, one hundred thousand bayonets in the hands of dusky soldiers, and then see if the Copperheads will dare to revile the brave soldiers of the Union. (Cheers.)

[¶] Quite recently the country has heard the glad things of the series of successes in East Tennessee. The flag of our country has been planted upon the highest pinnacle of Lookout Mountain, in the very heart of the so called Southern Confederacy, in the midst of a country where your brethren have been held in bondage. The flag placed there may be looked up to, floating from that eminence, as an ornament to future generations. The great Proclamation of Freedom is being made a fact. It was written about a year ago, that all man held in bondage in those States, remaining in rebellion up to a certain time, should hereafter be free. Daily we are witnessing the beneficial and holy effects of that document. Victory over the entire armed host of the rebellion is not far distant, and foreign governments are beginning to recognize the fact. The British lion, that a year ago was endeavoring to hem us in, preparatory to swallowing us whole, is now as calm as a sucking dove. The Frenchman, whose ideas were fast becoming wedded in favor of the rebels, is changing his tune, and now that he felt secure in his newly-effected foothold in Mexico, he is quite willing to let us alone.

[¶] Learn thoroughly the duties of a soldier. Take care to be manly and well informed upon your duties and responsibilities. Learn well the character you have assumed. Observe good and orderly regulations. Avoid vicious and dissipated habits, and all immoral practices. Obey your officers, and the result will be that you will come out of the contest better informed of what you really are, and what you can do. Remember that you have a dignity to maintain. We have committed to your care the flag of our country. That you will fight for it no one doubts, and if perchance any of you should fall, there will be a consolation that you will find honorable graves. It is my earnest wish you may escape unharmed, and that you may be able to return to your families. Such shall be my prayers, as well as of all those who love their Country. Hoping to see you again ere you depart for the seat of war, I bid you good bye.

The Governor's speech, which was delivered in his usual earnest manner, was received with wild applause, and at its close three times three were proposed and given for him. The men were subsequently put through various movements before quitting the field, and were then marched to dinner. At 1 1/2 o'clock they go to Marshall.[177]

---

177. *Detroit Advertiser & Tribune*, Dec. 10, 1863, 1.

Proclamation Convening Legislature
December 15, 1863

The president issued a call for more troops in October to make up losses and in anticipation of enrolled volunteers not reenlisting.[178] Blair responded two months later once the State's quota had been fixed.

Whereas, The President of the United States, by his proclamation, of the date of the 17th October last, has called upon the Governors of the different States to raise and have enlisted into the United States service, for the various companies and regiments in the field from their respective States, their quotas of three hundred thousand men;

And whereas, It has been judged necessary by many of the counties, towns and cities of this State, that provision should be made for the payment of bounties to volunteers, by such counties, towns, and cities, to enable them to fill their several quotas with volunteers, and that further legislation is necessary, in order to give full faith and credit to the acts and obligations of such municipal bodies;

Therefore, believing that such an extraordinary occasion exists, as is contemplated by the Constitution, I, Austin Blair, Governor of the State of Michigan, in virtue of the power vested in me by the Constitution, do convene the Legislature of this State, hereby requiring the Senators and Representatives to assemble in their respective Chambers, at the Capitol, in Lansing, on Tuesday, the 19th day of January next, at twelve o'clock, noon, then and there to consider and determine upon the measures proper to be adopted in regard to the payment of such bounties to volunteers, and the legalization of acts already done for that purpose, and all such other subjects as may be brought before the Legislature in pursuance of the Constitution.

---

178. *OR*, III, III, 892.

In testimony whereof, I have hereunto set my hand, and caused to be affixed the Great Seal of the State, at Lansing, this 15th day of December, in the year of our Lord one thousand eight hundred and sixty-three.

By the Governor:

Austin Blair.

James B. Porter, Secretary of State.[179]

---

179. *Journal of the Senate of the State of Michigan, Extra Session, 1864* (John A. Kerr & Co., 1864), 3-4.

Message to the Legislature
January 20, 1864

Blair's address to the special session of the legislature covered several areas of the state's participation in the war. The first part dealt with fulfilling Michigan's quota for the 300,000 new troops summoned by Lincoln the previous October. Blair proposed enhanced bounties to spur volunteering. He also recommended a measure to enable soldiers on duty outside the state to be permitted to vote in the upcoming November election—which would decide whether the Lincoln presidency continued. The final item of report: Michigan's participation in the creation of a Soldiers' National Cemetery at the Gettysburg battlefield.[180] The message is approximately 5,600 words in length.

Fellow-Citizens of the Senate and House of Representatives:

I welcome you again to the Capitol. By virtue of that provision of the Constitution which authorizes the Governor to convene the Legislature upon "extraordinary occasions," your present assembling has been required. The period is itself revolutionary and altogether extraordinary. The rebellion still refuses to give us either peace or rest; and no human forecast seems sufficient to provide for all the exigencies of a single year. At your last session, after having tried the hard experiences of war for nearly two years, and learned somewhat of the requirements of the occasion, it was hoped that all had been done which would be required during the term for which you had been

---

180.   Unlike at Gettysburg, where sentiment quickly materialized to set aside large portions of the battlefield as a park, the ground at Antietam awaited national protection until an act of Congress on August 30, 1890. The state of Maryland commenced the process of setting aside a burying ground for the Union dead in 1864, and a March 1865 law specified that any state could participate by funding its share. Michigan began its involvement via the appointment of future Governor John J. Bagley in 1866. *Michigan at Antietam*, 157-159.

elected, and for the fulfillment of the obligation owed by the people of Michigan to the National Government, in its great effort to protect the Union and save the nation entire. All the measures of that session were, I believe, wisely adapted to the purposes had in view; but some changes made by acts of Congress in the methods of recruitment of the National forces, and the failure of those acts to accomplish the object in the manner and to the extent anticipated, have rendered further legislation expedient and even necessary.

[¶] The enrollment act was evidently intended to dispense with the system of volunteering, and to rely mainly, if not entirely, upon drafting, to reinforce the National armies. No further appeals were to be made directly to the State authorities, to furnish their quotas of volunteers, as had been previously done; but the Government would at once lay its hands upon the men required, by means of the Provost Marshals and the machinery of the draft. It resulted, of course, that local and State bounties would be no further required, nor would any further agitation by the local authorities be necessary, in any part of the country. This project has been tried, apparently with results not altogether satisfactory, whether for the reason that the law itself was crude and defective, or that the system was not in accordance with the habits and genius of our people, it is not necessary now to inquire. The President has, for whatever reason, in his proclamation of October last, "calling upon the Governors of the different States to raise and have enlisted into the United States service, for the various companies and regiments in the field from their respective States, their quotas of three hundred thousand men," returned to the old system, which looks to recruiting as the chief reliance for strengthening the military forces. The demand that the enlistments should all be "for the various companies and regiments in the field," also indicates a determination to cease ornamenting ambitious civilians with the insignia of military command, and in its stead to reinforce the veteran corps by enlistments into their well trained ranks, under officers of tried courage and skill; a policy so wise that it is only wonderful that it was not adopted long before.

[¶] As soon as practicable after the issue of this call, the quotas of several States were made known to them, that of Michigan being a little in excess of eleven thousand. It was the duty of the State to respond to this call for volunteers with the promptness and energy which has characterized our people since the war began, and has made Michigan soldiers a pride and a glory in every army in which they have served. To do this required that all our recruiting machinery which had been laid aside for the draft, should be again brought into full operation. Some little delay was unavoidable occasioned in consequence of the draft being at the time in actual progress; but all things considered, the success has been more than equal to the most sanguine expectations. Recruiting has been brought back to the standard of enthusiasm of the first year of the war, and the ability of the State still to fill its quotas by the process of voluntary enlistments, has been proved beyond doubt.

Bounties.

This has been accomplished mainly by the offering of liberal bounties to the volunteers, and a thorough agitation and canvass of the communities, consequent upon it. The people have generally taken the matter directly in hand themselves. Without any adequate laws directing their action in a uniform course, they have come together in their local municipal corporations, and in the various ways which seemed best to them, have raised the money to enable them to offer such bounties as seemed sufficient to induce the enlistment of the requisite number of men to fill the quota and escape the draft. As a general thing they have aimed at levying the amount raised, finally, by a uniform tax, in order that all those who ought to contribute to it, should be made to do so, however unwilling any might be; and to this there seems to be no solid objection. If any interest is more indebted than another for protection, to the maintenance of stable government, it is the property upon which the taxation will fall. And inasmuch as the war is waged for the preservation of such government, it may justly demand that the property of the country shall contribute, by fair assessment, to its success in every proper way. What more effectual way than by filling the ranks of the army under the immediate action of the people themselves?

In many instances, county, township and city bonds, and other evidences of debt, have been issued, which lack the necessary statutory sanction, and do not therefore possess, in the hands of the holders, their proper and legitimate value.

These obligations have been entered into in good faith, and in good faith received, presuming upon the patriotism and justice of the Legislature. They have been incurred for the most patriotic object, and have accomplished most honorable and beneficial results, both to the State and the Nation.

I have no hesitation, therefore, in recommending that the legislative sanction be given to the action of the people in the raising of money for the payment of bounties to volunteers since the passage of the act of 1863, under such guards and restrictions as may be thought necessary for protection against frauds and pretended claims.

In this connection, I wish also to call the attention of the Legislature to the question of the propriety of providing by law, a uniform rule, by virtue of which bounties may hereafter be raised without the irregularities which have heretofore occurred, and without the necessity of another resort to an extra session.

It is extremely desirable that whenever bounties are offered, they should be uniform in amount throughout the State, in order that different localities may be prevented from a heated competition and bidding against each other, in a manner alike disastrous to themselves and the service, resulting in too many cases in downright deception and fraud, both upon the volunteers themselves and the towns and cities from which they enlist. For this purpose, it has been thought best by many patriotic persons that bounties should be offered only by the State, and that the smaller municipal corporations should be entirely forbidden to do so. In this opinion I do not concur. After considerable observation and experience, I am convinced that no contrivance has yet been adopted which can compare in efficiency with the local bounty for procuring enlistments into the military service.

The same amount of money offered in any other way, either by the State or General Government, will not begin to equal it, and the reason is obvious. When the people of a town, or ward of a city, are called together to consider of the propriety of raising a bounty to fill the quota of that town or ward, a very great interest is awakened in the question at the very first step, and when it is finally determined to do so, and to assess the amount in some way upon the little community, the interest is so greatly enhanced that every individual of that community feels thoroughly committed to the project, and lends his utmost influence to accomplish it. This influence is worth even more than the money itself. Few will enlist from a cold, lifeless community, no matter for the money that may be offered. But let the whole people rise up to cheer on those who enter the service of their country, offering generous bounties, not to buy an unwilling soldier, but as an earnest of hearty good will towards a gallant defender of a most righteous cause, in which all the blood is shed shall be sacred, and the case is "bravely altered." The ambitious, enthusiastic young men will go shouting with joy to the ranks, and take up their arms with the spirit of heroes.

In whatever laws may be enacted upon this subject, the object should be to aid the action of the people by giving legal force and validity to such measures as they may decide upon, as being most likely to accomplish their purpose. At the same time it will be wise to fix some well defined limits, beyond which it shall not be lawful to go to prevent inconsiderate rashness. In fixing such limits, care should be taken to avoid extremes. It is not only important that the object should be pursued with great enthusiasm and patriotic energy, but that it should at the same time be continuous and not transitory. The losses of the companies and regiments in the field are constantly and steadily occurring. The men drop out of the ranks one by one into the hospital. Large numbers of them never return to active duty, disappearing in the invalid corps, or being finally discharged to return to civil life. Their places in the ranks ought to be supplied by a steady influx of new recruits. It is better every way that the number required to keep up the numbers of the Michigan regiments in the field should be obtained by a steady and constant recruitment of new men, than that all should have to be done in a period limited to a few days, and consequently by a spasmodic exhausting effort which will soon need to be repeated. Under the present system of credits to the sub districts, any surplus is always carried forward, in fact the enrollment law requires that, and any town may, by a steady system of recruiting, keep its quota constantly filled, thus avoiding the extra expenses and effort occasioned by haste and strong competition on the eve of a draft.

We owe a great debt of gratitude to the companies and regiments we have put in the field, and can repay it in no way so well as keeping their ranks full. It ought not to be considered a fulfillment of our whole duty merely to raise the quotas assigned us. It is a sacred obligation resting upon the people to sustain the troops in the field; and for this purpose it is essential that the action be unremitting and steadily sustained. When bounties are offered, the offer should be continued after the immediate exigency is past, thus providing a surplus to meet another call.

The State bounty which was provided by the act approved March 6th, 1863, was withdrawn soon after the late call was made. This action was rendered proper by two considerations: First, the war loan fund was insufficient in amount to pay it to so large a number of men as the call embraced; and secondly, because the United States Government had so largely increased its bounties, that its payment was considered unnecessary so long as those should continue to be paid.

It will be remembered that this State bounty was recommended in the message of a year ago to supply the place, to some extent, of the local bounties which it was apprehended would cease as soon as the draft then progressing was over, which proved to be the case. And this was for the purpose of preventing the entire abandonment of the recruiting service, which it also has accomplished. This is a case which is very likely to occur again, and I wish to reserve the amount still remaining in the war loan fund to be used when and where other bounties are withheld, or there is some especial reason for their being paid, as in the case of the veterans who re-enlist, having never received any bounty from the State. The payment of this bounty was also confined by express words of the act to those who should "enlist in any regiment, battery or company heretofore mustered from this State into the military service of the United States, or now [then] organizing in this State for such service." The purpose of this was to encourage enlistments in the old regiments, and to discourage the formation of new ones, a policy which has now been adopted by the General Government. To prevent misconstruction, this act will require some slight amendment, more especially in regard to the discretion which was vested in the Executive. In its main object, however, I believe it to have been a very beneficial law, and trust it may be retained.

Enabling Soldiers in the Field to Vote.

At your session a year ago, a bill passed the House of Representatives, providing for the exercise of the right of suffrage in our elections by our soldiers absent from the State in the service of the United States. This bill reached the Senate at the very heel of the session and failed, it was understood, for want of time to consider it. The subject was one of great importance and surrounded with grave doubts and difficulties.

Perhaps the minds of members were not altogether settled at that time as to the rightfulness or policy of such a law. The Constitutions of the States have all been framed without any view to such a condition of things as the present; and there has always been in this country, as in England, great jealousy of the army mingling in the affairs of civil administration. During the past year, however, very great consideration has been given to the subject in nearly all the loyal States. It has come into judgment before the highest tribunals of several of them, eliciting very learned and patriotic opinions from the judges, which have thrown great light upon it, and gone far to establish the legal principles which must guide all proper legislation in that direction.

The patriotism, justice and sound policy require the passage of such laws, wherever they can be constitutionally enacted, seems to be now generally agreed. The volunteer army of the United States is composed of the people of the United States. They have left their various occupations in civil life and taken up arms at the call of their country, not to become professional soldiers, but to defend their country and government from destruction, and their homes and property from desecration and pillage. Not to renounce civil life and the pursuits of peace, but to establish, upon an enduring basis, the right to both, for themselves and their posterity. With a patriotism and courage worthy of everlasting remembrance they have periled everything, that their country and its free institutions may continue to exist. They are absent from the polls of the elections in their several towns and wards, beating back the power of a causeless and cruel rebellion in order that those very elections may be held in peace, and that the right to hold them and to have their results respected and obeyed shall continue forever. If these volunteer citizen soldiers should not have a voice in the civil administration of the government for which they fight, then it would be well to inquire who is worthy of it. Though soldiers, they have not ceased to be citizens and residents, nor is their stake less in the country than that of those who remain in peace at home. Surely, he who stands faithfully by his country in the shock of battle, may be safely trusted at the ballot box, though it should be carried to him at Vicksburg or Chattanooga.

Is it, then, within the constitutional powers of this Legislature, to enact a law granting the exercise of the right of suffrage elsewhere than in the town or ward where the voter is a resident? It is not a question of the right to vote, but only of the place where the ballot shall be received. No change of qualifications in the voter, nor in the manner of his exercising the right, will be required. All the case demands is the establishment of a pool for the reception of votes in or near the camps of the troops. No right of challenge will be denied, nor any safeguard which the utmost prudence may enact. If such power exists in your body, then by every consideration of justice and right let it be done; but if not, then however much we may regret it, we must not move a step in that direction, since they would not be fit to make laws who will not obey the fundamental law. It becomes us, therefore, to examine carefully and judge dispassionately.

That the Legislature has the power to fix the time, place and manner of holding elections, and to establish the qualifications of voters, unless prohibited by the Constitution from doing so, need not be doubted.

Justice Butler, in delivering the unanimous opinion of the Supreme Court of Connecticut, declaring unconstitutional and void the act of the General Assembly of that State, approved December 24th, 1862, "providing a mode of taking the votes in the election of State and other officers, of persons absent from the State as volunteers in the military service of the United States," remarks as follows:

"The Constitution establishes an elective government, and under it there must of necessity be a fixed time, place and manner of holding elections. If these are clearly and sufficiently fixed and prescribed by the Constitution, and nothing is expressly delegated, or by implication left to the Legislature, that body cannot interfere to alter, extend or suspend them, or either of them, in the slightest particular. If they are not thus fixed and prescribed by the Constitution, it is by implication incident to the general legislative power to do it, so that the government may be perpetuated and sustained.

"Our simple inquiry, therefore, is whether the Constitution has so fully and clearly prescribed the time, place and manner of holding elections, or either of them, as to leave by implication no power in the General Assembly to prescribe them, or either of them, in the way and to the extent they have attempted to do, in the act in question.

"In relation to the time, place and manner of holding elections, the Constitutions of the several States differ. In some of them all these are prescribed with that particularity which forbids all action of the Legislature. In others, neither are prescribed, but the qualifications of the voters are fixed, and the power to regulate the time, place and manner, committed to the Legislature; and in such States the reception of votes out of the State may be constitutionally authorized."

This doctrine of the Connecticut Court is sustained, substantially, by all the cases which have met my observation. It seems to me, also, the doctrine of good sense. Taking these principles as a guide, it will not be difficult, I think, to determine whether the Constitution of Michigan "has so fully and clearly prescribed the time, place and manner of holding elections, as to leave by implication no power in the Legislature to prescribe them, or either of them." It has certainly so prescribed the time. In section 34 of article 4, section 3 of article 5, and section 1 of article 8, the Tuesday succeeding the first Monday of November, in the year 1852, and of every second year thereafter, is established as the time of holding the general biennial election. And it is clear that every election of State officers and members of the Legislature must be upon that day, and no other, in spite of any legislative enactment whatever.

If the Constitution is equally explicit as to the place and manner of holding the elections, then we may dismiss the discussion at once, and obey the prohibition; but I am confident it will be found otherwise.

That instrument has no where required that the election shall be held in any particular place or number of places, nor in any particular manner. No election districts are established or required to be established, nor are any rules prescribed for the form or extent of such districts. They may be formed of entire counties if the Legislature so choose, unless the requirement that Senators and Representatives shall be elected by single districts affects the question. Neither is the manner of holding the election prescribed, except that the vote shall be by ballot. All these things have been left to the Legislature, unless the concluding words of section 1, article 7, should be held to provide otherwise. This article is headed "Elections," and deals entirely with the qualifications and privleges [sic] of electors, except that in the second section the vote is required to be given by ballot, "except for such township officers as may be authorized by law to be otherwise chosen." The words of section 1, referred to, are as follows: "But no citizen or inhabitant shall be an elector, or entitled to vote at any election, unless he shall be above the age of twenty-one years, and has resided in the State three months, and in the township or ward in which he offers to vote ten days next preceding such election." These are fit words to establish the qualifications of voters, but not to control the Legislature as to the places where polls of election shall be established and votes offered and received. They speak directly as to age and residence, and only to those qualifications. All else is incidental and explanatory. The elector must be twenty-one years of age, and he must have had a residence in some place, or any number of places in the State, of three months, and in some particular township or ward ten days next preceding the election at which he offers to vote. Can any greater scope be fairly given to this clause than that. If it was intended to forbid the Legislature from authorizing the reception of a vote in any other place than in town or ward where the elector resided, it is not conceivable that it should have been left by the convention to a merely casual expression which does not directly either command or forbid anything. The words no doubt, pre-suppose that the offer to vote will be made in the township or ward in which the elector resides, but they neither require it to be so, nor forbid it to be otherwise.

In the same article, at section 5, this Constitution is at the pains to declare that "no elector shall be deemed to have gained or lost a residence by reason of his being employed in the service of the United States." Did the people, in establishing this Constitution intend, while preserving the residence of the soldier, and consequently his right to vote, at the same time to forbid the Legislature to enact such laws as might enable him to exercise the right? The Constitution, like any other act, must be taken together, as a whole, and have such a reasonable construction as will carry into full and beneficial effect the system of government established by it. The usual and reasonable powers of the Legislature will not be held to be abrogated unless by clear and distinct enactments to that effect.

The government established is in all its branches elective, and the suffrage universal, or nearly so. Great care seems to have been taken to preserve for all white male citizens, of proper age, the exercise of the right to vote, and I think this manifest intention ought to have great weight in the determination of the present question. Unquestionably the present contingency is one not contemplated by the convention which framed the Constitution, or by the people in adopting it; and there is, on that account, all the more reason for declining to adopt any narrow construction which would make it accomplish what no one at the time designed it should do.

In several of the States laws of the sort proposed have been enacted and put into practical operation without much inconvenience, and with no apparent danger of public injury. In some of these States, with Constitutions similar to our own, the question of the validity of such laws has been before their highest courts, and they have been there sustained. Such, I believe, has been the case in Iowa and Wisconsin.

After giving the subject considerable attention, I do not hesitate to recommend the passage of such a law, by this Legislature, as will enable the soldiers of Michigan, while absent from the State in the service of the United States, to avail themselves of the right which they have never forfeited to vote in all the State and local elections. It will be only just towards them, and their votes will be dangerous to traitors only.

Military Road from Fort Wilkins to Green Bay.

[omitted; Blair recommended action to construct the road]

Soldiers' National Cemetery at Gettysburg.

On the 3d day of July, in the year 1863, was fought at Gettysburg one of the most memorable battles of the war. When we take into account all the circumstances surrounding and attending the campaign which culminated there, it is impossible not to feel that that field is historic and famous forever. The army of the Potomac, the largest and best appointed of the Union armies in the field, had then lately, under the command of Gen. Hooker, crossed the Rappahannock river successfully, in the face of the enemy, and marched to Chancellorsville, with high hopes and the congratulations of the whole country, to offer him battle; but only to return with hopes disappointed, and congratulations turned to doubts and discouragement. The rebel general, the most trusted and skillful of them all, immediately made his preparations to improve the occasion of his great advantage. Collecting with great rapidity the largest and best disciplined army that the Confederacy has ever put in the field, he assumed the offensive. Taking up his line of march straight for the middle States, the wealthiest and most populous portion of the Union, he left the Union army behind him, or merely covering the Capital and the great cities now most seriously menaced with pillage and destruction. His troops, flushed with victory, and meeting with no serious obstacles to their advance, were already in the midst of Pennsylvania. Washington, Baltimore, Philadelphia, and even New York, are all within his grasp, unless this triumphant march can be interrupted. The great struggle can no longer be delayed. The army of the Potomac, humiliated by partial defeat, less in numbers, but still indomitable in spirit and courage, approached rapidly, and prepared to accept the offered gage of battle. The mightiest of human interests hang upon the issue. The prize to be fought for is the life of the country and the liberties of a whole people, perhaps of mankind, for generations to come. The whole nation looks with troubled anxiety towards that field. If Lee is victorious, where will his march be stayed? Then Hooker is removed and Meade takes the command. The apprehensions of the people are increased. Will he be equal to the occasion? Yes, he will be equal to it; and the nameless heroes under his command will be more than equal to it. They meet in the quiet country village of Gettysburg, and there, in the shock of terrific battle, for three days is the great stake fought for, and won. Won for liberty and the Union. The proud rebels turn and flee back across the Potomac, over the Rappahannock, and beyond the Rapidan. And there, at Gettysburg, was the nation preserved, and the power of the rebellion broken, never to be reconstructed. It may linger yet awhile, and burn, and destroy, and kill, and murder, but its fate is none the less sure.

On that great field of Gettysburg, after the roar of battle had ceased, and the smoke had cleared away, there lay the unburied dead. They were 2,271 in number, exclusive of all such as were removed by friends for burial among their kindred—eight hundred of them were entirely unknown. Of the remainder, one hundred and twelve were from Michigan; and there she stands on that sad roll of honor, the fourth in point of actual numbers, but first in the comparison of the numbers of her slain with the ratio of population. The Governor of Pennsylvania proposed to purchase a portion of the battle-field, a picturesque, beautiful ground, and to establish there "The Soldiers' National Cemetery, at Gettysburg," the State of Pennsylvania holding the title in trust for all the States having soldiers buried there, each bearing a proper share of the expenses. All the States concurring, this has been done, and the remains of the dead soldiers have been gathered up "tenderly" and buried by States together. And there they rest, who saved their country with their blood.

The accompanying papers will show the details of the plan of the cemetery and the estimates of the expenses. I have ventured to promise that Michigan will not fail to do her proportion with alacrity, and I now recommend that the requisite appropriation may be made, and authority given to appoint an agent to proceed to Gettysburg and direct the proper arrangement and ornamentation of the portion of the grounds which have been set apart for this State. This cemetery will be a Mecca of patriotism as long as the country exists.

[Conclusion]

Gentlemen of the two Houses, I congratulate you upon the happier auspices under which we re-assemble. We have reason to be thankful not only for bountiful harvests and the material wealth and prosperity which surrounds us, but also for the bright hopes which promise the speedy return of peace to our country.

Unwearied by three years of continued war, the people are still faithful to the free institutions under which we have grown to be great. With unabated courage and ever-increasing confidence, they march steadily forward under the "starry flag" of freedom, "keeping step to the music of the Union." Since our last assembling, the arms of the Republic have been victorious at all points. A just cause has added to our strength the smile of the benignant Heavens. The madness and desperation of rebellion has not been able to maintain its ground. With sullen rage and gnashing teeth it yields up its most cherished strongholds. The bloody usurper in Richmond, with alternate prayers and curses, calls upon the civilized nations for help, even for recognition, and calls in vain. There are none so base as to keep him company.

Nor have our victories been those of the field alone. The loyal and true men of the country have crushed and silenced, at the ballot boxes, those more insidious enemies, who, under specious political pretences, plead the cause of the more manly traitors who are in arms.

The great and necessary measure of emancipation—the measure of justice and God-like charity—has, the past year, won triumphs of no less importance than the greatest military success. The great mistake and wrong of the nation is being put away. We return to our own great and immortal declaration. In spite of scorn, contempt and the pride of caste—of the lust of power and the love of money—of stupid ignorance and intellect without conscience, all men in America will be free. Let us thank God, bind up our wounds and fight on.

Austin Blair.

January 20, 1864[181]

Blair continued to rejoice "in the Emancipation Proclamation for its future implications as well as for its present application as a necessary war measure." It was also a "measure of justice and God-like charity."[182]

---

181. *Messages*, 479-490.
182. Jean J.L. Fennimore, "Austin Blair: Civil War Governor, 1863-1864" in *Michigan History*, Vol. 49, No. 4 (Dec. 1965), 344-345, 347-348, 350-352, 358-359 ["Fennimore IV"].

Messages on Approval of Legislation
February 3 & 5, 1864

During the final session of the legislature while governor, Blair as per custom signed and communicated on the disposition of bills. Several related to the war. At the same time, his solicitude for prisoners of war was demonstrated by correspondence later recorded in one of the classic accounts involving Private John L. Ransom (see Appendix). The House of Representatives adopted a resolution of praise for the governor.[183]

Executive Office
Lansing, February 3, 1864.
To the Senate:
I have this day approved, signed and deposited in the office of the Secretary of State, the following:

…

An act to provide for the preparation of the soldiers' national cemetery, at Gettysburg, in the State of Pennsylvania; …
Austin Blair.[184]

Executive Office
Lansing, February 5, 1864.
To the Senate:

---

183.   "*Resolved,* That this House entertain the highest confidence in the ability, integrity and patriotism of his Excellency Governor Blair, and that his administration of the affairs of the State, meets our full approval, and that for his care and fidelity to our citizen soldiery in the field, he is entitled to the thanks of all loyal citizens of the State. *Resolved,* That the course pursued by his Excellency in paying the reenlisted veteran volunteers, the State bounty, meets our approval." *Journal of the House of Representatives of the State of Michigan, Extra Session, 1864* (Lansing: John A. Kerr & Co., 1864), 220-222.
184.   *Journal of the Senate,* Extra Session 1864, 254.

I have approved, signed and deposited in the office of the Secretary of State, the following, viz.:

...

An act to amend section 1 of an act entitled an act to authorize the payment of a State bounty to volunteers, mustered from this State into the military service of the United States, approved March 6, 1863;

...

An act authorizing a war bounty loan;
Also,
An act authorizing the payment of bounties to volunteers in the service of the United States;

...

An act to provide for the interest on the war bounty loan.
Austin Blair.[185]

The first bill enacted into law in the extra session was to approve Michigan's participation in the national cemetery at the Gettysburg battlefield. The sum of $3,500 was appropriated for that purpose, and the governor was authorized to appoint a commissioner to represent the interests of the state. The measure became effective on February 3, 1864.[186]

When commissioners met on December 17, 1863, in Harrisburg, Pennsylvania, to carry the cemetery work forward, authority to participate had not yet been secured by Blair given that the Michigan legislature was in adjournment during July and for the remainder of the calendar year. Nonetheless, Blair sent a letter expressing "disposition to approve any reasonable action ... in reference to the completion of the cemetery at Gettysburg."[187]

---

185. Id. 263-264.
186. *Acts of the Legislature of the State of Michigan Passed at the Extra Session of 1864* (Lansing: John A. Kerr & Co., 1864), 1-2.
187. *Report of the Select Committee Relative to the Soldiers' National Cemetery, Together with the Accompanying Documents, as Reported to the House of Representatives of the Commonwealth of Pennsylvania, March 31, 1864* (Harrisburg: Singerley & Myers, 1864), 12-14.

Blair appointed Thomas White Ferry as the Michigan member of the board of managers of the Soldiers' National Cemetery for 1865.[188] *Born in the old Mission House on Mackinac Island in 1827, Ferry served in both houses of the legislature in the 1850s and as a member of the Republican state central committee.*

After adjournment, Blair traveled to Washington in late April.[189] *He remained away from Michigan for several days while the Overland campaign commenced and was not home on May 5. He paid a visit to the White House, and, on the afternoon of May 1, Lincoln took Congressman Francis W. Kellogg and Governor Blair riding.*[190] *A letter of July 26 (see Appendix) indicated* "I go to Washington Monday next the 29th just to be gone perhaps 10 or 12 days."

188.   *Revised Report of the Select Committee Relative to the Soldiers' National Cemetery, Together with the Accompanying Documents, as Reported to the House of Representatives of the Commonwealth of Pennsylvania* (Harrisburg: Singerley & Myers, 1865), 13.

189.   *OR*, III, IV, 251.

190.   *CW*, Vol. VII, 326; *OR*, III, IV, 265.

Call for Convention
February 22, 1864

On Washington's birthday, the Republican national committee issued a call for an assembly to nominate candidates for the fall presidential election. As the Michigan party representative, Austin Blair attached his name to the text.

The undersigned, who by original appointment, or subsequent designation to fill vacancies, constitute the Executive Committee created by the National Convention held at Chicago, on the 16th day of May, 1860, do hereby call upon all qualified voters who desire the unconditional maintenance of the Union, the supremacy of the Constitution, and the complete suppression of the existing rebellion, with the cause thereof, by vigorous war, and all apt and efficient means, to send delegates to a Convention to assemble at Baltimore, on Tuesday, the 7th day of June, 1864, at 12 o'clock noon, for the purpose of presenting candidates for the offices of President and Vice-President of the United States. Each State having a representation in Congress will be entitled to as many delegates as shall be equal to twice the number of electors to which such State is entitled in the Electoral College of the United States.[191]

---

191.   D.F. Murphy, *Proceedings of the National Union Convention Held in Baltimore, Md., June 7th and 8th, 1864* (New York: Baker & Godwin, 1864), 3.

Union National Convention
June 7, 1864

Blair attended the Baltimore convention in the Front Street theater as chairman of the Michigan delegation. It opened with remarks by the party chairman, governor Edwin D. Morgan of New York, who disclaimed intent to set an agenda for the assembly but hoped the convention "shall declare for such an amendment of the Constitution as will positively prohibit African slavery in the United States. (Prolonged applause, followed by three cheers.)"

Omar D. Conger, a member of the state military board with which Blair worked closely, represented the delegation in the committee on resolutions. He supported the committee report, which was reported thus:

Resolved, That as Slavery was the cause, and now constitutes the strength, of this Rebellion, and as it must be, always and everywhere, hostile to the principles of Republican Government, justice and the National safety demand its utter and complete extirpation from the soil of the Republic (applause):—and that, while we uphold and maintain the acts and proclamations by which the Government, in its own defence, has aimed a death-blow at this gigantic evil, we are in favor, furthermore, of such an amendment to the Constitution, to be made by the people in conformity with its provisions, as shall terminate and forever prohibit the existence of Slavery within the limits or the jurisdiction of the United States. (Tremendous applause, the delegates rising and waving their hats.)

A companion resolution addressed the discriminatory treatment given to black soldiers by the Confederacy:

Resolved, That the Government owes to all men employed in its armies, without regard to distinction of color, the full protection of the laws of war—(applause)—and that any violation of these laws, or of the usages of civilized nations in time of war, by the Rebels now in arms, should be made the subject of prompt and full redress. (Prolonged applause.)

The measures were approved by acclamation. When the roll was called for nomination of a candidate for president, Blair announced "Michigan gives sixteen votes for Abraham Lincoln." The incumbent received all but twenty-two votes, cast by Missouri for U.S. Grant, before the nomination was made unanimous. In response to the roll being called for the vice-presidential nomination, three names were presented: incumbent Hannibal Hamlin of Maine; Andrew Johnson of Tennessee; and Lovell H. Rousseau of Kentucky. Votes were cast for ten candidates. When called upon, Blair announced support of the incumbent abolitionist: "Michigan gives her sixteen votes for Hannibal Hamlin." *After word circulated that Lincoln favored Johnson, the delegations began to change their votes. Michigan was last to do so.*[192]

To manifest the national character of the proceedings, the term "'Republican' was not mentioned, nor was 'Republican Convention' referred to by any of the speakers."[193] In part, this approach occurred because on May 31, the "Radical Democracy Party" had met in Cleveland and nominated John C. Fremont for president and John Cochrane of New York as vice-president. Fremont withdrew his candidacy in September after the capture of Atlanta. Blair had not supported this splinter group, which "received little support from Michigan Republicans,"[194] and he never publicly denounced the Administration.

On September 2, Blair received a letter from New York publisher

---

192.   Id. 4, 24, 31, 57-58, 65-66, 72, 75.

193.   Joseph B. Oakleaf, *National Union Convention of 1864 and Why Lincoln was not Nominated by Acclamation* (Moline: n.p., 1924), 4. "Republican," in fact, was employed.

194.   Harris, *Public Life of Zachariah Chandler*, 89 n.23.

Horace Greeley questioning Republican prospects in the fall. Nine days later, the governor gave his thoughts:

Blair responded that Lincoln could be elected, that he could carry Michigan, and that it would be unwise to substitute at this time another candidate in place of Lincoln. He felt that a substitution would create a disaster and give the election to the Democrats.[195]

Only ten days prior, Lincoln wrote "it seems exceedingly probably [sic]" that he would not win a second term. He did, and he won Michigan. At Camp Blair in Jackson County at a "draft rendezvous," the soldiers' tally was: Lincoln, 141; McClellan, 81.[196]

---

195.   Harris, *Austin Blair*, 172, citing a letter in the Tilton Materials, New York Historical Society.
196.   *DFP*, Nov. 9, 1864, 1.

Proclamation on Conscription
July 21, 1864

On July 18, 1864, President Lincoln issued a call for 500,000 men pursuant to an act of Congress approved on the fourth of July. Quotas that were not filled would be completed by a draft to take place on September 5. Blair promptly responded by asking for "early and earnest efforts to meet the Presidential requisition." His proclamation laid out "in explicit terms the readiest and most feasible plans of doing so."[197]

The President of the United States, in pursuance of a law of Congress, has issued his call for five hundred thousand (500,000) volunteers for the military service, and has directed that immediately after the fifth day of September, 1864, a draft for troops, to serve for one year, shall be held in every town or sub-district, to fill the quota which shall be assigned to it, which shall remain unfilled on the said fifth day of September, 1864.

I believe this call to have been eminently proper and necessary for the public service, and being such, to demand the patriotic, earnest, and hearty response of the people. That it will be met in the same spirit that has put Michigan thus far largely in excess of all previous calls, there can be no doubt. The rebellion, as it approaches its final overthrow, grows steadily more desperate, wicked and hateful. Covered with the blood of patriots, cursed with the dying breath of starved prisoners, and abhorred by all good men for its barbarous butcheries of the unarmed who have ceased to fight, it must perish utterly. The people of this State, remembering their past sacrifices only as an additional motive to greater exertions in the future, will, I know,

197.   Robertson, 50.

enter upon this present duty with the activity and energy which does not admit of failure.

The quota assigned to the State is eighteen thousand two hundred and eighty-two, (18,282,) of which only a little over twelve thousand (12,000) remain to be recruited, or drafted if the recruiting fails. For the purpose of filling the quota, only two resources are available, viz: 1st. Recruiting in the States declared to be in rebellion, under the act of July 4th, except the States of Arkansas, Tennessee and Louisiana; and 2d. Recruiting among our own people. The first of these, I believe, will be found of no substantial value to us at present for obvious reasons. The points at which this recruiting is to be carried on are so remote that the period of fifty days will not be sufficient to enable agents to accomplish very much during that time, and they would meet the active competition of the older States, paying much larger bounties than our laws enable us to do. I shall not therefore appoint any such agents to be paid by the State, but will, under proper regulations, appoint such agents for the benefit of any counties, towns or sub-districts which may request it, paying the expenses of the agencies for themselves. They will, of course, also be entitled to the credits. This course is also justified by the fact that the State has no funds appropriated by law for this purpose.

Substantially, then, our only resource will be that which has always heretofore been found sufficient, the patriotism of our own people.

Recruits will be allowed to enlist for one, two, or three years, as they may prefer, and as far as practicable each recruit may select the regiment in which he will enlist. This will always be allowed in the regiments in the field, so long as such regiments are below the maximum number. As an inducement to enlist, the Government of the United States will pay a bounty of one hundred dollars to recruits enlisting for one year, two hundred dollars for those enlisting for two years, and three hundred for those enlisting for three years. Such local bounties will be paid as the people of the several towns, wards, and sub-districts may authorize in pursuance of law. No State bounty can be paid, for the reason that the appropriation made for that purpose is exhausted. For the purpose of aiding the recruiting service, and giving direction to the public efforts, six new regiments will be authorized, one of them being located in each Congressional District, and I will receive all the new companies that may be offered during the fifty days of recruiting. All the recruits offered for the new regiments and companies, however, must be enlisted for three years or during the war. Those who enlist for a shorter term than three years will go into the regiments now in the field.

I earnestly recommend to all those who enlist under this call, whether in the new organizations or the old ones, to do so for the war. This State has thus far raised no troops for a less term than three years. Both for the Government and the soldier, the longest term is the best. Let us continue to adhere to this policy, which has given us a most honorable position in the service, and the reputation of the Michigan soldiery, which is now unsurpassed, will continue to grow.

The work of filling up the quota of the State is for the people. The close of the war visibly approaches, and the sure triumph of the Union cause grows manifest.

Our troops are now led by tried and victorious Generals, leaving nothing to be desired in that direction. Conquering Union armies are in the very midst of the Confederacy, progressing steadily towards the final victory. Let the people of the country stand firmly by the lawful Government, and they can safely meet what is to come.

Given under my hand at the Capitol, in Lansing, the 21st day of July, eighteen hundred and sixty four.

Austin Blair.

James B. Porter

Secretary of State.[198]

Recruiting another 12,000 volunteers encouraged strictly limiting exemptions. Under date of August 2, 1864, Battle Creek members of the

---

198. *Annual Report of the Adjutant General of the State of Michigan, for the Year 1864* (Lansing: John A. Kerr & Co., 1865), 10-12.

pacifist "Seventh-day Adventists" leadership wrote Blair seeking his public endorsement that the denomination qualified for conscientious objector status. The letter presented the group's principles as "rigidly antislavery, loyal to the government, and in sympathy with it against the rebellion." Agreeing to the request would complicate achievement of the state's quota. Blair responded:

The Governor's Reply

I am satisfied that the foregoing statement of principles and practices of the Seventh-day Adventists is correct, and that they are entitled to all the immunities secured by law to those who are conscientiously opposed to bearing arms, or engaging in war.

Austin Blair,
Governor of Michigan
<u>Dated</u>, Aug. 3, 1864.

The state's representative at its military agency office in Washington "On E, near 7th Street North," wrote to the U.S. Army provost-general to confirm the governor's endorsement of conscientious objector status.[199]

199.   Francis McLellan Wilcox, *Seventh-Day Adventists in Time of War* (Washington: Review and Herald Pub. Assn., 1936), 58-59, 63. See Ahlstrom, 480-481.

Remarks at Michigan State Sanitary Fair
September 21, 1864

In September 1864, the Michigan state sanitary fair convened in Kalamazoo to provide support to the tens of thousands of soldiers at the front, both veteran and recently enrolled. It was "a great success," according to the Detroit Free Press, *which also reported on the remarks delivered in person by the governor to "an immense crowd."*

The address of Gov. Blair was quite brief, and confined to the objects and progress of the Sanitary Commission. On this subject he was quite eloquent, picturing the many blessings derived by the suffering soldiers from the sums donated by individuals, and raised by sanitary fairs, aid societies, &c. He remarked that England had its Florence Nightingale, other countries had their individual instances of devotion to the cause of humanity, but to the United States was reserved the picture of a nation whose women were all Nightingales who rose up in a body to the godlike work of relieving suffering. He eulogized the army, saying no country but our own could boast an army formed upon the same basis. Our gallant army had honored itself in all the battles it had participated in. He referred to South Mountain, Antietam, Gettysburg, Shiloh and Vicksburg. He spoke of the campaign in the Shenandoah Valley now almost triumphant, alluded to the late gallant Brewer, of the 7th Michigan Cavalry, in terms of deep feeling alluding to his fall in the recent battles in that locality. In conclusion, he remarked that, although in peace and quiet at home, we should remember the wants of those fighting for the preservation of these blessings; that it was a duty to do all that could be done; that money exhausted in this cause was not given away; that it would bring a blessing upon both giver and receiver.[200]

---

200. *DFP,* Sept. 24, 1864, 3. Lieutenant-colonel Melvin Brewer of Almont

Blair lauded the contributions to the cause by the female population of the Great Lakes state:

The ladies of Kalamazoo have inaugurated this Fair with great zeal for the one grand and noble purpose of alleviating the horrors of war … There is no other land which can say that the whole body of its women have risen up so gloriously as ours have done.[201]

was killed in action in the Battle of Winchester, Sept. 19, 1864. *Record of Service*, Vol. 37, 23.

201.   *Museography, the Official Magazine of the Kalamazoo Valley Museum*, Vol. 4, Issue 2, Winter/Spring 2005, 5.

Proclamation of Thanksgiving
November 16, 1864

Blair's fourth and final thanksgiving message followed by eight calendar days the national canvass that included election of the U.S. president. Lincoln defeated his Democrat opponent, George B. McClellan, with an Electoral College tally of 212-21. Just as he had promised to deliver the state for Lincoln in 1860, Blair was able to feel proud of the Michigan results: Lincoln/Johnson, 79,149 votes; Democratic ticket, 68,513. Blair was not a candidate for reelection but took satisfaction at the elevation of Henry H. Crapo over William M. Fenton. Republicans also took all six seats in the U.S. House of Representatives.

A long established custom, beautiful in itself, and sanctioned by the dictates of a pure religion, calls upon us to observe the Annual Thanksgiving Festival.

The year that is past has been filled with the bounties of Providence. The homes of the people have been the abodes of health and plenty, and though the nation has been engaged in war, no hostile forces have touched our border. The virtue, intelligence and courage of the people have been found a sufficient reliance in every emergency. Civil government has been maintained, and our rights and liberties protected.

The hosts of the rebellion have been beaten back by the victorious Union arms, and the smile of Heaven has rested upon the heroes who have carried our banners in battle.

I do therefore appoint Thursday, the 24th day of November instant, as a day of public thanksgiving and praise to Almighty God for his great mercies to us, both as individuals and as a nation, and I request the people of this State that, laying aside their usual employments, they will assemble in their places of public worship and around the family firesides, and keep this day with reverence and devout thankfulness, not forgetting the poor and wretched, but with kindly charity towards all, let us acknowledge our entire dependence upon the Giver of all Good, rendering willing praise to Him for all His mercies, and especially that He hath given victory to the nation, and well grounded hopes of freedom and peace to all.

In testimony whereof I have hereunto set my hand and caused to be affixed, the great seal of the State, this 16th day of November, A. D. 1864.

Austin Blair

By the Governor, James B. Porter, Secretary of State.[202]

---

202. *DFP*, Nov. 19, 1864, 1.

Retiring Governor's Message
January 4, 1865

Blair gave his last State of the State address as Crapo was sworn into office. The message was a triumphant valedictory: Union military affairs had reached the most positive point since the war began, and the end appeared in sight. The war-related portions are set out below.

Fellow-Citizens of the Senate and House of Representatives:

I appear before you to perform my last act as Chief Executive of the State. It is made my duty by the Constitution, at the close of my official term, to give to the Legislature "information by message of the condition of the State, and to recommend such measures to them as I shall deem expedient." In the performance of this duty, I shall be led, to some extent, over the history of the past four years—years full of great events, and destined to shape the course of our country through all times—years of bloody strife, of heroic endeavor, of sufferings courageously endured, and of triumphs nobly won. Upon the threshold of this work, I congratulate you upon the generally prosperous condition of the State. The people are in the enjoyment of health and plenty. Though in the midst of war, and subject to the trials and difficulties incident to that condition, public order has prevailed, and the rights and securities provided by the civil law have been maintained. Earnest patriotism and manly courage have a healthy growth, and a generous charity has given of our great abundance most liberally for the aid of the sick, the wounded and the needy. The State has increased in population and in wealth, in its educational facilities and in reputation, both at home and abroad. For all these blessings, let us give thanks to Almighty God, whose omnipotent hand hath led us safely through all perils.

When I came into office, in January, 1861, there had already begun to be heard the distant mutterings of that terrific storm that subsequently burst upon us in the attack upon Fort Sumter, and has raged with unabated fury during my entire term. The duties of the Executive office have in consequence been so greatly increased, as to seem to be almost entirely of a military character—and in giving the Legislature information of the condition of the State, I shall be necessarily occupied very much in that field, and upon those subjects which connect themselves more or less intimately with it. The whole energies of our people have been taxed to the uttermost in the constant effort to raise their quotas of the volunteer troops, to supply the necessary funds to pay bounties, and meet the other financial requirements of the crisis, while at the same time they had to bear the ordinary burdens of civil government. That we have been enabled to bear at all this immense increase of the public burdens, is a subject for congratulation, while the fact that the State has grown and prospered in spite of them, should excite the most intense satisfaction, not unmixed with wonder. It has been demonstrated beyond cavil, that freedom is the best basis of power.

Finances.

The first, and one of the most important duties of every government, is the care of its finances. If these fail, or get into disorder, all its operations must either cease entirely, or be carried forward in such an imperfect manner, as to realize but a share of the benefits which are the objects of its institution. Success in this field is success everywhere while to fail here is disastrous to the same extent. On coming into the administration four years ago, we found ourselves confronted at the outset with most serious difficulties. The treasury was empty, and the Treasurer himself a defaulter in a large sum, and absent from his post and from the State, having made no report, and not being likely to make any of value. The Auditor General told us that we were in debt largely to the counties, to the asylums, and other public institutions, and recommended a temporary loan of one hundred and fifty thousand dollars, to meet these present pressing claims. His warrants had been sold in the eastern money markets at a heavy discount to carry on the ordinary operations of government. This state of things was the plain result of the want of a proper financial policy for many previous years.

...

The following extracts from the report of the State Treasurer for the year ending Nov. 30th, 1864, show the present financial condition of the State:

The total receipts of the office, including last year's balance, are $2,444,242.25

The total payments for the same period is $2,004,194.98

Leaving a balance in the Treasury of 440,047.27

War Expenditures and Receipts.

The "War Fund" was overdrawn at the close of the last fiscal year, $120,387.04

The amount of expenditures for the current year, charged for to this fund is, 823,216.75

Making a total of $943,603.79

Under the provisions of act No. 109, approved March 14, 1863, I have sold War Loan Bonds to the amount of $571,000.00

On which I received for premium and accrued interest, 15,316.36

By the provisions of "an act authorizing a war bounty loan," approved Feb. 5, 1864, a loan of $500,000.00 was authorized for bounty purposes, the money arising from the loan to be credited to the war fund. Under the provisions of this act I have issued bonds to the amount of $230,000.00

All of which were taken up by this office for the sinking funds.

Of the amount levied for interest on the "War Loan," I have credited the war fund for the amount of interest actually paid, 54,019.00

Amount of State bounty refunded, 50.00

The war fund is now overdrawn,   73,218.43

$943,603.79

. . .

State Debt.

. . .

This exhibit is most satisfactory. The State has met all her obligations promptly, and will continue to do so, having now in the treasury a surplus of near $450,000. The Sinking Fund is rapidly absorbing the public debt, and but for the necessary increase from war loans, would soon make an end of it. We hope, of course, that this cause for increase will quickly pass away.

I have thus contrasted the present condition of the finances with that existing at the time of my coming into office, not for the mere purpose of comparison, but to emphasize the recommendation that the present policy should be continued without material change. It consists simply in paying off the public debt as rapidly as possible, by means of the Sinking Fund, and of creating no new obligations, either to the "trust funds" or otherwise, except in great emergencies; and uniformly laying taxes sufficient to meet appropriations. I have the satisfaction of adding, that the finances of the State have not suffered in any degree within the last four years from the frauds or peculations of public officers. The defaulting Treasurer was legally prosecuted, convicted and punished, and it is to be hoped that that wholesome example will be efficient to prevent the occurrence of like crimes hereafter.

. . .

Swamp Lands and Roads—The Military Roads.

. . .

By an Act of Congress, approved June 20, 1864, a large grant of lands was made to the State of Michigan for the construction of two wagon roads for military and postal purposes. One of them to run from Saginaw City, by the shortest and most feasible route, to the Straits of Mackinaw, and the other from Grand Rapids, through Newaygo, Traverse City and Little Traverse, to the same point. The grant is a liberal one, being of three sections to the mile, and should result in the construction of a good road. The act provides that the roads shall be located, surveyed, and constructed under the direction of such commissioners as the Governor may appoint, but has made no provision for the payment of the commissioners or their expenses. It seems to have been supposed that the State would be willing to do this. And the supposition was reasonable. Inasmuch as Congress has freely granted the land, it is not too much to ask of the State to pay the expenses of location and superintendence. I recommend that an appropriation of money be made for this purpose. It is reasonable to anticipate great benefits to the State to arise from the construction of these roads.

. . .

The Soldiers' Vote.

The "Act to enable the qualified electors of this State in the military service to vote at certain elections," approved February 5, 1864, requires some amendment. The authority to open polls at hospitals is not expressly given, as it should be, though I think it is, by fair inference. Some confusion has also occurred among the boards of canvassers of the several counties as to their duties in making returns to the Secretary of State, some supposing that no returns should be made until the final completion of their entire canvass. I recommend a careful revision of the law in these respects, and in any others in which the law may be found to lack in directness and clearness of language. In its main features the law has been found to operate admirably. The voting under it was done with as much order and propriety as at any of the polls in the State, and I hear of no complaint, from any quarter, of unfairness, or undue influence exercised over the soldiers. The voting was free, open, fair and intelligent, completely answering every objection to the policy of such a law. That volunteers in the military service shall vote in the field has become the settled policy of the whole country, and care should be taken to perfect our laws upon the subject.

National Cemetery at Gettysburg.

At the extra session in 1864, an Act was passed "to provide for the preparation of the Soldiers' National Cemetery at Gettysburg, in the State of Pennsylvania." For that object the sum of $3,500 of the war fund was appropriated, and a commissioner was authorized to be appointed to superintend the disbursement of the money. Such a commissioner has been appointed, and I have drawn from the appropriation the sum of twelve hundred and sixty-five dollars, which has been paid to the treasurer of the corporation created by the statute of Pennsylvania for the preparation of the Cemetery. The money will be called for from time to time as the work progresses. My vouchers for the payment of this money I have filed in the office of the Auditor General, though the Act did not prescribe any place for such filing.

The Cemetery is in rapid progress towards completion, upon such plans as could be produced by the best artistic skill of the country. I am satisfied that when finished it will be worthy of the great event it is intended to commemorate, and a fitting tribute to the gallant men who offered up their lives there for the salvation of their country. The column of victory will tower there through the ages, over the resting place of the heroes who fell in its grandest hour. The report of Hon. T.W. Ferry, Commissioner, is herewith submitted, containing a recommendation of an additional appropriation of twenty-five hundred dollars, which I think should be made. It has been rendered necessary by the immense increase in the price of labor and all the articles used in the construction of the work. For a more full statement of the condition and progress of the work, I refer you to the report itself and accompanying documents.

Military.

Since my last biennial message, great activity has prevailed in all military operations. Very large calls have necessarily been made upon the State for volunteers, all of which have been filled with great promptness but at very heavy expense; and still this work is by no means finished. A call is now impending, under which the quota of the State has lately been assigned, and does not vary much from six thousand men. The whole number raised and organized in the State since the beginning of the war, is now a little in excess of eighty thousand, (80,000). Of these, thirty-five thousand have been raised since January, 1863, though there have been added to the permanent organizations of the State only four new regiments of Infantry, five of Cavalry, and six batteries of Light Artillery. The State has now organized and in service thirty regiments of Infantry, eleven regiments of Cavalry, one regiment of Light Artillery, and one regiment of Mechanics and Engineers, besides two independent batteries of Light Artillery, and fifteen companies for various arms of service. It is not probable, and certainly it is not desirable, that any more new regiments will be formed. Many of the veteran regiments are much reduced in numbers and sound policy requires that their ranks should be speedily filled. It has been my steady effort since the war begun to fill up old regiments rather than to form new ones. The advantages of this course are obvious, even to those who are unacquainted with military affairs, and they apply with double force where the men are enlisted for short terms. The new recruit very quickly learns his duty if placed in an organization among veterans; but put a thousand of them together, under officers like themselves, and the case is different as possible. The policy of the Government of the United States has also been adapted to the strengthening of the old organizations, and as there are now in the field regiments more than enough to contain all the quotas called from the State, I think we may regard it as settled that few, if any, new ones will hereafter be formed.

The question most important for the Legislature now to settle, is the mode hereafter to be pursued in filling the quotas of volunteers for the State. Thus far, no very fixed and steady method has been pursued. Our action has been spasmodic. Sometimes we had paid a State bounty, and sometimes not. Some localities have paid a local bounty, and some none at all, and this has been in some towns very unreasonably large in amount, and in others quite small; and sometimes it has been raised in accordance with the laws, but quite as often without much reference to the law, and the Legislature has been appealed to for the purpose of legalization. In my message to the extra session of 1864, my views are fully stated upon this question of bounties, and they are still in the main unchanged. The Legislature did not then altogether agree with me, but in opposition to my recommendation, authorized a State bounty to be paid to all volunteers alike, of one hundred dollars, and at the same time authorized the towns to raise a like amount. A half million was appropriated to pay this State bounty, but we had only begun to raise our quotas when the appropriation was exhausted. I believe that so far as getting an additional volunteer is concerned, it is very questionable whether this expenditure has accomplished anything; and now this Legislature will find that all the men who have volunteered since the State bounty ceased to be paid for want of money, will request that an appropriation be made sufficient to pay them the same amount that the others have received, and for that purpose alone not less than seven hundred thousand dollars would be required. I shall not recommend it, though it will be very difficult for you to give a satisfactory reason for a refusal, which would not be equally a reason for rejecting the law itself.

[¶] In my judgment, this whole business of bounties has been carried to a great excess, resulting in excessive taxes, with great demoralization of the people, and with no corresponding benefit to the government or to the soldier himself. Reasonable bounties, enabling the soldier to place his affairs in a thrifty condition, with proper provisions for the care and support of his family while absent, are wise and well-timed, but they should never reach the point where the service of the country becomes a matter of merchandise. The citizen owes service to his country as a patriotic duty, and his true reward consists in the laurels which adorn the hero's brow. These cannot be bought with money, nor will any soldier ever wear them worthily who enters the service merely for a bounty. My own judgment has been that a moderate local bounty, added to that paid by the United States, is all sufficient; but if any State bounty was paid at all, it should be only to those old soldiers who will reenlist, after previous term has expired. It is a great object to retain these veterans in the service. It is not too much to say that one of them is worth three new recruits. The local districts will not usually make any distinction, because they are intent only on the filling of quotas. Such a State bounty might possibly do good. The system of bounties, as practiced in the country generally, has filled it with a set of desperate villains, who, as substitute brokers or middle men, rob and plunder the soldiers and the people alike. I do not know as it is possible to be rid of them, but they are a set hard to bear with. I must leave this whole subject to the careful consideration and matured judgment of the Legislature, satisfied that the true interests of the soldiers and the people will be safe in their hands.

Certainly, I shall be the last man in the State to find fault with any sacrifice, however great, that may be thought necessary for the welfare of the Michigan soldier in the field. The true soldier, who, with earnest devotion to his country, has taken up arms in her defence, and enduring all hardships, has periled everything for the service, not regarding his own life, deserves much more than we are able to pay. His service is of that priceless sort which cannot be measured with money.

By an act of Congress, approved July 4, 1864, "further to regulate and provide for enrolling and calling out the national forces," it is enacted: "That it shall be lawful for the Executive of any of the States to send recruiting agents into any of the States declared to be in rebellion, except the States of Arkansas, Tennessee and Louisiana, to recruit volunteers under any call under the provisions of this act, who shall be credited to the respective sub-divisions thereof which may procure the enlistment."

Under the provisions of this law, and the orders of the War Department issued in accordance with it, I have issued letters of appointment to a considerable number of recruiting agents, requested by various sub-districts, for the purpose of filling their quotas under the call of the President previous to the one issued recently. As a general rule, these agents were unsuccessful. They went out, of course, entirely at the expense of the localities procuring their appointment, as I had no fund that could be used for that purpose. I have not much confidence in the beneficial results to be derived from the operations of this law, and, therefore, shall make no recommendation in regard to it.

But it is obvious that if the State wishes to take advantage of its provisions, it will be necessary to provide by law for the appointment of a number of permanent agencies in the rebel States, with ample means to compete with other States which will meet them with like agencies at every point. Whether this course is advisable, your honorable bodies must decide.

[¶] By the Act approved Feb. 18, 1863, "for the relief of sick, disabled and needy soldiers," there was appropriated the sum of twenty thousand dollars from the war loan fund, and it was set apart as the soldiers' relief fund. This fund the Governor was authorized to use in his discretion for the class of persons mentioned in the title of the Act, and for the purpose to appoint one or more agents. In carrying into effect the wise and benevolent intention of this law, five permanent agencies have been established, employing six agents, as follows: One in the city of Washington, employing two agents, and one each in the cities of Nashville, St. Louis, Louisville, and Detroit, employing each one agent. In addition to these, some special agents and many volunteer surgeons have been employed, being paid expenses only. I have drawn from the Treasury, out of the fund, the sum of eighteen thousand dollars and probably the remainder will be required to pay outstanding liabilities. My statement of the expenditures, and vouchers for the same, are on file in the Auditor General's office. I am satisfied that in no other way could the soldiers have been benefitted to an equal degree by this amount of money. The number relieved has been very great, and in most instances at a small expense. The agencies have become homes for the soldiers, when separated from their commands, and they resort to them for information and assistance in every emergency—to break them up would occasion deep regret among all our troops. I earnestly recommend that a like appropriation be made for the next two years.

Gentlemen—Again and for the last time I commend the Michigan troops to your continued care and support. They have never failed in their duty to the country or to the State. Upon every battle-field of the war their shouts have been heard and their sturdy blows have been delivered for the Union and victory. Their hard-earned fame is the treasure of every household in the State, and the red blood of their veins has been poured out in large measure to redeem the rebellious South from its great sin and curse. At this hour they stand under the flag of their country, far away from home, in every quarter where the enemy is to be met—along the banks of the father of waters—in the great city at his mouths—on the Arkansas—in the captured forts of the Gulf—by the waters of the Cumberland, the Tennessee, and of the Savannah—in the chief city of the Empire State of the South— among the conquering columns in the Valley of the Shenandoah, and in the trenches under the eye of the Lieut. General in the great league of Petersburg and Richmond. Alas, that they are also perishing of cold and hunger, and disease, in the filthy rebel prisons and pestilential camps of the South. In every situation their bravery has won the approval of their commanders, and their heroic endurance of hardships has added lustre to their name. It is my sole regret at quitting office that I part with them. My earnest efforts for their good shall follow them while I live, and now from this place I bid them hail, and farewell!

The Union and Liberty.

The great conflict has had its useful lessons. Under the hard experiences of the past four years, the relations sustained by the State and National governments towards each other have come to be more clearly understood and more accurately defined. We understand now the full meaning of that pernicious phrase "sovereign States," which had stealthily crept its way into so many public documents, political speeches and platforms, and finally into the common language of the people, until it came to teach and be understood to mean that there was no other sovereign in this country but the States, and that whatever they decided to do, it was lawful to perform. Under this teaching, the foundations of loyalty and fidelity to the National Government were sapped, and insensibly the false theory grew and extended itself, until, under the shadow of that upas tree,[203] the whole body of the rebellion found shelter and protection. It had in it just enough of truth to conceal its fundamental errors. When applied simply to the authority of the States over their own domestic affairs, there is no objection to it, though even then the word sovereign is not very correctly applied. A sovereign, without authority to make war or conclude peace, to make treaties or contract alliances, or even to coin money or levy duties and imposts, is certainly not a very dignified one, nor is he likely to have the nations much in awe.

There is and can be, under the Constitution of the United States, only one paramount sovereign authority, and to that every other is subordinate. Nor does this theory in the least interfere with the proper and harmonious working of our system. On the contrary, it is essential to it. The rights reserved to the States are not in any respect interferred [sic] with, though some of the claims which have been set up for them may be. It is not surprising that some of the powers assumed at this time by the National Government should startle the unreflecting by their apparent departure from former precedents. The fact that the exigencies of the country have not previously called for their exercise, does not, however, prove that they do not exist. A state of war necessarily calls for the exercise of the utmost powers of sovereignty, which are wholly disused in time of peace. More especially is this true of a domestic war like the present. The whole war power is conferred by the Constitution upon the National Government, and the propriety of its exercise at such a time as this will hardly be questioned. In fact the imperative necessity for its exercise is one of the propositions made too clear for argument by the condition of the country. The people of the Loyal States have acquiesced in it with great unanimity. They have disregarded the unreasonable and factious complaint that the liberties of the country were endangered by the encroachments of

---

203. The "upas" tree (*Antiaris toxicaria*), reputed to be productive of a poisonous substance.

the general Government, and have most emphatically sustained the Administration.

They know that the liberties and existence of the country are threatened together by the rebellion, and that they can only look for union and peace through the total destruction of that rebellion. For this purpose they have rallied around and upheld the government of the United States, and they will continue to uphold it. The march of events has made many things clear which have been considered doubtful. Four years ago, when we assembled here, the discussion turned upon the repeal of the personal liberty laws, and the propriety of sending commissioners to meet John Tyler and his Virginia traitors to endeavor to effect another compromise. Michigan spurned both, to the great grief of timid conservatives, and declared that she demanded her rights under the Constitution, and intended to accept nothing less; that she would abide by the law, but the day of compromises was over; she would not meet Virginia to consider whether by further abasement we could win her to remain in the Union; the Union was a fixed and eternal fact, and if any should attempt to destroy it, and our birthright in it, then she offered the national government her entire military and monetary power to maintain it by force of arms. And she has kept her pledge. Who now would have had it otherwise? Many a brave hero has bit the dust maintaining that pledge; many a household has been draped with mourning, and many a heart has broken. But who would take it back? That is priceless which is bought with blood.

Thus has our national Union been made sacred, and its emblems endeared in the hearts of the people. Thus we restore national sentiments, national honor and national faith. Have we paid too high a price for it? We do more; instead of casting down any of the safeguards of liberty we rebuild the ancient landmarks of freedom and destroy forever the bulwarks of slavery. Prejudices made venerable by age, which nothing else could have made respectable; time-honored stupidity, once called statesmanship, and even the religion of mammon, are being swept away in the earnestness of the conflict, which every one now knows to be irrepressible. Men drive at once at the root of the matter, and having found the infamous author of all our troubles, they recognize our old acquaintance, "the peculiar institution," and prepare a fitting end for him. As he has lived and increased in power and become bloated with pride, through hypocritical pretence of reverence for the Constitution and impudent demands for its protection, so let him perish by the Constitution which he has insulted and defied. By the glorious amendment of universal freedom, we are about to break every yoke, wipe away the last spot from the national banner, and stand forth a nation of freemen indeed. And the people cry amen and amen! Who now would have this otherwise?

The close of the great drama approaches. The skies of the Southern horizon are lighted up with the glow of Union victories. The proud and boastful chivalry fly before despised mudsills, "the greasy mechanics and small fisted farmers" of the North—nay, before the dark-skinned bondmen of their own household. No part of their territory is longer safe from invasion. The army that started to avenge the fall of Atlanta by planting its victorious banners upon the banks of the Ohio, routed and broken, is fleeing to hide itself south of the Tennessee. Deprived, to a great extent, of its transportation, its arms and munitions, it is not likely that it will ever be really formidable again. At the call of their Commander-in-Chief they have "pressed the soil of Tennessee," but all in vain. Tennessee has thrust them forth from her loyal bosom in the smoke and flame of battle, and henceforth she is free. The Empire State of the South has been traversed by a Union army from border to border, from mountains to the sea. The shell of the rebel power is broken, and its hollowness laid bare. The fairest fields of their sunny South are laid waste, and there are none to defend them. Cotton is no longer King, but a fallen captive. The army that was to recapture the valley of the Shenandoah and carry the war across the Potomac upon Northern ground, thrice beaten, has consulted its safety by giving up its work and seeking safer and more quiet camping ground. Only a single army remains to the Confederacy and that under its boasted "invincible Chief," has fled to its intrenchments around the besieged capital. How long can it stand?

Only until the Union armies, flushed with victory, and strengthened by reinforcements, at the command of the Lieut. General, from every point of the compass, commence their triumphal march upon the doomed place. It will fall, and in its fall the Confederacy, black with treason, stained with blood, and abhorred by all good men throughout the world, will perish miserably. Upon the blackened spot where it fell will rise in resplendent beauty the re-established Union, purified in the heated furnace of its fierce trial; consolidated in unity and affection by common sufferings and dangers; adorned with the garlands of victory and peace, it will start upon its new career. It is the career of liberty to all men. This is proclaimed to whom it may concern. In fancy we might seek to penetrate the future, and proclaim the triumphant progress of our country in its new path. But not now. It is enough that it is clear and bright. Peace approaches, following victory. Its dawning is already visible, and its full blaze will fulfill our utmost desire.

Austin Blair.

Jan. 4, 1865.[204]

Perhaps the best measure of the governor's success in contributing Michigan's troops on behalf of the Union came in the year-end report of the adjutant-general that concluded Blair's term of office. It summarized the work during 1864:

The striking fact is exhibited by these figures that during ten months only of the present year, the State of Michigan has furnished more than half as many men for the service as were sent from the State during the whole of the first three years of the war; and of this large number of men actually furnished, only 1,600 were drafted.

---

204. *Messages*, 495-512.

The grand total as of the end of 1864 amounted to 83,347 soldiers.[205]

Blair retired from the Governor's position with hope that he would be chosen by the legislature to serve in the U.S. Senate. Instead, incumbent Jacob M. Howard was reelected. Blair went home to Jackson to earn a living through his law practice: he was "impoverished and worn out."[206] Just before the war, the Blairs' portfolio included $16,000 of real and $3,000 of personal property.[207] Having willingly made sacrifices in their public service, putting their finances on hold, the Blairs might anticipate better days ahead. Indeed, on April 9, the main Confederate army under Lee surrendered to Grant at Appomattox Court House, Virginia, prompting joyful celebrations throughout the Union.

One more heartbreaking chapter of the war remained.

205.   *Annual Report of the Adjutant General*, 1864, 17. Over 90,000 Michiganders served. *Documents Relating to the Erection of the New Capitol of Michigan. 1871 to 1879* (Lansing: W.S. George & Co., 1879), 71.

206.   Bingham, 106.

207.   Census of 1860, Jackson County, June 7, page 22.

Remarks on the Assassination
April 1865

Abraham Lincoln was murdered and died on the 15th of April. Whether the just-retired governor publicly delivered the following remarks has not been ascertained. Internal evidence suggests he wrote before assassin John Wilkes Booth was apprehended and shot to death on April 26th. Perhaps he wrote before the details of Lincoln's funeral train procession were published in Michigan on April 18th, along with news about the recovering condition of Secretary Seward, also an assassination target.

The words have an immediacy and passion that characterizes a writing made very soon after news arrived of the president's death. It is consistent with the judgment that "Lincoln had no supporter more loyal than Austin Blair."[208] It appears that the surrender of the second most important Confederate army, in North Carolina on April 18, finalized on April 17, had not yet occurred. The pages are numbered 2 through 4 and begin with four crossed out lines forming a single sentence; a few other words were also revised by their scribe.

Pausing in the midst of weightiest affairs the American people have been suddenly, startlingly summoned to attend the funeral of the President of their Choice and to consider what is fitting to be done upon such a mournful occasion. [crossing out ends here]

On the 14th day of April, a day memorable in our annals hereafter forever more, the day on which there had been again uplifted upon[209] Sumter the very same flag of the Union which just four years before had been pulled down in disgrace by traitors in armed rebellion, and while that flag was being saluted by salvos of artillery from the very

---

208.   George I. Reed ed., *Bench and Bar of Michigan: A Volume of History and Biography* (Chicago: The Century Publishing and Engraving Co., 1897), 136.
209.   The original "unfurled over" is crossed out.

guns which had previously compelled its surrender, while the whole land was aglow with bonfires & illuminations in honor of the complete triumph of the arms of the Republic over the rebellion and the surrender of its principal army with its most trusted leader and the air was rent with the acclimations of the people at these wonderful events and the near approach of peace and while the doomed President was meditating the great & magnanimous amnesty by which he fondly hoped to illustrate the dignity & God like charity of a great forgiving Christian people, being oblivious of all past treasons with grateful long sought peace to all our war worn land, he was struck dead by the bullet of an assassin, a mean cowardly wretch who shall be nameless here, and I trust elsewhere while time lasts. To our great national jubilee there came mourning and sadness. Into to [sic] our joyous song of victory entered the toll of the funeral bell and the muffled drum. The salute was exchanged for the minute gun, and the nation bowed its head and wept, as only they weep who sorrow for the good & great.

Death by assassination is always appalling. In this instance it was doubly so, both from the illustrious character and position of the victim and the boldness and audacity of the act, having been performed in the very faces of hundreds of people in the full glare of the gas lights of a theater accompanied by the most insulting bravado of the criminal. The plan had been carefully arranged by more cunning brains and a fit instrument was chosen for its execution. Probably[210] we are to regard it as the beginning of that system of organized murder called guerilla warfare with which we have all along been threatened in case the rebel armies were beaten. I am not alarmed by it. It was only the sense of perfect security which rejected all precaution that made it successful in this instance. The Nation has been roused by it as the ocean wave is lashed by a tempest. The feeling of brotherhood which was rapidly gaining ground has been swept away and the true nature of this rebellion is better understood in the light of this bloody & inhuman act than ever before since its commencement. It will now

---

210. The original "No doubt" is crossed out.

be dealt with as it only can be dealt with successfully. Rejecting with inhuman hate & bloody revenge every approach towards a speedy & peacefully termination of the contest, they who continue to wage it must be treated as the devouring wild beast of the forest is treated, hunted down & killed. Do you say this is inhuman? then look on the gory head of Lincoln and tell us what milder measures you propose. It was not the vulgar tool who slew him that was the party really guilty of his murder. It was the spirit of the rebellion which found a true interpreter in his act.

And the beloved President was no more murdered than has been every soldier of the Republic slain by rebel bullets or starved and frozen to death in a rebel prison since this monstrous work of Carnage began. For the first time in our history the bullet[211] of the assassin has been thrown into the political scale. We seem suddenly transported backward to the times of Henry the 4th & William the Silent. The country is not only overwhelmed by the sudden Cruel death of its Chief Magistrate but men are appalled at the shadow cast upon the future by the bloody and infamous precedent. Will it have imitators? and must we hereafter count assassination as one of the political institutions of the country? If we are not to do so it will be only because the malevolent & baleful system which has given us this example is perishing from the Country forever. Let it perish and with its fetters and its weapons of cruelty and murder and all its paraphernalia of oppression & crime be buried close by the place where the smoke of the pit which is bottomless ascendeth up forever and ever. And all the people shall cry Amen! and Amen! Crimes of this character come of bloody instructions. The education of the school of the dagger and the pistol are essential to them. It is the code of the duello and the license for slaughter in single Combat for fancied affronts which teach the turbulent and unprincipled that they are allowable. In a community ruled by law, they are well nigh impossible—but where violence is the

---

211. The original "dagger" is crossed out.

rule without restraint over the servile class it shortly overrules the law in regard to all and legal restraints are regarded as tyranny—[212]

The 900-word document ends here, and "it" and "restraints" are each dotted with an atypical vertical downstroke mark.

In mourning, Blair now "faded into private life and worked to recover the financial losses he had endured as governor." He had been "The Soldier's Friend," but that legacy did not earn an income.[213] The forthcoming supplemental volume in this series will recount Blair's postwar years.

---

212. Blair Collection, Bentley.
213. Engle, *Gathering*, 440; Patton, 13.

I commend the Michigan troops to your continued care and support.
They have never failed in their duty to the country or to the State.
Upon every battle-field of the war their shouts have been heard
and their sturdy blows have been delivered for the Union and victory.
Their hard-earned fame is the treasure of every household in the State

Appendix

Italicized sentences below represent editorial commentary; non-italicized text is original to the author/speaker.

I. The Amazing Mrs. Blair

Sarah Louisa Horton (1824–1897) was the third (and final) wife of Austin Blair. They married in 1849 in Jackson, and together they built there a twenty-four room house within a few years of their wedding. After a dozen years of marriage, she was called upon to do more than had been expected of the spouses of previous governors. When the Civil War commenced, she "devoted much of her time to helping young soldiers camped in Jackson as well as throughout the state." *On at least one occasion (May 1863) she accompanied the governor for visits to the front. She worked in relief efforts for those in prisons and hospitals, endearing herself* "to the soldiers by her kind deeds." *When the Jackson Ladies Soldiers and Sailors Monument Association formed in 1867, Sarah Blair continued her service to Michigan by becoming its first president. She raised money, assisted in soldiers' relief work, and—most poignant of all—engaged personally with soldier volunteers. Vignettes give a hint of her efforts:* "When the Ninth Michigan deployed from Jackson, with no fanfare, she walked through the crowd ('quiet and unobtrusive') to distribute food to the soldiers." *She was* "credited with ably assisting her husband" *in his war work.*[214]

The 26th Michigan Infantry was largely raised and mustered in Jackson, and a special bond developed with the Governor's spouse. One soldier recorded details: "Their house was between our camp and the city, and we were all welcome there at any time. Mrs[.] Blair was

---

214. Willah Weddon, *First Ladies of Michigan* (Lansing: NOG Press, 1994), 40-43.

intensely patriotic, and any thing she could do for us was cheerfully done. When we left the state the officers of the Regiment presented them with a Beautiful span of Black horses and an elegant carriage." *The purchase included a "silver-plated harness, side-saddle and blanket" in recognition of her care for the ill. Upon return from service, the men presented her with regimental colors, a gesture that expressed their affection more than words.*[215]

Several years later, the veterans wrote Mrs. Blair to request a return of the flag for their annual reunion:

As we now have a permanent organization and meet regularly every year the members thought it would add greatly to the interest of these re-unions if they had the flag in their possession, that it would remind them as they looked upon it, of the dangers thro' which they had passed, of the Battles where they had followed it, and that as they meet year after year, they could show it to their children, and teach them the principles it represented and embodyed and thus they would have ever before them an incentive to holier Patriotism, and they thought, perhaps, for such a purpose you would be willing to return it to them.

The mails soon brought a handwritten reply:

Dear Sir:

Mrs[.] Blair has received your letter of the 4th inst on the subject of the Flag, presented to the 26th Infty by the Ladies of Jackson, and desires me to acknowledge the receipt of it for her, and to assure you that she will, with great pleasure, accede promptly to the wish of the surviving members of the Regt to have the flag again in their possession. Our recollections of the 26th are of the most pleasant kind, and we rejoice in every opportunity to show our sense of their gallantry in the most trying exigencies of our great struggle. The flag you carried so honorably thro' so many battles shows the rough usage of actual war. It is torn and rent in almost every part, but you will recognize it

---

215.   Richard F. Miller, *States at War: A Reference Guide for Michigan in the Civil War* (Ann Arbor: University of Michigan Press, 2020), 10-11.

as the same you carried through bloody sacrifices to beneficent victory. It will be sent by express to your address immediately, and may the brave men who fought under it live long to enjoy the ripe fruits of their victory.

Your obt servant—

Austin Blair—

When the regiment held its annual reunion in 1881 in Howell, the assembly enjoyed the reading aloud of Governor Blair's letter, which "was received with cheers." Then the Corresponding Secretary read another that had accompanied the banner upon its return:

Dear old tattered and war-worn flag, good-bye. The brave boys who followed where you led, "on to victory or death," and who would have died to save you from dishonor, have recalled you, and into better hands, or a more loyal or patriotic organization I <u>could</u> not deliver you.

The flag-staff stands alone with barely enough of the blue and gold to cover it. Like its brave supporters, its fragments are scattered on the hard fought battle-fields from Bull Run to the bloody battle of the Wilderness.

As you stand in their midst yearly, you will refresh their memories with the faces of the comrades who went out from Camp Blair, and whose last salute in front of the old brown house on the hill, as you passed the last time for the front, still rings mournfully in my ear.

Boys, for the sake of those who did not return, cast your eyes up to the scarcely discernible figures 26 and remember the <u>widows</u> and <u>orphans</u>, and be assured you will ever hold a warm place in the heart of you[r] war mother.

Mrs. Austin Blair.

The veterans cheered her letter. Not long before her death in 1897, when Mrs. Blair was enfeebled by a stroke and the same veterans held a reunion in Jackson, they did not forget their "war mother":

After the banquet was over—50 of us marched up to the Governors Home to pay our respects to Mrs Blair. We formed in line in the front Yard, and Saluted her as she came to the door. Major Church explained that we had learned with deep sorrow of her serious illness and wished (?) and had called to express our sympathy in her affliction and that we had not better disturb her by coming into the House, but she would not have it so—we must come in, and she insisted on being introduced to all and actually <u>kissed</u> every one of the <u>Fifty</u>, telling us what great honor we had conferred on her and the State by upholding the integrity of the Union. She would be glad to have us write her at any time. Some time after I wrote her about my being wounded and my experiences in Andersonville, Ga, She sent me a letter and a Beautiful Portrait of Gen Grant on Ivory.—She was loved by all the Soldier Boys of the State. I am glad to pay this feeble tribute to her Memory.[216]

According to one historian, "hundreds of letters in the Blair correspondence" were directed to the subject of Mrs. Blair's solicitude toward soldier interests, and "she received hundreds of letters of gratitude for her services."[217]

II. Joint Resolution respecting Slavery in the Territories of the United States (1855)

On January 26, 1855, the legislature took a stand against the expansion of involuntary servitude into U.S. territories. The text of the measure, a succinct statement of grievances, is set out below. Both "Blair and Hussey were instrumental in the passage" of the document.[218]

[No. 6.]

---

216.   *DFP*, Nov. 11, 1881, 4; *Memoirs of Newton Thorne Kirk*, Michigan State University Archives and Historical Collections, Collection C-28, Folder 1, Ch. Two, 6-11 (research, transcription by K.K. Chartkoff).

217.   Harris, *Austin Blair*, 161-162.

218.   *Acts of the Legislature of the State of Michigan, Passed at the Regular Session of 1855, with an Appendix* (Lansing: Geo. W. Peck, 1855), 483-485; Fennimore II, 153.

JOINT RESOLUTION respecting Slavery in the Territories of the United States.

Whereas, Slavery is regarded by the people of this State as a great moral, social and political evil, at war with the principles of the Declaration of Independence, and the great object contemplated by our fore-fathers in establishing the constitution of the United States; an impediment to the prosperity of our common country, and an element of domestic weakness and discord; and

Whereas, The people of Michigan owe it to the early and prudent exercise of the power of Congress over the Territories of the United States, in applying the anti-slavery restriction contained in the ordinance of 1787, that she is not now a slaveholding State; and

Whereas, The people have heretofore, through their Legislature, repeatedly and earnestly remonstrated against the further extension of slavery in the National Territories; and

Whereas, Our present Senators, and two of our Representatives in Congress, did, at the session thereof now last past, vote for the repeal of the Missouri Compromise, so called, and for the passage of an act organizing the Territories of Kansas and Nebraska, thereby permitting slavery to be introduced into a region equal in extent to the thirteen original States, from which territory, by the solemn legislative compact of 1820, it was forever excluded; and

Whereas, Such repeal has been effected without petition, without discussion by the people, and in defiance of the well known wishes and opinions of a large majority of the people of this State and of the United States; and

Whereas, The violation by Congress of the compact of 1820, has released the people of this State from all obligation to respect Congressional compromises for the extension or perpetuation of slavery; therefore

Resolved by the Senate and House of Representatives of the State of Michigan, That we hold the said repeal and the permission granted by said Territorial act, to introduce slavery into said Territories, to be a violation of a mutual covenant between the free States and the slave-holding States of the Union, justified by no necessity, present or prospective, injurious to the rights of the former, tending to interrupt the internal harmony of the country, and to frustrate the well known purpose of the framers of the constitution, who by gradual legislation designed ultimately to put an end to slavery.

Resolved, That we are opposed to the further extension of slavery, or the recognition or permission thereof in any territory now owned or which may hereafter be acquired by the United States.

Resolved, That we hold it to be within the constitutional power of Congress to abolish slavery and the slave trade in all the Territories of the United States, including the District of Columbia, and that it is their duty, in view of the great and permanent interests of the nation, to pass laws for its immediate suppression and extinction in all such Territories and in said District.

Resolved, That our Senators in Congress be and they are hereby instructed, and our Representatives requested, to vote for and use their best exertions to procure the passage of an act of Congress that shall prohibit the introduction or existence of slavery in any of the Territories of the United States, and especially in Kansas and Nebraska, and to introduce, without delay, a bill for this latter purpose.

Resolved, That the act of Congress of 1850, known as the Fugitive Slave Law, was, in the opinion of the people of this State, an unnecessary measure; that it contains provisions of doubtful constitutionality; that the mode of proceeding under it is harsh, unjust, and repugnant to the moral sense of the people of the free States, cruel and despotic towards the person claimed as a fugitive, and that we are in favor of its immediate repeal; therefore,

Resolved, That our Senators in Congress be and they are hereby instructed, and our Representatives requested, to use their best exertions to procure the immediate repeal of the act of 1850, known as the Fugitive Slave Law.

Resolved, That the Governor be requested to forward copies of the foregoing preamble and resolutions to our Senators and Representatives in Congress.

Approved January 26, 1855.

III. Testimonial in 1858

Apparently, one of the editors of the Lansing State Republican *had his first encounter with Blair at the state Republican convention in the summer of 1858. Soon thereafter appeared this article.*

AUSTIN BLAIR—Among the pleasant incidents of the late State Convention was meeting this eminent speaker and true man, who is so soon we trust, to be transferred to the halls of Congress in accordance with the general expectation of the last two years.

True to his convictions of principle and duty, faithful to the extreme of scrupulousness towards his friends, untiring in his labors in the great cause of freedom, freely and frequently sacrificing all personal considerations for the general good, Mr. Blair has called around him a body of devoted personal friends such as it is rarely the fortune of man to possess. These men remember his faithful devotion to the Republican cause; they recall with emotion his thrilling eloquence and his self-forgetting and successful labors on the stump, and they rally around him at this time as a man under whose banner they feel certain of being able to march to victory in the Congressional District so closely contested two years ago. That they are right in this conviction, no one can for a moment reasonably doubt.[219]

IV. Stature in 1859

Blair's position within the Michigan Republican party just before the 1860 gubernatorial and presidential elections is revealed by this statement:

Michigan has a right to feel proud of her distinguished Republican citizens—her Howards, her Blair, her Walbridge, and many others whom she might have called to this distinguished post of trust and honor ....

The "post" was U.S. Senator, and the person called was Kinsley S. Bingham, eleventh governor of Michigan from 1855-1859, who would

---

219. *LSR*, Sept. 7, 1858, 2.

replace Senator Charles E. Stuart. Others cited: Jacob M. Howard and William Alanson Howard; and David S. Walbridge of Kalamazoo. W.A. Howard was serving his second term in the U.S. House of Representatives and was future party chairman. Walbridge had served in the Michigan House and Senate before becoming chairman "under the oaks." He thereafter served two terms in the U.S. House of Representatives. When Lincoln paid his only personal visit to Michigan in 1856, wife Eliza Walbridge served as his hostess. He recalled the event four years later in a letter to Zachariah Chandler: "I very well remember the jovial elderly lady, and wife of an M.C. with whom we took tea, calling you "Zach Chandler."[220]

V. Blair, Willcox, Richardson, and Williams (1861)

Despite a lack of experience in assessing military leadership, the governor quickly chose three men who went on to fashion records that arguably were unsurpassed by any other three from any other jurisdiction. He did so, in part, by seeking advice, a trait exhibiting good leadership qualities. As part of forming the second infantry regiment, Blair sought the counsel of the colonel chosen to lead the 1st Michigan Infantry. The dialogue went something like this:

Austin Blair: "The Pontiac people think he is crazy. Do you know the man?

Orlando Willcox: "Not personally, but I know something of him as a West Point graduate. He has seen service in Mexico."

Blair: "Well, he is modest anyway. He says he had resigned a captaincy in the regular army and thinks he might fill the office of major in the volunteers. Will you please see him?"

Willcox arranged a meeting and found that Israel B. Richardson was slouchy and slovenly and quite absentminded—but also clear and alert and up to the occasion. Returning to the governor, Willcox reported:

---

220. *LSR*, Jan. 25, 1859, 3, republishing item from *Clinton Republican*; *CW*, Vol. IV, 102-103.

"That is your man, not for major, but for colonel, the man to drill your Second regiment."

Showing how much he relied on this input, Blair gave the appointment as colonel to Richardson. He led the 2nd Michigan Infantry capably at First Bull Run, received promotion to major-general, commanded a brigade and then a division, and became known as "Fighting Dick" for his offensive mindset, He was mortally wounded during a key advance at the Battle of Antietam. It might never have happened so, for Richardson at first declined the appointment as colonel. But "he was promptly overruled by the governor," an assessment sustained by his mettle under fire.[221]

As for Alpheus Starkey Williams, Blair appointed him brigadier-general of the 1st Michigan Brigade and helped achieve Williams's commission on August 12, 1861, as brigadier-general of U. S. Volunteers, the state's first citizen-general officer in the war.[222]

VI. Correspondence with War Department (1861)

On August 19, 1861, Secretary of War Simon Cameron sent two telegrams to northern governors regarding organization of volunteer units in their jurisdictions. The second urged them to forward all units in whatever status, "whether under your immediate control or" not, including independent regiments.[223] *Blair responded, though the correspondence had really begun a week before, and a back-and-forth ensued.*

Executive Office,
Jackson, Mich., August 12, 1861.
Adjt. Gen. L. Thomas,
Washington:

---

221. Jack C. Mason, *Until Antietam: The Life and Letters of Major General Israel B. Richardson* (Carbondale: Southern Illinois University Press, 2009), 79, relying on Scott, *Forgotten Valor*, 250.
222. See Jack Dempsey, *Michigan's Civil War Citizen-General: Alpheus S. Williams* (Charleston: The History Press, 2019).
223. *OR*, III, I, 425-426.

Sir: The First Regiment, reorganized, the Fifth, Sixth, Seventh, and Eighth Regiments of the new levy, Michigan infantry, will all be in rendezvous and ready to be mustered into the service of the United States within the next ten days. Colonel Backus, the present mustering officer, is in poor health, and I think will need assistance. Brig. Gen. A.S. Williams, lately appointed, would be willing to render such assistance, and would like to be assigned to duty here in charge of these five regiments, sending on the First as soon as ready, and the others as the Department may desire. I think this would be well. It would be agreeable to [the] regiments themselves to be brigaded under his command, and I trust it may be so.

Very respectfully, your obedient servant,

Austin Blair,

Governor.

Jackson, Mich., August 19, 1861.

Hon. Simon Cameron,

Secretary of War:

I have your second dispatch of last night and will proceed to obey its instructions at once, and will inform you from time to time as the troops move. Hope to send 5,000 men within six days. Can Brig. Gen. A.S. Williams be detailed to aid in the mustering?

Austin Blair,

Governor.

Jackson, Mich., August 19, 1861.

Hon. S. Cameron:

We have no military organization in the State of any consequence now, except the three-years' regiment. It would be no use to call for troops for temporary service at present. We can furnish three-years' men just as easily, and prefer it. I can furnish more regiments than have been required if you wish on pretty short notice.

Austin Blair,

Governor.

War Department,

August 19, 1861.

Governor Blair,

Jackson, Mich.:

Fill up all regiments authorized as rapidly as possible and hold yourself in readiness for more. We may require them.

Simon Cameron,

Secretary of War.

Jackson, Mich., August 19, 1861.

Hon. Simon Cameron,

Secretary of War:

Sir: I desire to say a word which is not appropriate for the telegraph. It is to make an earnest appeal to you to recognize no more independent regiments in this State. They are introducing confusion and discord into all our affairs. Companies are divided and officers in unseemly quarrels. I will furnish all the troops you call for much sooner and in better order than these independent regiments can do, and thus avert a great amount of local ill feeling.[224]

I remain, most respectfully, your obedient servant,

Austin Blair,

Governor of Michigan.

Executive Office,

Detroit, Mich., August 21, 1861.

Hon. Simon Cameron,

Secretary of War:

Sir: I have the honor to inform you that the Sixth Regiment of Michigan Volunteer Infantry, numbering at date of last report 950

224.   Blair was not alone in lodging this complaint about "a struggling War Department overwhelmed by the volume of demands and directed by a wholly incompetent secretary." Engle, *All the President's Statesmen*, 11. Lincoln soon confirmed the primacy of State recruitment under Cameron's successor, Edwin Stanton. *OR*, III, I, 898.

officers and men, and mustered into the service of the United States, will leave their regimental rendezvous at Kalamazoo on Thursday, the 29th instant, and proceeding by rail to Detroit, thence by steamer to Cleveland, and thence by rail to Pittsburg and Harrisburg, will arrive at Washington about Sunday morning, the 1st proximo. The regiment will be supplied before their departure with uniforms (of blue), undershirts, drawers, forage-caps, stockings, and shoes, and with tents, cooking utensils, haversacks, and canteens. I request that provision may be made for furnishing them with arms and accouterments immediately on their arrival at Washington, and that I may be notified thereof by telegraphic dispatch before they leave Detroit.

[¶] The Seventh Regiment of Michigan Volunteer Infantry, numbering at date of last report 900 officers and men, will leave their regimental rendezvous at Monroe, via rail for Cleveland, and thence by the same route to Washington, as above designated for the Sixth, supplied with clothing and camp equipage similar to that furnished the Sixth Regiment, on the 2d proximo, and will arrive at Washington about the 5th proximo.

[¶] The Fifth and First Regiment of Michigan Volunteer Infantry, now being rapidly concentrated at their respective regimental rendezvous at Detroit and Ann Arbor, will be forwarded to Washington at as early a day as will be possible to supply them with the clothing indispensably necessary to enable them to leave their respective rendezvous. This clothing is under contract, and is being pressed forward with all possible dispatch.

I will hereafter report the earliest possible day at which I can forward the Eighth Regiment of Michigan Infantry, now being concentrated at Grand Rapids. I have organized the Ninth Regiment, which will be filled to its complement at an early day succeeding the completion of the organization of the Eighth. Lieut. Col. E. Backus, mustering officer for the State of Michigan, who has been charged by your Department with the organization of Stockton's independent regiment of infantry and of Brodhead's independent regiment of cavalry (both now being concentrated at Detroit), will report to you the day on which these regiments will be prepared to leave Detroit.

Your obedient servant,

Austin Blair,

Governor of Michigan.

War Department,

Washington City, D.C., August 26, 1861.

Governor Blair:

(Care Adjutant-General Robertson, Detroit, Mich.)

You can retain your men ten days in camp to fully uniform and equip them. Do not delay beyond that period.

Simon Cameron,

Secretary of War.

War Department,

Washington City, September 7, 1861.

Hon. A. Blair,

Governor of Michigan:

What number of volunteer regiments can you have ready for marching orders on a few hours' notice, if required to meet an emergency? It is desirable that organizations and equipment should progress as rapidly as possible, and in such manner as will enable the Government to use the forces actually mustered in. Please advise fully and immediately.

Simon Cameron,

Secretary of War.

Jackson, Mich., September 7, 1861.

Hon. Simon Cameron,

Secretary of War:

The Sixth Regiment Michigan Infantry left for Washington last week and must have arrived. The Seventh is now on the way. The Fifth can march full and uniformed in a few hours' notice. The First, reorganized, can march with about 700 strong. Stockton's, about the same, and the Eighth also about the same. We are proceeding with the greatest dispatch. The two new cavalry regiments have driven away recruits from the infantry badly.

Austin Blair,

Governor of Michigan.

War Department,

Washington City, September 10, 1861—8.45 p. m.

Governor Blair, Lansing, Mich.;

William P. Innes, chief engineer and superintendent of Grand Rapids, offers a regiment of mechanics and engineers. I have telegraphed him the matter would be referred to you, and if you deem it advisable for the interests of Government the organization may be made under your direction.

Simon Cameron,

Secretary of War.

War Department,

September 12, 1861.

Governor Austin Blair,

Lansing, Mich.:

You are desired to put in rapid march to this place all organized regiments under your control.

Simon Cameron,

Secretary of War.

War Department,

September 12, 1861.

Governor Blair:

Report to Colonel Berdan, here, all your sharpshooters. Special uniforms furnished here.

Simon Cameron,

Secretary of War.

Detroit, Mich., September 13, 1861.

Hon. Simon Cameron,

Secretary of War:

In your dispatch of yesterday by the words "organized regiments" do you intend me immediately to forward all State regiments, whether full or part full, and also independent infantry and cavalry regiments raising within the State by direct instructions to colonels from the War Department?

Austin Blair,

Governor of Michigan.

Jackson, Mich., September 13, 1861.

Hon. Simon Cameron,

Secretary of War:

Sir: I have received your telegram containing the directions to William P. Innes, esq., in regard to raising a regiment of mechanics under my direction if in my judgment the interest of the Government will be promoted thereby. Finding that several companies have already been formed for this purpose, I have cheerfully authorized the formation of the regiment and will assist in it to the utmost of my ability.

I am, sir, respectfully, your obedient servant,

Austin Blair,

Governor of Michigan.

War Department,

September 14, 1861.

Governor Blair:

Start all the regiments you can to Washington to-day. Important. Answer immediately, and let me know what can be done.

Simon Cameron,

Secretary.

War Department,

September 14, 1861.

Governor Blair,

Jackson, Mich.:

Start to-day for Washington the First and Colonel Stockton's regiments. Use such authority as may be necessary to fill these regiments from any men now mustered into service. Secure transportation and forward immediately. Answer what we may expect from Michigan.

Simon Cameron.

Detroit, September 15, 1861.

Hon. Simon Cameron,

Secretary of War:

The First Michigan Regiment and Colonel Stockton's regiment leave to-morrow for Washington.

A. Blair,

Governor of Michigan.

War Department,

September 16, 1861.

Austin Blair,

Governor of Michigan, Lansing:

We intend that you shall use your discretion in forwarding all regiments, and put them in such shape as to be serviceable.

Simon Cameron,

Secretary of War.

Executive Office,

Jackson, Mich., September 27, 1861.

Hon. Simon Cameron,

Secretary of War:

Sir: The regiments now raising in Michigan are all nearly full, and arrangements are perfected to fill them entirely, and I am constantly requested to receive new companies, which I cannot do unless your Department will receive them when organized. I wish, therefore, to know as soon as may be whether I shall continue to receive as many men as may volunteer and organize them as I have so far done. And if so, within what time? Michigan can easily furnish several more regiments if desired. I hope you take them.

I am, sir, your obedient servant,

Austin Blair,

Governor of Michigan.

War Department,

Washington City, October 5, 1861.

Governor Blair,

Detroit or Lansing, Mich.:

Have you two regiments armed, uniformed, and equipped that can be prepared for marching orders to-day? Get them ready and answer immediately.

Simon Cameron,

Secretary of War.

Jackson, Mich., October 7, 1861.

Hon. Simon Cameron,

Secretary of War:

I have two regiments which might march in about five days. Neither of them are armed, there being no arms in the State. One of them is fully equipped, except the arms; the other will be in the time stated unless the uniforms are delayed on the way.

Austin Blair,

Governor of Michigan.

War Department, Washington, October 11, 1861.

His Excellency Austin Blair,

Governor of Michigan, Jackson, Mich.:

Sir: You are hereby authorized to raise and organize five additional regiments of infantry for the service of the United States, to serve for three years, or during the war. The acceptance is with the distinct understanding that this Department will revoke the commissions of all officers who may be found incompetent for the proper discharge of their duties.

I am, sir, very respectfully,

Thomas A. Scott,

Acting Secretary of War.

Detroit, October 12, 1861.

Hon. Simon Cameron,

Secretary of War:

General Sherman telegraphs that Michigan Volunteers are of no use to him unless armed and equipped. He has no arms there. Can arms and equipment be forwarded here for two regiments now ready to march?

Austin Blair,

Governor of Michigan.

War Department,

Washington City, October 12, 1861.

Governor Blair, Detroit, Mich.:

We have not arms and equipments on hand to furnish you now. We expect them every day. As soon as they arrive you shall be provided.

Thomas A. Scott.

War Department,

Washington, October 22, 1861.

Hon. Austin Blair,

Governor of Michigan:

Sir: Mr. John McDermott, now commanding the Mulligan Regiment of the State of Michigan, desires authority to raise a battery of artillery to be attached to his regiment. You may consider yourself authorized to form a battery of six guns for the purpose aforesaid, if in your discretion you should see proper so to do, with the distinct understanding, however, that said battery may at anytime be detached from said regiment if the wants of the service require it.

Respectfully,
Thomas A. Scott,
Assistant Secretary of War.

War Department,
Washington City, October 28, 1861.
Major Hagner, U.S. Army,
New York:

Governor Blair, of Michigan, wants 3,000 arms. If the 2,500 arms in Moller's control, at $10, can be had, and meet your approval as suitable for service, buy them and send 500 rifles for flanking companies. They are wanted immediately. Do the best you can. Answer.

Thomas A. Scott,
Assistant Secretary of War.

New York, October 28, 1861.
Thomas A. Scott,
Assistant Secretary of War:

I have bought Moller's 2,500. Will send when altered—probably to-morrow: also 500 rifles.

P.V. Hagner.[225]

VII. Joint Resolution in Reference to the Rebellion (Jan. 15, 1862)

Whereas, The Government of the United States is engaged in putting down a causeless and wicked rebellion against its authority and sovereignty, inaugurated by ambitious men to obtain political power; a Government, the safety and perpetuity of which must ever rest upon the loyalty of its citizens, and in an adherence to the Constitution.

---

225.   *OR*, III, I, 407, 428, 450-451, 456, 489-490, 497, 501, 508-510, 513, 516, 521, 544, 563, 567, 572, 574, 587, 603. On August 25, General McClellan requested Cameron to instruct the governors not to send any units "uniformed in gray." Id. 453.

And whereas, The welfare of mankind, the usefulness and power of the nation, are involved in the events and issues of the present conflict; therefore, be it

Resolved, (the House concurring,) That Michigan, loyal to herself and to the Federal Government, re-affirms her undying hostility to traitors, her abiding love for freedom, and her confidence in the wisdom and patriotism of the national administration.

Resolved, (the House concurring,) That the people of Michigan deem it the imperative duty of the Government, to speedily put down all insurrection against its authority and sovereignty by the use of every constitutional means, and by the employment of every energy it possesses; that Michigan stands firm in her determination to sustain by men and treasure the Constitution and the Union, and claims that the burthen of loyal men should be lightened as far as possible, by confiscating to the largest extent, the property of all insurrectionists; and that as between the institution of slavery, and the maintenance of the Federal Government, Michigan does not hesitate to say, that in such exigency, slavery should be swept from the land, and our country be maintained.

Resolved, That the Governor be requested to forward a copy of the foregoing preamble and resolutions to each of our Senators and Representatives in Congress.[226]

VIII. Early 1862 State of Affairs

The following article appeared in the Lansing State Republican *of February 2, 1862 (p. 2), under the heading "The State Administration Vindicated."*

Col. Scott, assistant Secretary of War, has been to Detroit on a visit of inspection. He has been detailed by Secretary Stanton, to examine into the number, condition and wants of the various regiments now organizing in the Northern States, and to learn when they

---

226. *Journal of the Senate,* Extra Session of 1862, 130-131.

will be ready to take the field. He had a satisfactory interview with Governor Blair, and Adjutant General Robertson, obtaining all the information required. He thinks that within sixty days blows will be struck not only upon the Potomac, but in other quarters, which will speedily put an end to the Rebellion.

The <u>Advertiser</u> says, "Col. Scott expressed himself in the warmest terms of admiration with the condition in which he found everything connected with military affairs in this State, and was emphatic in his approval of Gov. Blair's conduct. He declared that in no State had he found matters in so favorable a condition. . . . his impression was that there had been, and could have been, none of those frauds in the contract department of which we have heard so much. The remarks of Col. Scott were, therefore, most complimentary to the Governor, the Quartermaster, and the Contract Board; and until something is <u>proved</u>, it should silence the clamors to which we refer. The people of Michigan have reason to feel proud of their State, and of the officers who have had control of military interests. They have escaped those gross frauds which have so disgraced almost every department of the Government. Coming from a man who has had such favorable opportunities for correct comparisons, it is a high compliment to the integrity of our Governor, and other officers connected with military affairs here."

IX. Resolution in Reference to the Rebellion, 1862 State Convention

The Republican state convention held in Detroit on September 24, 1862, adopted the following policy statement.

Resolved, That the existing rebellion is without justifiable cause. It has no parallel in the world's history, in its <u>magnitude, extent, power</u> and <u>atrocity</u>. Its wickedness can be measured only by the beneficence of the Government it [unreadable].

Resolved, That our national existence, the interest of unborn millions, the hopes of constitutional freedom throughout the world, all

4 ★ RADICAL OF RADICALS

depend upon the utter annihilation of this nefarious rebellion and it must and shall be subdued, whatever be the cost in treasure and in blood. That it is the paramount duty of the Government to accomplish this object without qualification or compromise. Unconditional surrender is the only terms to armed traitors.

Resolved, That the proclamation of the President of the United States of the 22d of Sept., meets our unqualified approbation, as a war measure, right and proper in itself, and necessary and effective for destroying this wicked rebellion, and since the Administration is the only legal and constitutional agent of the people for maintaining the existence of the Government, we as good citizens will sustain them in the use of all appropriate means for preserving the constitution whether they are measures of our choice or not—with or without our choice of measures, we are for the Government.

Resolved, That the constitution of the U.S. is the free act and deed of the people in convention assembled. It provides on its face the only mode of change, equally free and sovereign. It may be destroyed, but cannot be changed by violence or war—therefore when the rebellion shall cease, we shall have still intact the constitution of our fathers.

Resolved, That while this rebellion threatens the life of the Government, we tender no other issues to political friends or foes, and accept no other from them.

Resolved, That we cordially approve the administration of our State affairs for the last two years. That in times of unprecedented difficulty and embarrassment it has performed the difficult task of raising and equipping our noble regiments, in a manner which has elicited the admiration of the country, and at an expense far below that of our sister States—that it has presented a financial record, without a parallel, and leaves the State in time of war, in a condition of credit at home and abroad, unusual even in time of peace.

Resolved, That we tender to our soldiers in the field our hearty thanks for the noble manner in which they have at the same time upheld the honor of Michigan and the glory of our common country, and while Michigan is justly proud of the name for valor and heroism they have won for her, she will never forget the wounds they have received, and the blood they have spilled in her service.

The reading of the resolutions was accompanied with immense applause, and the report was accepted and adopted.[227]

X. Re-election Message

Central Michigan's Republican party organ, the State Republican, *sought to make a case for Blair's reelection as the November balloting drew near. The following editorial comment appeared on October 29 (p. 2); deleted is the paper's comments about Byron G. Stout, the Democratic challenger.*

Once more before the election takes place, we desire to call the attention of the voters in this State, to the two tickets which are presented for their suffrages.

At the head of the Republican ticket we have the name of Austin Blair, who has been Governor of the State for nearly two years, in the most trying time which it has ever been the lot of the people of this country to experience; and we submit to the people of Michigan, if he has not discharged the arduous duties of his office ably and faithfully? Has he not stood up like a true man and patriot, in the exigencies of the hour, and nobly won for himself and the State, the honor of having placed in the field better troops, at less expense, than any other State in the Union? Has he not in all things shown himself the man of executive ability, exactly suited to the position which he occupies, in these perilous times? Has he not done all in his power, and in the power of the State, in complying with the demands of the General Government? Has he not faithfully, honestly, zealously supported the Government in the suppression of the rebellion? Is he not now doing it? Does anybody doubt his disposition to do so in the future? Why should any patriotic supporters of the Government now abandon him and his friends, to try a new and untried man?

227.   *LSR*, Oct. 1, 1862, 1-2.

XI. Election Charges

A key issue in the November 1864 balloting was the soldier vote. Would they have to return home, or could they vote while on duty at the front lines of the war? Charges were levied about manipulation; the chief Democratic newspaper in the state had this to say.

The Soldiers Vote in the Army Thus Far

A very interesting column will be found in to-day's issue of how the army votes for President. The New York regiments vote by proxy, and during the past ten days these votes have been taken and forwarded to their respective localities. It is immensely for McClellan, in the proportion of more than five to one. The terrible frauds which the telegraph informs us have been committed, it is safe to believe are so many stories put afloat to break the force of the news that the army is for McClellan.

In this State, Governor Blair informed those who were present to hear him speak on Friday evening, that he had an order for every Michigan man who could leave, to return home and vote. We are rejoiced to hear this, because no one who has examined our law can believe it constitutional, and it would be wrong to deprive our soldiers of the privilege of voting, because the republicans preferred to trample on the Constitution rather than amend it. Governor Blair also said that every soldier who dared to cast a vote for McClellan, should be arrested as a traitor. We are inclined to think it would take more men than would be left to furnish a guard for them, for if we are not misinformed, a majority of the men from Michigan will vote for their old General.

The skies are bright, and the indications are that we shall not only carry Michigan for McClellan on the home vote, but the soldiers vote will add largely to the majority.[228]

---

228. *DFP*, Oct. 31, 1864, 2.

McClellan did not receive a five to one margin; indeed, he lost the Army vote.

XII. Joint Resolution on the State of the Union

Whereas, The existing rebellion, in its strength, extent and ferocity, in its baseness, enormity and wickedness, is without parallel in the history of mankind—is waged against a government the most beneficent on the face of the earth—and is without any justifiable cause, or even plausible pretext;

And whereas, The National Administration is the only legally constituted authority to direct the means and agencies to be employed in the prosecution of the war;

And whereas, The safety and perpetuity of the Government can only be secured by the utter and complete overthrow of the rebellion; therefore

Resolved by the Senate and House of Representatives of the State of Michigan, That it is the solemn and imperative duty of the Administration, to direct all the energies of the nation, to employ all the means recognized and sanctioned by the laws and usages of civilized nations, to speedily and effectually crush the rebellion, restore an honorable and enduring peace to the nation, preserve the Constitution of our country, the Union of all the States, and the government of our fathers;

Resolved, That for the accomplishment of the objects expressed in the foregoing resolution, we do hereby pledge to the National Administration the cordial, united, unfaltering support of the people of the State of Michigan, till rebellion shall be overthrown, till law and order shall triumph, till the authority of the Government shall be restored over every State, and a permanent and enduring peace be established throughout the land.

Resolved, That to weaken the enemy, by cutting off his supplies, taking away his means of support, stripping him of his property and depriving him of his slave, is no less a duty than actually fighting him in the field, and is demanded alike by the priceless blood of the gallant soldiers of our army, and the sacredness of the cause in which we are engaged; and we therefore approve the proclamation of the President, emancipating the slaves in the insurgent States, as a war measure eminently fit and proper, sanctioned by the usages of civilized warfare, and therefore warranted by the Constitution; and emanating thus from the President, by virtue of his authority as Commander-in-Chief of the army, it becomes the duty of all good citizens at home, as well as soldiers in the field, to sustain and enforce it.

Resolved, That we are unalterably opposed to any terms of compromise or accommodation with the rebels, while under arms, and acting in hostility to the government; and in this we express but one sentiment—unconditional submission and obedience to the laws and the constitution.

Resolved, That while we mourn over the desolations of war, brought upon the country by this most iniquitous rebellion, we still trust and rejoice in the hope that God will so order events as to promote the interests of humanity, place upon a firmer and more enduring basis our free institutions, and thus secure the highest good and glory of the nation.

Resolved, That we feel a just and glowing pride in the honor which has been reflected on Michigan by the promptitude with which her citizen soldiers have rallied to the standard of the country, and by their noble gallantry on the battle-field, which has given them an undying fame.

Resolved, That the Governor be requested to forward a copy of the foregoing preamble and joint resolutions to each of our Senators and Representatives in Congress, and to the Governors of the several loyal States.[229]

---

229.   Introduced as Sen. J. Res. 7 on Jan. 17, *Journal of the Senate of the State of Michigan, 1863* (Lansing: John A. Kerr & Co., 1863), 75; substitute reported by committee on Feb. 5, at 186; reported without amendment by Committee of the Whole, Mar. 3, at 493-494; placed on third reading, Mar. 10, at 610; and adopted same evening, at 615; notice of concurrence by House of Representatives, Mar. 14, at 694; enrollment on Mar. 17, at 750.

XIII. Prisoners of War

As shown in his remarks welcoming Orlando B. Willcox home after months in captivity, Blair regarded those taken prisoner as every bit worthy of commendation as any soldier at the front. In February 1864, he received a letter from behind Confederate lines, from someone he knew. It is a remarkable correspondence, recorded on February 23rd in a prison diary.

Have heard that a box came for me, and is over in Richmond. Hope the rebel that eats the contents of that box will get choked to death. I wrote to the Governor of Michigan, Austin Blair, who is in Washington, D.C., some weeks ago. He has known me from boyhood. Always lived in the neighborhood at Jackson, Mich. Asked him to notify my father and brothers of my whereabouts. To-day I received a letter from him saying that he had done as requested, also that the Sanitary Commission had sent me some eatables. This is undoubtedly the box which I have heard from and is over in Richmond.[230]

XIV. Blair's Military Secretaries

To be his right-hand man in the role of military secretary, Blair chose two individuals from Jackson. The first, who was appointed effective May 15, 1861, and served until September 13, 1862, was William K. Gibson, his law partner. The second, who served until March 10, 1865, was Eugene Pringle. Gibson was a leader at the Jackson bar for many years. He served as city attorney and prosecutor and "held many offices of trust." Pringle, born December 1, 1826, in Richfield, N.Y., came to Jackson in 1850 to practice law. He served in local offices, attended the meeting "under the oaks" in 1854, and was elected to the Michigan House of Representatives in November 1860. He died June 16, 1908, and was buried in Mount Evergreen Cemetery in Jackson. Both performed services for the governor,

---

230.   John L. Ransom, *Andersonville Diary, Escape, and List of the Dead* (Auburn: 1881), 33, republished as *John Ransom's Andersonville Diary* (Middlebury: Paul S. Eriksson, 1963), with introduction by Bruce Catton.

the state, and its people that were important for the war effort out of three locations: Detroit, Jackson, and Lansing.[231]

XV. Wounded and Ill Soldiers

Among the issues that continually concerned the governor was the condition of hospitalized soldiers. Blair was particularly mindful of the wounded and ill, making "numerous trips" to battlegrounds and medical wards. His call upon the legislature to underwrite commissioning of "active agents" to visit Michigan soldiers in hospital and provide them with financial support was approved. Armed with appropriations, the governor appointed state agents in Detroit, Louisville, Nashville, and Washington. Joseph Tunnicliffe Jr., born near Monroe and educated at Jefferson Medical College, held the post in the national capital from 1863-1865 together with his wife, Caroline E. Davis of Plymouth Township (1823-1910). Married since 1842, the couple provided aid to numerous wounded Michiganders at the Gettysburg battleground and participated in lobbying the War Department to create a general military hospital in Detroit. Together with Blair, the Michigan congressional delegation, and Dr. Charles S. Tripler of Detroit, those labors were rewarded when Harper Hospital opened its doors to patients in 1864. Blair—and Tripler[232]—insisted that soldiers convalesced better when near home rather than distant from family and friends.[233]

---

231.   Robertson, 5; *DeLand's History*, 343, 497-503; *History of Jackson County*, 248; *Official Records* mentions him as "W.J. Gibson," III, I, 287; Vanacker, 33.

232.   Michigan Civil War Association, *His Sword a Scalpel: General Charles S. Tripler MD USA* (Traverse City: Mission Point Press, 2023).

233.   Both Tunnicliffes were involved in this great work: a near-contemporaneous source recorded that "the Governor appointed him, with his wife, as Assistant State Military Agent of Michigan, with head-quarters at Washington City. Their duties were: to look after the wants of Michigan soldiers," to procure passes, furloughs, or assignments to duty, to collect and forward funds to soldier families, and "a multitude of other duties. They continued in the faithful discharge of this work until the close of the war, in 1865." *American Biographical History of Eminent and Self-Made Men: Michigan Volume* (Cincinnati: Western Biographical Pub. Co., 1878), 94-95.

XVI. Blair and Stockton

Thomas Baylis Whitmarsh Stockton (1805-1890) graduated sixteenth out of thirty-eight cadets in the West Point class of 1827. He served in various capacities until resigning in 1836. He returned to the service during the Mexican-American War as colonel of the 1st Regiment of Michigan Volunteers. He was "Member of a Board to Organize the 'Volunteer Systems' of the State of Michigan, 1858" and "Captain, Michigan Militia, 1858-60—and Major, 1860-61." On September 8, 1861, he accepted a commission as colonel, 16th Michigan Volunteers, sometimes referred to as "Stockton's Regiment." At the Battle of Gaines' Mill in June 1862 he was taken as prisoner of war and incarcerated in Libby Prison until August 12. He commanded a brigade in the Maryland Campaign, being engaged in the Battles of Antietam and Shepherdstown, and also fought at the Battles of Fredericksburg and Chancellorsville. He resigned on May 18, 1863.[234]

The adjutant-general's compendium of Michigan's service in the war gave this account of the regiment's formation and designation:

The 16th, originally known as "Stockton's Independent Regiment," was organized at Camp Backus, Detroit by Colonel T.W.B. [sic] Stockton of Flint, under direct authority from the Secretary of War, and took the field as such, the officers being for some time without commissions, but finally, in order to make their status legal, it was found necessary to have commissions from the State of Michigan for them, which they received. Numerical designation of the 16th Infantry was given the regiment at the same time.[235]

---

234.   George W. Cullum, *Biographical Register of the Officers and Graduates of the U.S. Military Academy*, Vol. I, 2nd Ed. (New York: D. Van Nostrand, 1868), 394-395; *Official Army Register of the Volunteer Force of the United States Army for the years 1861, '62,' 63, '64, '65*, Vol. 5 (Washington: Government Printing Office, 1865), 321.

235.   Robertson, 359.

The Adjutant-General's annual report for 1861 lists the regiment as twelfth among the infantry units raised that year.[236]

According to the excellent modern regimental history of the 16th Michigan, this rather peculiar origination was due to the political sensibilities of Governor Blair, who did not provide Stockton with the commission and command he sought in April 1861.[237]

XVII. Blair and Shoemaker

When Michael Shoemaker of Jackson (1818-1895) was commissioned colonel of the 13th Michigan Infantry on January 28, 1862, eyebrows might have raised. Governor Blair approved the appointment despite having lost the Senate race to him in 1847. Democrat Shoemaker went on to serve five terms representing the district of Jackson, Livingston, and Washtenaw, becoming an influential member of the Senate and returning to it as a Democrat in 1876. He served in uniform with distinction until resigning in May 1863 on account of family illness. His performance at the Battle of Stones River was especially noted. He was taken prisoner and held for twenty days in September 1862.

The following Blair letter (postscript omitted) from the 1847 campaign can provide insight on whether he was one to hold a grudge.

Jackson Oct. 18. 1847

Hon. D[arius]. Pierce

Lima [Township]

Dear Sir

I trust you will pardon me for troubling you with a personal affair. I have the honor of being a candidate for Senator & am asking my old friends in the county of Washtenaw to help me in my troubles—My

---

236. *Annual Report of the Adjutant General of the State of Michigan for the Year 1861* (Lansing: John A. Kerr & Co., 1861), 4.

237. Crawford, 14-24. Republished with revisions in 2019 by Michigan State University Press, it begins with a new Preface that states the regiment was formed "over the objection of Michigan's governor" and submits that Blair's disaffection with Stockton lay in the latter's having been a slave owner (vii, 2, 5).

opponent Mr. Shoemaker is an old hunker[238] but almost entirely unknown in your County & for that reason expects the reformers to support him. Now I have suffering too much in the furnace of reform to allow him to do that so easily—Consequently I want to make the gentleman known in Washtenaw, & rend of all reformers there—Will not you take a little pains to bring about so desirable a thing—I shall thrash him here beautifully, but I am some afraid of Washtenaw. I was at Dexter the other day & thought the Whigs were too dull in that region. We doing bravely here in Jackson & shall give Edmunds a heavy vote.

   Yours for Auld Lang Syne
   Austin Blair[239]

XVIII. The Adjutant-General

For his chief military administrator, Blair chose John Robertson (1814-1887), born in Portsoy, Aberdeenshire, Scotland. Unsuccessful in seeking a military career within the United Kingdom, Robertson looked to America:

[H]e concluded to immigrate to the United States and enter the army. Arriving at Montreal, he started on foot for the nearest American rendezvous, which he reached at Burlington, Vermont, where, on the 2nd of July, 1833, he entered as a private in the United States Army.

   In the spring of 1834 he was sent to the 5th United States Infantry, stationed at Fort Howard, Green Bay, then in Wisconsin Territory. Soon after joining the regiment he was appointed a non-commissioned officer, and served the most part of six years as Quartermaster-Sergeant and Sergeant-Major of the regiment. After his term of service

---

238.   An "Old Hunker" was a conservative Democrat. https://www.loc.gov/ resource/cph.3b35971/ Pierce was a Whig member of the Legislature.
239.   Blair Collection, Bentley; Robertson, 332-338, 928; *Record of Service,* Vol. 13, 128; *Manual,* 1846, 20; *DeLand's History,* 162; *Portrait and Biographical Album of Jackson County* (Chicago: Chapman & Bros., 1890) 187-197 (contrast the two-page biography of Blair, 145-146).

expired, he was engaged in the Quartermaster and Commissary Departments at Prairie du Chien, and went with the regiment from that post to Detroit in 1840.

Soon after arriving at Detroit he was employed by Brady & Trowbridge, merchants of that city, and a few years afterwards went with one of the partners to Mexico, and engaged in mercantile business connected with the United States army, and remained there about eighteen months. Returning to Detroit, be rejoined Mr. Trowbridge, and a few years later became his partner, the two doing business as commission merchants, under the firm of C. A. Trowbridge & Co.

In March, 1861, he was appointed by Governor Blair, Adjutant-General of the State, serving in that capacity throughout the war of the Rebellion, and held the office until 1887. To his zeal and energy is due the history of the "Flags of Michigan," the "Roll of Honor," deposited in the state library, "Michigan in the War," and other works. To his efficiency and zeal the state of Michigan is greatly indebted, especially from 1861 to 1865.[240]

Michigan in the War (at 6) cites the date of his appointment as March 15, 1861, making it an act of prescience by the governor. The attack on Fort Sumter occurred twenty-nine days later. Robertson set up his headquarters in Detroit on the second floor at 122 Jefferson Avenue. It soon became "thronged" with volunteers and engulfed in "voluminous" correspondence.[241] Blair likely used it as an office when in the city.

Blair's right-hand man? Such is the term employed in a study of the parallel office within the U.S. Army:

the right arm of the military establishment,—the medium of its orders and commands, the custodians of its records and archives, the guardian of its documentary and best evidence, from the muster of the

---

240.   https://www.michigan.gov/dmva/about/history/military-personalities/team-listing-page/john-robertson
241.   *DFP*, Mar. 21, 1887, 5, Apr. 20, 1861.

humblest enlisted man to the commission of the commander-in-chief
....[242]

Michigan's current state flag was first unfurled at the laying of the corner-stone at the monument of the Soldiers' National Cemetery at Gettysburg on the fourth of July, 1865. The design was recommended by Robertson and approved by Governor Crapo.

Robertson's responsibilities concerning Civil War documentation enabled him to make his first written contribution in 1871. The compiler of the Red Book *ascribed him this credit:*

[T]he success of his present enterprise has been assured by the effective artillery of James H. Lanman and General John Robertson. To the first, who is a relative of the Compiler, he is indebted for the history of the Territory, from its earliest settlement down to the organization of the State; and the latter, who was the able and indefatigable Adjutant-General of Michigan during the War for the Union, has contributed a complete account of the important part which the State took in subduing the Rebellion. Not only has he chronicled the action of the Legislature, but he has taken special care to place upon the record, in compact form, the heroic achievements of the Officers and Soldiers who have honorably identified their names with the State of their nativity or adoption. [243]

With approval of the legislature and governor, Robertson compiled and published "a report, in one volume, from the reports in his office, and on

---

242.   Yael A. Sternhell, *War on Record: The Archive and the Afterlife of the Civil War* (New Haven: Yale University Press, 2023), 11, quoting L.D. Ingersoll, *A History of the War Department of the United States* (Washington: Francis B. Mohun, 1879). See Robert E. Mitchell, "The Organizational Performance of Michigan's Adjutant General and the Federal Provost Marshal General in Recruiting Michigan's Boys in Blue" in *Michigan Historical Review*, Vol. 28, No. 2 (Fall 2002).
243.   Charles Lanman, *The Red Book of Michigan: A Civil, Military and Biographical History* (Detroit: E.B. Smith & Co., 1871), iii.

file in the War Department at Washington, of the services of Michigan regiments, batteries, and companies in the late war." It drew upon his contributions to the Red Book. *The first version appeared in 1879, with a revised edition issuing in 1882. At over a thousand pages, it has for nearly a century and a half served as an essential resource in telling the story of Michigan in the war.*

Blair sent a telegram of sympathy and regret at not being able to attend Robertson's funeral in 1887. He must have remembered how his deputy felt about their partnership:

Michigan was extremely fortunate in her Executive. His example and utterances in public and private, full of loyalty, patriotism, and courage, gave an abiding tone to public sentiment, and inspired the troops. And although the intense prevailing patriotism of the people of Michigan was undoubtedly the main source of the high standard reached by her troops in this respect, yet it being so eminently inherent in her "War Governor," Austin Blair, and which he so eloquently imparted to them on every fitting occasion, impressed it on their minds with so much earnestness as to produce most beneficial and enduring effects.[244]

XIX. Blair's Portrait

By Shayla Croteau, Art Registrar, Michigan State Capitol.

The Michigan Senate website states that the capitol's portrait of Austin Blair "was begun during the Civil War, and was finished in 1865 at Blair's Jackson home. Michigan's Civil War veterans paid for the portrait and presented it to the state."

Begun during the Civil War.

Artist Alvah Bradish was born in New York and first began painting there. He later moved to Michigan and became a professor of fine art at the University of Michigan. Bradish traveled back and forth

---

244. *DFP*, Mar. 23, 1887, 5; Robertson, 13.

between the two states, staying in New York for several months at a time to paint prominent citizens there.

- On Dec. 2, 1863, the *State Republican* noted that Bradish would be coming to Lansing soon "for the purpose of painting some of our citizens," stating: "Prof. Bradish comes direct from New York city, where he has just finished a very fine portrait of Senator E.D. Morgan."

- On Jan. 13, 1864, the *State Republican* reported that Bradish has come to Lansing to paint portraits of some of the state's first citizens.

- A letter in the Burton Historical Collection, written in Jackson by Blair to Bradish on May 10, 1864, states: "You will find me at home now most of the time for a month to come. If it will suit you better I can meet you in Detroit without inconvenience." This suggests the men were meeting, possibly for sittings, between May and June 1864.

- In the July/Aug. 1990 *Michigan History*, author Maria Quinlan Leiby stated that the portrait was begun by Bradish "during the war, possibly as early as 1863."

- On Nov. 23, 1864, the *State Republican* reported that the Blair portrait was "recently painted" and quoted from a letter of June 6, 1864, by Daniel T. Grinnell of Jackson to Bradish, referring to a "full length portrait of Gov. Blair, which you have just completed in this city."

These sources suggest that Bradish had returned to Michigan by mid-January 1864 (possibly in Dec. 1863) and painted the Blair portrait, likely with several others, between then and June 1864—placing both its beginning and end dates during the war.

Likely finished before 1865.

Based on the *State Republican* article from Nov. 23 and Grinnell's letter, it is probable that the portrait was finished in 1864. The article noted that the portrait is currently placed in the governor's room at the capitol. It is possible that it was not formally presented until

1865, though a source has not been found that provides a date for its presentation.

Finished in Jackson (but not necessarily in Blair's home).

The Grinnell letter confirms that the portrait was finished in Jackson, and correspondence between Blair and Bradish suggests that Blair sat for the painting in his home. It is also possible that this reference only intended to refer to the city of Jackson as Blair's home, not his residence.

- The letter of May 10, 1864, suggests that Blair sat for the portrait in his home. The letter is written in Jackson and notes he will be "home now most of the time for a month to come." Blair also offers to meet the artist in Detroit if needed, however, and the letter does not directly refer to the portrait or a sitting. While this letter hints at the portrait being painted in Blair's home, it does not confirm the statement.

Michigan's Civil War veterans paid for and presented the portrait to the state.

- The *Michigan Manual* from 1879 (pp. 371-372) describes the Senate chamber in the capitol, including the portraits on its walls. It states that the Blair portrait "was painted at the solicitation of officers and soldiers of Michigan regiments, and by them presented to the State."
- The Nov. 23 *State Republican* article stated the portrait was painted "at the request of numerous friends of the Governor." It also noted that "the compensation paid the artist is one thousand dollars, while the frame, which is a very handsome one, cost one hundred and twenty-five dollars more."

—While the article does not directly state that the governor's friends provided the payment, it is a fair assumption that those who requested the portrait be painted also paid for it. The act of presenting a portrait to the state suggests that the state was accepting it as a gift, not paying for it, as well.

—The article does not state that the friends were veterans, but the *Michigan Manual* is a strong source for that claim.

- The *Michigan History* article states: "The painting was paid for and presented to the state by Michigan's Civil War veterans."

Other Notable Sources

The Burton collection contains three other letters written by Blair to Bradish from Jackson that are relevant:

- One on July 26, 1864: "Enclosed please find card. It has been long delayed by various causes but is for the whole a pretty good one. I go to Washington Monday next the 29th just to be gone perhaps 10 or 12 days." The card enclosed could be a photo of Blair for the artist to use, suggesting that Blair may have asked for a few finishing touches on the portrait. This is not certain, however, and there is no evidence that any changes were made to the portrait.

- Two others in 1879 involve Blair asking Bradish to touch up his portrait around the time that it was hung in the Senate chamber. Again, there is no evidence that changes were made.

– Jan. 31: "In reference of our conversation yesterday I enclose the photograph—It is a striking likeness & I hope you can reform the picture in the Senate Chamber in that respect."

– Jul. 10: "I send here with a picture taken during the war by Mr. Raymand (sp.) in Detroit and which I think will answer your purpose—It is all that Mrs. Blair had in a frame here and she says you must send it back when you get through with it."

XX. Speech Durations

Nineteenth century speeches could be lengthy. Abraham Lincoln's first inaugural address amounted to approximately 3,627 words. William H. Harrison's in 1841 stretched to 8,445 on an inclement day— and a month later, he died of illness. James Monroe's inaugural in 1821 lasted 4,400 words; James K. Polk's in 1845 was 4,800. Edward

Everett's "Gettysburg Address" on November 19, 1863, extended to 13,582 words. No one remembered it, finding Lincoln's 267-word remarks in that same ceremony to have more succinctly addressed the occasion.

XXI. The Conference of Loyal Governors at Altoona Pennsylvania in 1862

The document with this title is undated, but an internal reference to an article published in January 1892 suggests the year of its preparation.

First, though, is provided an 1883 newspaper story based on a Blair speech:

Lincoln and M'Clellan.

Gov. Blair's Recollections of the Convention of War Governors.

In a recent address at Bellevue, Mich., ex-Gov. Austin Blair gave an account of the convention of Governors of Northern States that met at Altoona, Pa., at the time of the issuing of the emancipation proclamation by President Lincoln in 1862. The convention was called to bring an influence to bear upon President Lincoln to induce him to issue a proclamation or do some act that should set at liberty the 4,000,000 slaves, but the President outwitted the twenty-two Governors by issuing the proclamation the same day their convention met. The Governors decided then to go on to Washington and present to the President, not the urgent resolutions they had intended, but an address complimenting him upon the step he had taken. This address was prepared in an able manner by Gov. Andrew, of Massachusetts, who read it to President Lincoln as he sat at his desk, while the Governors were seated around the room. After that an incident happened that Gov. Blair said he had never before related to anyone. Gov. Kirkwood, of Iowa, since a United States Senator and Secretary of the Interior, rose and said:

"Mr. President—I should be delighted could I return to my home and say to the people of Iowa that the President of the United States believes Gen. George B. McClellan is a loyal man." He branched off upon other subjects connected with the war, and then closed by repeating with more emphasis: "I should be glad, Mr. President, to be able to tell the people of Iowa that you believe in the loyalty and patriotism of George B. McClellan."

Taking his feet down from the desk upon which they had been resting, Mr. Lincoln sprang to his feet and straightened up apparently two inches taller than usual, and said, with much force and apparent excitability: "Loyal! George B. McClellan is as loyal as any one of you." Then stopping a moment the President's face assumed its naturally pleasant look, and he continued in a natural and pleasing tone: "I'll tell you, gentlemen, Gen. McClellan is an exceedingly well informed general, and is very careful, in fact too careful, and the great trouble with him is that when he wins a victory he doesn't know what to do with it."

"Why not try somebody else?" mildly suggested Gov. Blair.

"We might do that and might lose an army by it," was the quick response of the President, which Gov. Blair admitted "completely unhorsed him."[245]

The Altoona Conference has been regarded as inconsequential by historians of classic studies, reflecting the judgment that issuance of the preliminary Emancipation Proclamation turned "a potentially harmful convention of Northern governors at Altoona, Pennsylvania, into an innocuous farce." Such an interpretation keeps faith with the trope that Lincoln outsmarted the governors, as per Hesseltine, supra.[246]

Perhaps the view that Lincoln took captive the loyal state executives lost sight of the contemporary political situation. Military failures led to demands "for a complete reorganization of the administration;" the

---

245. *DFP*, July 12, 1883, 4; *New York Times*, July 14, 1883.

246. Allan Nevins, *The War for the Union, Vol. II, War Becomes Revolution 1862-1863* (New York: Charles Scribner's Sons, 1960), 239. See also Kees D. Thompson, "'Altoona was his, and fairly won': President Lincoln and the Altoona Governors' Conference, September 1862" in *The Gettysburg College Journal of the Civil War Era*, Vol. 7, Article 7 (2017).

"approaching conference of Northern war governors would almost certainly demand an emancipation proclamation"; and foreign recognition of the Confederate States of America was "close" absent "a stand against slavery."[247] *Affairs in the Eastern Theater were in "chaos," and the gathering at Altoona perhaps could "bring pressure on the President ... to issue some positive declaration against slavery."*[248] *Other histories cite how "The conference had its origins in discontent with the Lincoln administration. There had been much to disturb the state executives in the weeks preceding the call for the conference."*[249]

Blair contended that the governors met in support of the Administration during a period of reverses (the Peninsula Campaign; the Battle of Second Bull Run; Lee's invasion of Maryland) and that it was, rather than farcical, a bracing for vigorous prosecution of the war. The leaders participating in this conference had shown initiative and a commitment to the Union that perhaps deserves more from posterity. The words are Blair's. All punctuation is as in the original copies.

It has been thought desirable that the story of this Conference should be told, by one of those who participated in it, and it is the object of this paper to meet that desire as fully as the material at the disposal of the writer will permit.

The Conference was wholly private and informal. No records seem to have been kept either of its objects or its doings and no reporters were present to give to the public press what was said or done there. Its history therefore rests mainly in the memory of the Governors who attended it.

There was no formal organization, no secretary, and no record made at the time even of the names of those who were present taking part in the Conference.

---

247. David H. Donald, *Lincoln* (New York: Simon & Schuster, 1995), 373-374.

248. Carl Sandburg, *Abraham Lincoln: The War Years*, Vol. II (New York: Harcourt, Brace & World, 1939), 514, 585.

249. Mark E. Neely, *The Abraham Lincoln Encyclopedia* (New York: Da Capo Press, 1984), 5.

The Governors of the loyal states were not all present, but a majority of them were present taking part in the conference. The names of thirteen of them appear attached to the address to President Lincoln, but some of these subscribed to it after the conference had adjourned.

The Call for the Conference

The Call originated with Gov. Andrew G. Curtin of Pennsylvania. The correspondence was by telegraph entirely and began by a message from Gov. Curtin to Gov. John A. Andrew of Massachusetts, dated September 6, 1862 as follows:

"In the present emergency would it not be well that the Loyal Governors should meet at some point in the border states to take measures for the more active support of the government?"

To this Gov. Andrew replied on the same day that should a meeting be called he would attend.

On the 14th day of September 1862 the call was issued in these words:

"We invite a meeting of the Governors of the Loyal states to be held at Altoona, Pennsylvania on the 24th instant.

Andrew G. Curtin, Pa.

David Tod, Ohio

F.U. Pierpont, West Virginia"

This call was sent to all the Governors by telegraph and was accepted by most of them. Governor Morgan of New York however declined to accept.

Gov. Curtin states no doubt correctly that he first suggested action by the governors to Mr. Seward secretary of state in a conversation between them in the city of New York immediately after the disaster on the Peninsula.

The Governor happening to be in New York, Mr. Seward sent for him to come to the Astor House and they met there. Mr. Seward had with him the Mayor of Philadelphia, had called on the Mayor of New York, and was intending to visit Boston to interest the Mayor of that city also, upon some plan for the increase of the Army, a more vigorous prosecution of the war.

At this interview the suggestion was made that it would be better that action should be taken on this subject by the governors of the Loyal states. This suggestion was immediately telegraphed to the President and he warmly approved of the plan.

The Loyal Governors

The breaking out of the great war of the rebellion in April 1861, immediately brought the governors of the loyal states into great prominence. Upon them devolved at once the raising of all the troops called for by the President in defense of the Government. To them directly every call was sent and upon them rested the responsibility of meeting that call promptly and efficiently.

They enlisted the volunteers, organized them into regiments, commissioned all the officers and sent them so organized to the army at the front of battle.

The importance of this service could not be overestimated. It brought the Governors at once into very close and intimate relations with the President and Secretary of War.

They became many of them trusted advisers of the President in all matters relating to the war and especially as to the raising of troops in their several states. They were deeply interested in the quotas for their states and found it necessary to visit the departments in Washington very frequently when these quotas were under discussion. Consultations amongst themselves in an informal manner were very frequent as they came together in Washington upon similar errands and often the whole policy of the war came under discussion.

Before the actual commencement of the war a conference of the Governors of the North Western States was called by Gov. Dennison of Ohio at Cleveland which was attended by the Governors of Indiana, Illinois, Michigan and Wisconsin or their representatives.

It was at this conference that some of us heard for the first time of Gen. Geo. B. McClellan, who Gov. Dennison told us he had secured to be Major General of the Ohio troops. Conferences amongst the Governors therefore were not uncommon nor were they without influence upon the administration by any means, though they were always very careful to avoid anything that seemed likely to embarrass the Government.

Some of them were very eminent men and all of them were men of great influence & power in their states.

Mr. Greeley in his book, The American Conflict, has a plate containing portraits of seventeen "Eminent Loyal Governors" as he styles them, but the plate does not include quite all of them.

The Reason for the [Altoona] Conference

The situation of the country at the time undoubtedly occasioned this call and the conference that followed. The campaign of 1862 had opened in the spring with brilliant prospects for the Union Arms. Gen. McClellan with a great army carefully organized and drilled and splendidly equipped and supplied had started out to capture the Confederate Capital.

From this army and its commander the people of the country had expected the grandest results and no less than the speedy fall of the Confederate Capitol and the collapse of the rebellion. How completely those anticipations were disappointed. How failure was afterwards written upon every movement of this army to its final retreat to the James River and back to Washington is current history now.

The gloom that overspread the loyal states on account of these disasters and the movement of Gen. Lee's Army north for the invasion of the border states occasioned very great depression in the public mind. It was necessary to relieve this situation promptly and nothing could accomplish this so effectively as the energetic action of the war Governors unless it should be a victory of the National Arms.

The Conference

On the 24th day of September 1862 in pursuance of the Call the Governors met at Altoona. Meantime the situation had greatly changed. The skies had brightened and the hopes of the loyal people had revived.

On the 17th of September 1862 the great battle of Antietam had been fought and a substantial victory won.

Gen. Lee was retreating across the Potomac to his stronghold in Virginia and the emancipation proclamation of September 1862. The danger was not passed by any means for Lee had got away with his army in fair condition. That army ought to have been destroyed then and there, as we all believed but it was not, it was getting away to fight other battles & slay its other thousands of loyal men.

The conference was wholly informal. No records of its action were kept, but its results were embodied in an address to the President which was drawn up by Governor John A. Andrew and signed by most of the Governors who were present. It was afterwards sent to those who were not able to attend the conference with a request to sign if they approved of it, which most of them did.

Many subjects were discussed that are not mentioned in the address. Gov. Kirkwood of Iowa in an article recently published in the "Iowa Historical Record" says, "We discussed the condition of Military affairs and especially the fitness of Gen. McClellan for military command. On this point there was some difference of opinion but my recollection is that a decided majority were of opinion that the public welfare would be promoted by his retirement from the command of the army of the Potomac. But as there was not the same accord of opinion on this point as there was in regard to the emancipation proclamation it was decided that the address should not include any expression of opinion in regard to Gen. McClellan.

That we should go to Washington and have an interview with the President at which such of us as chose so to do might say what we thought on that subject."[250]

---

250. The article is a letter written on Dec. 20, 1891: Samuel J. Kirkwood, "The Loyal Governors at Altoona in 1862" in *The Iowa Historical Record*, Vol. VIII, No. 1, Jan. 1892 (Iowa City: A.J. Hershire & Co., 1892), 210-214. Kirkwood stated the purpose of the meeting was "for consultation in regard to the then critical condition of public affairs," and that while the statement of the Governors had been "published at the time" an account of their meeting with Lincoln "so far as I know has not hitherto been made public." Id. 210. The article focused

The conference at Altoona adjourned on the same day of its meeting to meet again in Washington on the next day. In pursuance of this determination the Governors came together in Washington and in a body called upon the President at the White House.

The Interview with President Lincoln

The interview was entirely private. No reporters were present and I think none of the President's secretaries were there and no report of what occurred & what was said at that interview was published at the time but the address was made public.

The address was read to the President in full by Gov. Andrew and it is here given at length with the signatures which it then contained & those that have since been added. [see text, *supra*]

The writer of this article was present at the entire interview and has a distinct recollection of all the more striking things that occurred and of the discussion that took place in regard to Gen. McClellan.

After the President had made a very short & pleasant reply to the address some conversation was had upon the then all engrossing subject the military situation. Gov. Kirkwood of Iowa then rose from his seat and addressing the President said, substantially:

"Now Mr. President as I suppose the business for which we came here as a body has been concluded, there are a few words that I desire to speak for the people of Iowa & on my own account. That in the opinion of our people George B. McClellan is unfit to command the army of the Potomac. The people of Iowa fear & I fear that the administration is afraid to remove Gen. McClellan from his command, and I know it would be a great comfort to the People of Iowa if on my return I can say to them that the President believe in the loyalty of George B. McClellan."

At the conclusion of this speech President Lincoln immediately arose, showing more excitement than was usual to him and proceeded to reply. He said:

on Kirkwood's criticisms of McClellan and the President's response.

"Do I believe in the loyalty of Gen. McClellan? Of course I believe in his loyalty. I have the same reasons to believe in his loyalty that I have to believe in the loyalty of you gentlemen before me now. I suppose you to be loyal & I believe he is loyal. I cannot dive into the hearts of men and find what is there." Then pausing for a moment, he said, "Now gentlemen, after having said so much in favor of Gen. McClellan I don't want you to think that I do not know his deficiencies. I think I do know them. He is over cautious and lacking in confidence in himself & in his ability to win victories with the forces at his command. He fights a battle about as well as any of them when he does fight, but when a substantial victory is won he seems incapable of properly following it up so as to reap the fruits of it, and it does not seem to do us any good. But if I remove him some one must be put in his place. Who shall it be?"

As he sat down Gov. Blair of Michigan said, "Why not try another man Mr. President" to which, he replied, "Ah: but I might lose an army by that."

The little excitement that arose out of this discussion had already disappeared and the interview closed pleasantly.

The hopes of the President were high and his confidence unshaken. This was equally true of the Governors and they immediately returned to their states to fulfill the promises of the address and they did fulfill them to the letter as the country knows.

The Effect of the Conference

What effect the Conference had upon the country and upon the administration is mainly a matter of inference. The publication of the address to the President at once made known to the people the vigorous policy recommended by the Governors, that it had some influence in restoring confidence in the ability of the government to sustain itself is undoubted. That it promoted enlistments in the states and infused greater activity into the recruiting service and tended greatly to strengthen the armies in the field and to silence discontent amongst the disloyal elements in the loyal states there can be no question.

It was also very evident at this time that the unanimous agreement of the loyal Governors to sustain the administration, its efforts to increase the army rapidly and promote its strength both in number and activity was very grateful to the President and not by any means without its influence upon the future policy of the administration.

There had existed from the commencement of the war a considerable party in the Northern States that preferred to believe that the South could not be conquered; but that at last a compromise would have to be made that would leave to the South its institution of Slavery intact, with more effectual guarrantees for its protection in the future. This party was greatly encouraged by the failure of McClellan in the peninsular campaign and the disasters that followed it.

The unanimity of the Governors and the vigorous address of the conference in favor of a more energetic prosecution of the war together with the emancipation proclamation of the president had a great effect to shut the mouths and paralyze the efforts of the so called peace party. The conference showed no signs of discouragement, but its action on the contrary proved its absolute confidence in the ability of the country to put down the rebellion as well as a determination to employ the entire power of the loyal states to that end.

Some illy informed persons have asserted that the Call for the Conference had occasioned the issue of the Emancipation Proclamation though the proclamation itself was issued & published to the country two days before the Conference assembled.

That assertion was certainly not true. It was well understood by all men at all corners and with the views of President Lincoln that he had for a long time contemplated the proclamation and only waited for a favorable occasion to put it forth.

On the 25th of June 1864 the emancipation bill well being under consideration in the House of Representatives in Washington, a discussion arose upon this subject. It was argued by Mr. Mallory a member of the House from Kentucky. He was attacking the policy of the administration in regard to slavery and in that connection he said:

"A set of factious Governors of Northern States, after having in conjunction with leading radical traitors in vain urged and pressed the president to change his policy met at Altoona in the state of Pennsylvania and informed the President that unless his policy was changed, unless the extermination of slavery was made, the object and purpose of the war and not the restoration of the authority of the constitution & laws over the rebellious states. That if slavery was not put in process of exterpation they would stop the war.

That not one of their states would rally to the standard we had raised for the purpose of vindicating the constitution & the laws. Then as if by magic the policy of the Government changed.

I say Mr. Speaker that it was the meeting of factious Governors at Altoona and this pressure they brought to bear & had previously with others brought to bear on the President who sits at the head of our government and holds the reign of power in a nation like the United States, that caused him to abandon his original policy, which was successful, which was admirable, and to take up that other policy which has failed and which gentlemen on the other side acknowledged to have failed."[251]

How utterly ridiculous this was fully appears in the preceding portions of this article. It is evident that Mr. Mallory knew nothing accurately concerning the conference at Altoona, had never read the address to the President nor considered this fact, that the proclamation was issued before the conference assembled & was in fact the act of the President alone, though it met with a hearty response from the Conference and the people of the loyal states as well and now has become one of the principal supports of the great and increasing fame of Abraham Lincoln.

Mr. Mallory was merely talking politics and very much at random but before the discussion closed, Mr. Boutwell of Massachusetts corrected the error of the "gentleman from Kentucky" very fully in substance, though falling himself into the error of admitting that the

---

251. This recollection and quote, while not completely accurate, is correct in a general sense. *Congressional Globe*, June 25, 1864, 3272, 3279-3280. Ironically, chosen for its rail location and ready access, Altoona was in Blair County, Penn.

conference assembled at Altoons before the proclamation was issued which was a mistake by the space of two days.

But the statement of Mr. Boutwell that the conference had nothing to do with the issuing of the proclamation was entirely correct.

The whole history of that proclamation, its consideration by the President & his Cabinet and its final issue on the 22nd day of September 1862 is now well known & has become a matter of current history.

The conference at Altoona had a distinct purpose and that purpose it fully accomplished. A small number of the Governors of the loyal states for reasons of personal prudence declined to sign the address, but there was substantially no opposition to the policy it set forth.

That the government was to be triumphant in the end and that chattel slavery would perish with the rebellion none of them doubted and they immediately returned to their states and again set in more active motion all the powers they possessed to fill up the ranks of the army, add vigor and strength to the Government and hasten the downfall of a rebellion that was both causeless & wicked.

Austin Blair[252]

---

252.   Blair Papers, Burton; typescript version, Bentley.

"No State won a brighter record
for her devotion to our country than the Peninsula State,
and to Gov. Blair, more than to any other individual
is due the credit for its untiring zeal and labors in the Nation's behalf,
and for the heroism manifested in its defense."[253]

---

253.   *Portrait and Biographical Album of Ingham and Livingston Counties, Mich-igan* (Chicago: Chapman Bros., 1891), 146.

Bibliography

A Protest Against American Slavery, by One Hundred and Seventy-three Unitarian Ministers (Boston: B.H. Greene, 1845)

Act to confiscate Property used for Insurrectionary Purposes, Pub. L. 37-60, 12 Stat. 319

Acts of the Legislature of the State of Michigan, Passed at the Regular Session of 1855, with an Appendix (Lansing: Geo. W. Peck, 1855)

Acts of the Legislature of the State of Michigan Passed at the Extra Session of 1862 (Lansing: John A. Kerr & Co., 1862)

Acts of the Legislature of the State of Michigan, Passed at the Regular Session of 1863 (Lansing: John A. Kerr & Co., 1863)

Acts of the Legislature of the State of Michigan Passed at the Extra Session of 1864 (Lansing: John A. Kerr & Co., 1864)

Ahlstrom, Sydney E. *A Religious History of the American People* (New Haven: Yale University Press, 2004)

Ambler, Charles H. *Francis H. Pierpont: Union War Governor of Virginia and Father of West Virginia* (Chapel Hill: University of North Carolina Press, 1937) (reprinted 2012)

American Biographical History of Eminent and Self-Made Men: Michigan Volume (Cincinnati: Western Biographical Pub. Co., 1878)

An Address by [former U.S. Senator] *John Patton, Delivered at Lansing, Mich., October 12, 1898, at the Unveiling of the Statue, Erected by the State of Michigan, in the Capitol Grounds, to the Memory of Austin Blair, War Governor* (Lansing: 1898)

Ann Arbor Journal

Annual Report of the Adjutant General of the State of Michigan for the Year 1861 (Lansing: John A. Kerr & Co., 1861)

Annual Report of the Adjutant General of the State of Michigan, for the Year 1864 (Lansing: John A. Kerr & Co., 1865)

Archives of Michigan

Austin Blair Collection, Bentley Historical Library

Austin Blair Papers, Burton Historical Collection, Detroit Public Library

Barber, E.W. *Reminiscences of Governor Austin Blair*, Blair Papers, Burton Historical Collection

Basler, Roy P. ed. *The Collected Works of Abraham Lincoln* (New Brunswick: Rutgers University Press, 1953)

Bierce, Ambrose. *The Collected Works of Ambrose Bierce, Vol. VII: The Devil's Dictionary* (New York: Neale Pub. Co., 1911)

Bingham, S.D. *Early History of Michigan with Biographies of State Officers, Members of Congress, Judges and Legislators* (Lansing: Thorp & Godfrey, 1888)

Bitter, Rand K. *Minty and His Cavalry: A History of the Saber Brigade and Its Commander* (2006)

Blair, Austin. *Address in Honor of Loyal Governors: Their Claim to Grateful Remembrance*, Reunion, New York, Grand Army of the Republic, February 1888

Boatner, Mark M. III. *The Civil War Dictionary* (New York: David McKay Co., 1987)

Braun-Hass, Linda. *Charles Victor DeLand: Wheelhorse of the Republican Party, 1852 to 1854* (East Lansing: Michigan State University, 1988) (Master's thesis)

Brodie, Fawn M. *Thaddeus Stevens: Scourge of the South* (New York: W.W. Norton & Co., 1959)

Camp Blair: A Civil War Camp 1864-1866 (Jackson County Michigan Historical Society: 2024)

Carmichael, Peter S., Lorien Foote, Jennifer M. Murray & Craig L. Symonds. "The Fortenbaugh Lecture: A Panel Discussion on Military History" in *The Journal of the Civil War Era*, Vol. 14, No. 3 (Sept. 2024)

Cassidy, Michelle K. *Michigan's Company K: Anishinaabe Soldiers, Citizenship, and the Civil War* (East Lansing: Michigan State University, 2023)

Catalogue of the Officers & Students of the Michigan Central College at Spring Arbor, for the Year Ending July 1850 (Jackson: R.S. Cheney, 1850)

Catton, Bruce. *Reflections on the Civil War* (Garden City: Doubleday & Co., 1981), 8-9 (John Leekley ed.)

_____. *This Hallowed Ground: The Story of the Union Side of the Civil War* (Garden City: Doubleday & Co., © 1955-1956)

Chartkoff, Kerry. "Austin Blair & His Adjutant General" in *Michigan History Magazine*, Vol. 95, No. 2, Mar.-Apr. 2011

Chittenden, L.E. *A Report of the Debates and Proceedings in the Secret Sessions of the Conference Convention, for Proposing Amendments to the Constitution of the United States, Held at Washington, D.C., in February, A.D. 1861* (New York: D. Appleton & Co., 1864)

Cirillo, Frank J. *The Abolitionist Civil War: Immediatists and the Struggle to Transform the Union* (Baton Rouge: Louisiana State University Press, 2023)

Civil War Governors of Kentucky Project[254]

Claghorn, Charles E. "Maine Privateers during the Revolutionary War" in *Maine History* 28, 4 (1989)

Clark, Hovey K. *Under the Oaks. The Record of the First Republican State Convention. Which Was Held in Jackson, July 6, 1854. The Events Which Led To It, and the Results That Followed. Republished from the Detroit Post and Tribune of July 6, 1879.*

Cleveland Morning Leader

Clinton Republican

Correspondence between His Excellency, President Abraham Lincoln, with General Hiram Walbridge, of New York, in 1861 (New York: John F. Trow, 1865)

254. Online collection of historical documents about ordinary Kentuckians, not the five governors.

Cralle, Richard K. ed. *The Works of John C. Calhoun*, Vol. IV (New York: D. Appleton & Co., 1854)

Crawford, Kim. *The 16th Michigan Infantry* (Dayton: Morningside, 2002)

Cross, Whitney R. *The Burned-over District: The Social and Intellectual History of Enthusiastic Religion in Western New York, 1800-1850* (New York: Harper & Row, 1950)

Cullum, George W. *Biographical Register of the Officers and Graduates of the U.S. Military Academy*, Vol. I, 2nd Ed. (New York: D. Van Nostrand, 1868)

Curry, Leonard P. *Blueprint for Modern America: Nonmilitary Legislation of the First Civil War Congress* (Nashville: Vanderbilt University Press, 1968)

Curtis, O.B. *History of the Twenty-Fourth Michigan of the Iron Brigade* (Detroit: Winn & Hammond, 1891)

Daily National Intelligencer & Washington Express

DeLand, Charles V. *DeLand's History of Jackson County, Michigan* (n.p.: B.F. Bowen, 1903)

Democratic (Detroit) Free Press

Dempsey, Jack. *Michigan's Civil War Citizen-General: Alpheus S. Williams* (Charleston: The History Press, 2019)

_____. "Union Victory: The Midwest's Decisive Role in the Civil War" in *Middle West Review*, Vol. 10, No. 2 (University of Nebraska Press, Spring 2024)

_____ & Brian James Egen. *Michigan at Antietam: The Wolverine State's Sacrifice on America's Bloodiest Day* (Charleston: The History Press, 2015)

De Pree, Max. *Leadership Jazz* (New York: Dell Publishing, 1992)

"Descriptive List of the Papers of Governor Austin Blair" in *Michigan History Magazine*, Vol. I (Lansing: Michigan Historical Commission, 1917)

Detroit Advertiser & Tribune

Detroit Daily Advertiser

Dew, Charles B. *Apostles of Disunion: Southern Secession Commissioners and the Causes of the Civil War* (Charlottesville: University of Virginia Press, 2002)

Dilla, Harriette M. *The Politics of Michigan, 1865-1878* (New York: Columbia University, 1912)

Documents Accompanying the Journal of the House of Representatives of the State of Michigan at the Annual Session of 1846 (Detroit: Bagg & Harmon, 1846)

Documents Accompanying the Journal of the House of Representatives of the State of Michigan at the Biennial Session of 1861 (Lansing: Hosmer & Kerr, 1861)

Documents Relating to the Erection of the New Capitol of Michigan. 1871 to 1879 (Lansing: W.S. George & Co., 1879)

Donald, David H. *Lincoln* (New York: Simon & Schuster, 1995)

_____. *Inside Lincoln's Cabinet: The Civil War Diaries of Salmon P. Chase* (New York: Longmans, Green & Co., 1954)

Downey, Arthur T. *The Civil War Lawyers: Constitutional Questions, Courtroom Dramas, and the Men Behind Them* (Chicago: ABA Publishing, 2010)

Dubin, Michael J. *United States Gubernatorial Elections, 1776-1860: The Official Results by State and County* (Jefferson: McFarland & Co., 2003)

Dunbar, Willis F. *Michigan: A History of the Wolverine State* (Grand Rapids: William B. Eerdmans Pub. Co., 1975)

Durant, Samuel W. *History of Ingham and Eaton Counties, Michigan, with Illustrations and Biographical Sketches of Their Prominent Men and Pioneers* (Philadelphia: D.W. Ensign & Co., 1880)

Engle, Stephen. *All the President's Statesmen: Northern Governors and the American Civil War* (Milwaukee: Marquette University Press, 2006)

_____. *Gathering to Save a Nation: Lincoln and the Union's War Governors* (Chapel Hill: University of North Carolina Press, 2016)

_____. *In Pursuit of Justice: The Life of John Albion Andrew* (Amherst: University of Massachusetts Press, 2023)

Farmer, Silas. *The History of Detroit and Michigan or The Metropolis Illustrated*, 2d Ed., Vol. One (Detroit: Silas Farmer & Co., 1889)

Fearey, Thomas H. *Union College Alumni in the Civil War, 1861-1865* (Schenectady: n.p., 1915)

The Federalist, on the New Constitution, Written in the Year 1788, by Mr. Hamilton, Mr. Madison, and Mr. Jay: with an Appendix, Containing the Letters of Pacificus and Helvidius on the Proclamation of Neutrality of 1793; also, the Original Articles of the Confederation, and the Constitution of the United States, with the Amendments Made Thereto. A New Edition. The Numbers Written by Mr. Madison Corrected by Himself (Hallowell: Glazier, Masters & Smith, 1837)

Fennimore, Jean J.L. "Austin Blair: Pioneer Lawyer, 1818-1844" in *Michigan History*, Vol. 48, No. 1 (Mar. 1964)

_____. "Austin Blair: Political Idealist, 1845-1860" in *Michigan History*, Vol. 48, No. 2 (June 1964)

_____. "Austin Blair: Civil War Governor, 1861-1862" in *Michigan History*, Vol. 49, No. 3 (Sept. 1965)

_____. "Austin Blair: Civil War Governor, 1863-1864" in *Michigan History*, Vol. 49, No. 4 (Dec. 1965)

Findagrave.com

Finkelman, Paul & Martin J. Hershock eds. *The History of Michigan Law* (Athens: Ohio University Press, 2006)

First Fifty Years of Cazenovia Seminary, 1825-1875 (New York: Nelson & Phillips, 1877)

First Quinquennial Record of the Alumni Association of Hillsdale College (Hillsdale: Frank Sands & Co., 1876)

Foner, Eric. *Free Soil, Free Labor, Free Men: The Ideology of the Republican Party Before the Civil War* (London: Oxford University Press, 1971)

Formisano, Ronald P. *The Birth of Mass Political Parties: Michigan, 1827-1861* (Princeton: Princeton University Press, 1971)

Fuller, George N. ed. *Governors of the Territory and State of Michigan*, Bulletin No. 16 (Lansing: Michigan Historical Commission, 1928)

_____. *Messages of the Governors of Michigan*, Vol. II (Lansing: Michigan Historical Commission, 1926)

_____. *Michigan, A Centennial History of the State and Its People*, Vol. I (Chicago: Lewis Pub. Co., 1939)

Furniss, Jack. *Between Extremes: Seeking the Political Center in the Civil War North* (Baton Rouge: Louisiana State University Press, 2024)

General Committee, *Proceedings at Celebration of the Fiftieth Anniversary of the Birth of the Republican Party at Jackson, Michigan, July 6, 1904; together with a History of the Republican Party in Michigan* (Detroit: Detroit Tribune, 1904)

Gilbert, Arlan K. *Hillsdale College: The Civil War Experience* (Hillsdale: Hillsdale College Press, 1994)

Goodwin, Doris Kearns. *Team of Rivals: The Political Genius of Abraham Lincoln* (New York: Simon & Schuster, 2005)

Grand Rapids Eagle

Hamilton, Nigel. *Lincoln vs. Davis: The War of the Presidents* (New York: Little, Brown & Co., 2024)

Hamilton, Richard L. *"Oh! Hast Thou Forgotten." Michigan Cavalry in the Civil War: The Gettysburg Campaign* (2008)

Hardee, William J. *Rifle and Light Infantry Tactics; for the Exercise and Manoeuvres of Troops When Acting as Light Infantry or Riflemen* (Philadelphia: Lippincott, Grambo & Co., 1855)

Harriman, W.C. "The Late Gov. Blair of Michigan" in *The Unitarian: A Monthly Magazine of Liberal Christianity*, Vol. IX (Boston: George H. Ellis, 1894)

Harris, Robert C. *Austin Blair of Michigan: A Political Biography* (East Lansing: Michigan State University, 1969) (Ph.D. dissertation)

Harris, William C. *Lincoln and the Union Governors* (Carbondale: Southern Illinois University Press, 2013)

Harris, Wilmer C. *Public Life of Zachariah Chandler 1851-1875* (Lansing: Michigan Historical Commission, 1917)

Hershock, Martin J. "Copperheads and Radicals: Michigan Partisan Politics during the Civil War Era, 1860-1865" in *Michigan Historical Review*, Vol. 18, No. 1 (Spring 1992)

_____. *The Paradox of Progress: Economic Change, Individual Enterprise, and Political Culture in Michigan, 1837-1878* (Athens: Ohio University Press, 2003)

Hesseltine, William B. *Lincoln and the War Governors* (New York: Alfred A. Knopf, 1948)

_____. "Introduction" in Richard H. Abbott, *Ohio's War Governors* (Columbus: Ohio State University Press, 1962)

Hesseltine William B. & Hazel C. Wolf. "The Cleveland Conference of 1861" in *Ohio Archaeological and Historical Quarterly*, Vol. 56, No. 3 (July 1947)

Hillsdale Standard

History of the Amphictyon Society of Hillsdale College, Hillsdale, Michigan (Chicago: Smith & Colbert, 1890)

History of Jackson County, Michigan (Chicago: Inter-State Pub. Co., 1881)

History of the Ordinance of 1787 and the Old Northwest Territory (Marietta: Northwest Territory Celebration Commission, 1937)

Homer, Elizabeth A. *Pioneers, Reformers, & Millionaires* (Saline: McNaughton & Gunn, 2014)

House Doc. No. 12 in *Documents Accompanying the Journal of the House of Representatives of the State of Michigan at the Annual Session of 1846* (Detroit: Bagg & Harmon, 1846)

http://tompkins.nygenweb.net/cemeteries/blair_cem.htm

https://projects.kora.matrix.msu.edu

https://www.michigan.gov/dmva/

https://www.presidency.ucsb.edu/documents/1844-democratic-party-platform

https://www.tcpl.org/sites/default/files/content/archive/1860-74.pdf

https://www.trumanlibrary.gov/library/public-papers/378/presidents-farewell-address-american-people

Illinois State Journal

Ingersoll, L.D. *A History of the War Department of the United States* (Washington: Francis B. Mohun, 1879)

Jackson Citizen

Joint Documents of the State of Michigan, for the Year 1860, No. 2 (Lansing: Hosmer & Kerr, 1861)

Journal of the House of Representatives of the State of Michigan, 1846 (Detroit: Bagg & Harmon, 1846)

Journal of the Senate of the State of Michigan, 1855 (Lansing: Hosmer & Fitch, 1855)

Journal of the House of Representatives of the State of Michigan, 1861 (Lansing: Hosmer & Kerr, 1861)

Journal of the Senate of the State of Michigan. 1861 (Lansing: Hosmer & Kerr, 1861)

Journal of the House of Representatives of the State of Michigan, Extra Session of 1861 (Lansing: John Kerr & Co., 1861)

Journal of the House of Representatives of the State of Michigan, Extra Session of 1862 (Lansing: John A. Kerr & Co., 1862)

Journal of the Senate of the State of Michigan, Extra Session of 1862 (Lansing: John A. Kerr & Co., 1862)

Journal of the House of Representatives of the State of Michigan, 1863, Part II (Lansing: John A. Kerr & Co., 1863)

Journal of the Senate of the State of Michigan, 1863 (Lansing: John A. Kerr & Co., 1863)

Journal of the House of Representatives of the State of Michigan, Extra Session, 1864 (Lansing: John A. Kerr & Co., 1864)

Journal of the Senate of the State of Michigan, Extra Session, 1864 (Lansing: John A. Kerr & Co., 1864)

Kaplan, Fred. *Lincoln and the Abolitionists: John Quincy Adams, Slavery, and the Civil War* (New York: Harper, 2017)

Kidd, J.H. *Personal Recollections of a Cavalryman with Custer's Michigan Cavalry Brigade in the Civil War* (Ionia: Sentinel Printing Co., 1908)

Kirkwood, Samuel J. "The Loyal Governors at Altoona in 1862" in *The Iowa Historical Record*, Vol. VIII, No. 1, Jan. 1892 (Iowa City: A.J. Hershire & Co., 1892)

Kushner, Tony. *Lincoln: The Screenplay* (New York: Theatre Communications Group, 2012)

Lambert, Joseph Jr. *The Political Transformation of David Tod: Governing Ohio During the Height of the Civil War* (Kent: Kent State University Press, 2023)

Lanman, Charles. *The Red Book of Michigan: A Civil, Military and Biographical History* (Detroit: E.B. Smith & Co., 1871)

Lansing State Republican

Lauck, Jon K. *The Good Country: A History of the American Midwest, 1800-1900* (Norman: University of Oklahoma Press, 2022)

Leavitt, Emily Wilder. *The Blair Family of New England* (Boston: David Clapp & Son, 1900)

Levine, Bruce. *Thaddeus Stevens: Civil War Revolutionary, Fighter for Racial Justice* (New York: Simon & Schuster, 2021)

Lewis, Martin D. *Lumberman from Flint: The Michigan Career of Henry H. Crapo 1855-1869* (Detroit: Wayne State University Press, 1958)

Library of Congress

Lineage Book, National Society of the Daughters of the American Revolution, Vol. XLVII (Washington: Judd & Detweiler, 1919)

Livingstone's History of the Republican Party, Vol. I (Detroit: Wm. Livingstone, 1900)

Loomis & Talbott's Jackson City Directory, and Business Mirror, for 1860-61 (Detroit: George W. Hawes, 1860)

Luthin, Reinhard H. *The American Historical Review*, Vol. 54, No. 4 (Jul. 1949)

Manual, Containing the Rules of the Senate and House of Representatives, of the State of Michigan (Detroit: Bagg & Harmon, 1846)

Manual, Containing the Rules of the Senate and House of Representatives, of the State of Michigan (Detroit: Bagg & Harmon, 1848)

Manual for the Use of the Legislature of the State of Michigan, 1875-76 (Lansing: W.S. George & Co., 1875)

Mason, Jack C. *Until Antietam: The Life and Letters of Major General Israel B. Richardson* (Carbondale: Southern Illinois University Press, 2009)

Massachusetts Soldiers and Sailors of the Revolutionary War [Vol. 2] (Boston: Wright & Potter Printing Co., 1896)

May, George S. *Michigan and the Civil War Years 1860-1866, A Wartime Chronicle* (Lansing: Michigan Civil War Centennial Observance Commission, 1964)

McClellan, George B. *McClellan's Own Story: The War for the Union* (New York: Charles L. Webster & Co., 1887)

McPherson, Edward. *The Political History of the United States of America, During the Great Rebellion* (Washington: Philp & Solomons, 1864)

McWhiney, Grady ed. *Grant, Lee, Lincoln and the Radicals: Essays on Civil War Leadership* (Baton Rouge: Louisiana State University Press, 2001)

Memoirs of Newton Thorne Kirk, Michigan State University Archives and Historical Collections, Collection C-28, Folder 1, Ch. Two

Messner, Vivian Thomas. *The Public Life of Austin Blair, War Governor of Michigan (1863-1894)* (Detroit: Wayne State University, 1937) (Master's thesis)

Michigan Civil War Association. *His Sword a Scalpel: General Charles S. Tripler MD USA* (Traverse City: Mission Point Press, 2023)

_____. *Warriors for Liberty: William Dollarson & Michigan's Civil War African Americans* (Traverse City: Mission Point Press, 2024)

Michigan Historical Review

Michigan Legislative Manual and Official Directory for the Years 1897-1898 (Lansing: Robert Smith Printing Co., 1897)

Michigan Liberty Press

Miers, Earl Schenck ed. *Lincoln Day by Day: A Chronology, 1809-1865*, Vol. III (Washington: Lincoln Sesquicentennial Commission, 1960)

Miller, Richard F. *States at War: A Reference Guide for Michigan in the Civil War* (Ann Arbor: University of Michigan Press, 2020)

Mitchell, Robert E. "The Organizational Performance of Michigan's Adjutant General and the Federal Provost Marshal General in Recruiting Michigan's Boys in Blue" in *Michigan Historical Review*, Vol. 28, No. 2 (Fall 2002)

Monroe County Museum System

Moore, Charles. *History of Michigan*, Vol. I (Chicago: Lewis Pub. Co., 1915)

Mull, Carol E. *The Underground Railroad in Michigan* (Jefferson: McFarland & Co., 2010)

Murphy, D.F. *Proceedings of the National Union Convention Held in Baltimore, Md., June 7th and 8th, 1864* (New York: Baker & Godwin, 1864)

Museography, the Official Magazine of the Kalamazoo Valley Museum, Vol. 4, Issue 2, Winter/Spring 2005

Neely, Mark E. *The Abraham Lincoln Encyclopedia* (New York: Da Capo Press, 1984)

Nevins, Allan. *The War for the Union, Vol. I, The Improvised War: 1861-1862* (New York: Charles Scribner's Sons, 1959)

_____. *The War for the Union, Vol. II, War Becomes Revolution 1862-1863* (New York: Charles Scribner's Sons, 1960)

New York Historical Society

New York Times

New York Tribune

Nicolay, John G. & John Hay. *Abraham Lincoln: A History*, Vol. Six (New York: The Century Co., 1890)

Oakleaf, Joseph B. *National Union Convention of 1864 and Why Lincoln was not Nominated by Acclamation* (Moline: n.p., 1924)

Official Army Register of the Volunteer Force of the United States Army for the years 1861, '62, '63, '64, '65, Vol. 5 (Washington: Government Printing Office, 1865)

Official Directory and Legislative Manual of the State of Michigan for the Years 1893-94 (Lansing: Robert Smith & Co., 1893)

Plummer, Mark A. *Lincoln's Rail-Splitter: Governor Richard J. Oglesby* (Urbana: University of Illinois Press, 2001)

Portrait and Biographical Album of Ingham and Livingston Counties, Michigan (Chicago: Chapman Bros., 1891)

Portrait and Biographical Album of Jackson County (Chicago: Chapman & Bros., 1890)

Portrait and Biographical Album of the Members of the Legislature of the State of Michigan (1883.) Thirty-Second Session (Chicago: Chapman Bros., 1883)

Portrait and Biographical Record of Genesee, Lapeer and Tuscola Counties, Michigan (Chicago: Chapman Bros., 1892)

Prigg v. Pennsylvania, 41 U.S. 539 (1842)

Proceedings of the First Three Republican National Conventions of 1856, 1860 and 1864 (Minneapolis: Charles W. Johnson, 1893)

Proceedings of the National Republican Convention, Held at Chicago, May 16, 17 and 18, 1860 (Albany: Weed, Parsons & Co., 1860)

A Protest Against American Slavery, by One Hundred and Seventy-three Unitarian Ministers (Boston: B.H. Greene, 1845)

The Public Statutes at Large of the United States of America, Vol. I (Boston: Charles C. Little & James Brown, 1845)

The Public Statutes at Large of the United States of America, Vol. II (Boston: Charles C. Little & James Brown, 1845)

Quaife, Milo M. ed. *From the Cannon's Mouth: The Civil War Letters of General Alpheus S. Williams* (Lincoln: University of Nebraska Press, 1995)

Quist, John W. ed. *Michigan's War: The Civil War in Documents* (Athens: Ohio University Press, 2019)

Ransom, John L. *Andersonville Diary, Escape, and List of the Dead* (Auburn: 1881), republished as *John Ransom's Andersonville Diary* (Middlebury: Paul S. Eriksson, 1963)

Record of Service of Michigan Volunteers in the Civil War 1861-1865 (Kalamazoo: Ihling Bros. & Everard, 1903)

The Red Book for the Thirtieth Legislature of the State of Michigan, 1879–1880 (Lansing: W.S. George & Co., 1879)

Reed, George I. ed. *Bench and Bar of Michigan: A Volume of History and Biography* (Chicago: The Century Publishing and Engraving Co., 1897)

Report of the Secretary of War, Dec. 1, 1862, 10, in *Message of the President of the United States to the Two Houses of Congress at the Commencement of the Third Session of the Thirty-Seventh Congress*, Vol. IV (Washington: Government Printing Office, 1862)

Report of the Select Committee Relative to the Soldiers' National Cemetery, Together with the Accompanying Documents, as Reported to the House of Representatives of the Commonwealth of Pennsylvania, March 31, 1864 (Harrisburg: Singerley & Myers, 1864)

The Revised Constitution of the State of Michigan, Adopted in Convention, August 15, 1850 (Lansing: R.W. Ingals, 1850)

Revised Report of the Select Committee Relative to the Soldiers' National Cemetery, Together with the Accompanying Documents, as Reported to the House of Representatives of the Commonwealth of Pennsylvania (Harrisburg: Singerley & Myers, 1865)

Robertson, John. *Michigan in the War* (Lansing: W.S. George & Co., 1882)

Robison, W. Scott. *History of the City of Cleveland: Its Settlement, Rise and Progress* (Cleveland: Robison & Cockett, 1887)

Sandburg, Carl. *Abraham Lincoln: The War Years*, Vol. II (New York: Harcourt, Brace & World, 1939)

Scott, Robert G. *Forgotten Valor: The Memoirs, Journals, & Civil War Letters of Orlando B. Willcox* (Kent: Kent State University Press, 1999)

Seaman, Ezra C. *Gov. Blair's Speech*, reprint of *Ann Arbor Journal*, Nov. 1866, 1,2 (Library of Congress Control Number 11030886)

Seidule, Ty. *Robert E. Lee and Me: A Southerner's Reckoning with the Myth of the Lost Cause* (New York: St. Martin's Press, 2020)

Seilhamer, George O. *Leslie's History of the Republican Party* (New York: Publishing Society of New York, 1905)

The Semi-Centennial Celebration of the Organization of the University of Michigan, June 26-30, 1887 (Ann Arbor: University of Michigan, 1888)

Shoemaker, Henry W. *The Last of the War Governors; A Biographical Appreciation of Colonel William Sprague* (Altoona: Altoona Tribune Pub. Co., 1916)

Sikkenga, Raymond. *Doers & Dreamers: The Governors of Michigan* (Spring Lake: River Road Publications, 1987)

Smith, Theodore C. *The Liberty and Free Soil Parties in the Northwest* (New York: Longmans, Green & Co., 1897)

Spooner, Lysander. *A Defence for Fugitive Slaves, Against the Acts of Congress of February 12, 1793 and September 18, 1850* (Boston: Bela Marsh, 1850)

Stahr, Walter. *Seward: Lincoln's Indispensable Man* (New York: Simon & Schuster, 2012)

Stauffer, John. *Giants: The Parallel Lives of Frederick Douglass and Abraham Lincoln* (New York: Twelve, 2008)

Sternhell, Yael A. *War on Record: The Archive and the Afterlife of the Civil War* (New Haven: Yale University Press, 2023)

Stewart, Matthew. *An Emancipation of the Mind: Radical Philosophy, the War over Slavery, and the Refounding of America* (New York: W.W. Norton & Co., 2024)

Stocking, William ed. *Under the Oaks: Commemorating the Fiftieth Anniversary of the Founding of the Republican Party at Jackson* (Detroit: Detroit Tribune, 1904)

Streeter, Floyd Benjamin. *Political Parties in Michigan, 1837-1860: An Historical Study of Political Issues and Parties in Michigan from the Admission of the State to the Civil War* (Lansing: Michigan Historical Commission, 1918)

Thatcher, Marshall P. *A Hundred Battles in the West, St. Louis to Atlanta, 1861-65, The Second Michigan Cavalry* (Detroit: L.F. Kilroy, 1884)

Thomas, James M. *Jackson City Directory and Business Advertiser for 1867 & 1868* (Jackson: Carlton & Van Antwerp, 1867)

Thompson, Kees D. "'Altoona was his, and fairly won': President Lincoln and the Altoona Governors' Conference, September

1862" in *The Gettysburg College Journal of the Civil War Era*, Vol. 7, Article 7 (2017)

Tilton Materials, New York Historical Society

U.S. Census

Utley, Henry M. & Byron M. Cutcheon. *Michigan as a Province, Territory and State, the Twenty-Sixth Member of the Federal Union* (New York: Publishing Society of Michigan, 1906)

Vale, Joseph G. *Minty and the Cavalry: A History of Cavalry Campaigns in the Western Armies* (Harrisburg: Edwin K. Meyers, 1886)

Van Buren, A.D.P. "Michigan in Her Pioneer Politics; Michigan in Our National Politics, and Michigan in the Campaign of 1856" in *Michigan Historical Collections*, Vol. XVII, 2d Ed. (Lansing: Wynkoop Hellenbeck Crawford Co., 1910)

Van Santvoord, C. *Memoirs of Eliphalet Nott, D.D. LL.D. For Sixty-Two Years President of Union College* (New York: Sheldon & Co., 1876)

Vanacker, Matt. *Lansing and the Civil War* (Charleston: The History Press, 2023)

Vila, Bryan & Cynthia Morris eds. *Capital Punishment in the United States: A Documentary History* (Westport: Greenwood Press, 1997)

The War of the Rebellion: A Compilation of the Official Records of the Union and Confederate Armies (Washington: Government Printing Office, 1880-1901)

Ward Family Papers, Burton Historical Collection

Washington *Evening Star*

Weddon, Willah. *First Ladies of Michigan* (Lansing: NOG Press, 1994)

_____. *Michigan Governors: Their Life Stories* (Lansing: NOG Press, 1994)

Weeden, William B. *War Government, Federal and State, in Massachusetts, New York, Pennsylvania and Indiana, 1861-1865* (Boston: Houghton, Mifflin & Co., 1906)

Weeks, George. *Stewards of the State: The Governors of Michigan* (Ann Arbor: Historical Society of Michigan, 1991)

Wilcox, Francis McLellan. *Seventh-Day Adventists in Time of War* (Washington: Review and Herald Pub. Assn., 1936)

Williams, T. Harry. *Lincoln and the Radicals* (Madison: University of Wisconsin Press, 1941)

_____. "Lincoln and the Radicals: An Essay in Civil War History and Historiography" in Grady McWhiney ed., *Grant, Lee, Lincoln and the Radicals: Essays on Civil War Leadership* (Baton Rouge: Louisiana State University Press, 2001)

Wilson, Mark R. *The Business of Civil War: Military Mobilization and the State, 1861-1865* (Baltimore: Johns Hopkins University Press, 2006)

Woodford, Frank B. *Father Abraham's Children: Michigan Episodes in the Civil War* (Detroit: Wayne State University Press, 1961)

_____ & Philip P. Mason. *Harper of Detroit: The Origin and Growth of a Great Metropolitan Hospital* (Detroit: Wayne State University Press, 1964)

For more about the "radicals," see Stephen Puleo, *The Great Abolitionist: Charles Sumner and the Fight for a More Perfect Union* (New York: St. Martin's Press, 2024); LeAnna Keith, *When It Was Grand: The Radical Republican History of the Civil War* (New York: Hill & Wang, 2020); David W. Blight, *Frederick Douglass: Prophet of Freedom* (New York: Simon & Schuster, 2018); James M. McPherson, *The Struggle for Equality: Abolitionists and the Negro in the Civil War and Reconstruction* (Princeton: Princeton University Press, 2014); Robin Blackburn, *The American Crucible: Slavery, Emancipation and Human Rights* (London: Verso, 2013); James Oakes, *The Radical and the Republican: Frederick Douglass, Abraham Lincoln, and the Triumph of Antislavery Politics* (New York: W.W. Norton & Co., 2007); Frederick J. Blue, *Charles Sumner and the Conscience of the North* (Arlington Heights: Harlan Davidson Inc., 1994); David H. Donald, *Charles Sumner and the Coming of the Civil War* (New York: Alfred A. Knopf, 1961), and

Charles Sumner and the Rights of Man (New York: Alfred A. Knopf, 1970), republished together in *Charles Sumner* (New York: Da Capo Press, 1996).

Index

Acknowledgments

Grateful appreciation is expressed by the editor to the following, among others: Margaret O'Brien and Matt Vanacker for continuing invaluable thematic guidance, research assistance, and manuscript reviews; Brian James Egen for stalwart and inspirational leadership; fellow MCWA Board members, including Jacqueline Tinney for manuscript review; Dr. Marty Hershock for support of and insightful comments on this volume; Jeremy K. Moghtader of the University of Michigan for research assistance; Kerry Chartkoff, 2015 Milliken/ Adams/Kelley awardee by the Michigan Historical Commission, for consultative input; Shayla Croteau, Michigan State Capitol Art Registrar, for a special contribution; Lori N. Curtis, Archivist and Special Collections Librarian, Mossey Library, Hillsdale College; Harrison Marcott, Director of Curatorial Affairs, Ella Sharp Museum; Diana Bachman, Bentley Historical Library; Katherine Emrich and staff of the Burton Historical Collection; Linda Hass, Jackson County Michigan Historical Society; the excellent and earnest staff at the Plymouth District Library for "MeL" and other assistance; the professionals at Mission Point Press; Dave Dempsey for extensive research contributions; and Suzzanne Dempsey for guidance and support. And, invoking our subject's words, "acknowledging our entire dependence upon that Divine Providence which is constantly over us."